KNOWLEDGE, SPIRIT, LAW

BOOK I: RADICAL SCHOLARSHIP

KNOWLEDGE, SPIRIT, LAW

BOOK I: RADICAL SCHOLARSHIP

Gavin Keeney

punctum books ⓟ brooklyn, ny

KNOWLEDGE, SPIRIT, LAW // BOOK 1: RADICAL SCHOLARSHIP
© Gavin Keeney, 2015.

All rights reserved. No part of this publication may be reproduced, distributed, or transmitted in any form or by any means, including photocopying, recording, or other electronic or mechanical methods, without the prior written permission of the publisher, except in the case of brief quotations embodied in critical reviews and certain other noncommercial uses permitted by copyright law.

First published in 2015 (in a limited print-on-demand edition of 500 copies) as a co-imprint of

punctum books
Brooklyn, New York
http://punctumbooks.com

CTM Documents Initiative
Center for Transformative Media
Parsons School of Design
http://ctm.parsons.edu/

Cover image: Detail from Gavin Keeney, *James Joyce Café, Via Roma, 14, Trieste, Italy* (2014). Photo © Gavin Keeney, 2015. Photo-editing by Ed Keller, Claudio Palmisano, and Chris Piuma. Cover Design by Chris Piuma. Book design by Eileen Joy.

ISBN-13: 978-0692558447
ISBN-10: 0692558446

Facing-page illustration by Heather Masciandaro.

For Chris Marker

For want of a real object, by the power of my vague desires, I evoked a phantom which never quitted me more.
François-René de Chateaubriand

Whatever may happen next, we will always have had this. For the first time, and forever, there will be other memories floating around these heavy machines than silence, coercion and submissiveness.
Simone Weil

Nothing is, nothing is the same. /And I won't go back the way I came.
Lhasa de Sela

TABLE OF CONTENTS

// i

Preface

// v

Acknowledgments

// ix

Notes on the Edition

// 1

Introduction: **Radical Scholarship**

// 25

Essay 1: **Re-universalizing Knowledge**

// 43

Essay 2: **Estranged Dawns**

// 61

Essay 3: **The Film-essay**

// 83

Essay 4: **Film Mysticism and "The Haunted Wood"**

// 105

Essay 5: **Circular Discourses**

// 123

Essay 6: **Verb Tenses and Time-senses**

// 149

Appendix A: **Agence 'X' Publishing Advisory**

// 183

Appendix B: **Perpetual Petition for the Right of the Author to Have *No* Digital Rights**

// 189

Appendix C: **Symptom "A": The End**

// 195

References

PREFACE

Knowledge, Spirit, Law—as project—is a summary and analysis of current and past textual and visual practices and their relationship to parallel arts and discourses where greater risks may be taken, inclusive of categorically "useless" high-discursive disciplines such as theology and philosophy, plus consideration of methodologies and venues for the dissemination of works critical of, or at odds with, both the neo-avantgarde culture industry (Benjamin H.D. Buchloh's term, updating Theodor W. Adorno) and intellectual orthodoxy in neo-liberal humanistic studies. As a phenomenology of scholarship (by way of the chiasmus, scholarship as work of art, and art work as form of scholarship), it seeks to condition future forms of avant-garde scholarship through an analysis and critique of past practices and how they inform and/or deform present-day practices.

The six essays presented here cover topics and circle themes related to the problems and crises specific to neo-liberal academia, while proposing creative paths around the various obstructions. The obstructions include metrics-obsessed academia, circular and incestuous peer review, digitalization of research as stalking horse for text- and data-mining, and violation by global corporate fiat of Intellectual Property Rights and the moral rights of authors and artists. These issues, while not addressed directly in a sustained manner in the main text, inform the various proscriptive aspects of the essays and, via the Introduction, underscore the necessity of new means to no obvious end in the production of knowledge—a return to forms of non-instrumentalized intellectual inquiry.

The overarching theme is the necessity for the re-universalization of knowledge, arguably underway regardless of the dramatic increase in pseudo-empirical studies in present-day academia and still-born aesthetic *frisson* in the arts, plus the penchant for the so-called Digital Humanities in concert with aspects of Cognitive Capitalism.

The six essays therefore survey various arguments and discussions underway in the multiple arts but collect such only as preliminary means for determining possible outcomes for the late "post-contemporary" world (George Steiner's term, from *Real Presences*). These arguments and discourses primarily concern political and socio-economic conditions but also intersect with cultural anthropology, theology, and aesthetics (via art, architecture, and art history). While Alain Badiou and Slavoj Žižek (the main influences in the author's previous synoptic works, *Art as "Night": An Art-theological Treatise* and *"Else-where": Essays in Art, Architecture, and Cultural Production 2002-2011*), Giorgio Agamben (the main influence in more recent focused studies, *Dossier Chris Marker: The Suffering Image* and *Not-I/Thou: The Other Subject of Art and Architecture*), Antonio Negri (father of the Multitude), and Jacques Rancière (all-purpose post-Marxist *bête noire*) et al. are implicated, they are also not always directly mentioned. The collective sense of this episodic critique via essays is that each of these figures is a manifestation of a persistent late-modernist critique of cultural production, one which is passing away, quite naturally (but also begrudgingly). High-Marxist and post-Marxist world-views, while addressed obliquely through the body of the essays and the supporting discursive currents within the footnotes, are also implicated as mostly passé in the stalemate of the twenty-first century capitulation of nearly all forms of cultural production to Capital. Far from re-introducing "epigones of irrationality," the book considers the intuitive and mystical aspects of the production of knowledge contra the dictates, biases, and prejudices of Cognitive Capital, or that which Tom Conley (Harvard University) has recognized, in his examination of *Dossier Chris Marker*, as always present in the Arts and Sciences (whether or not addressed and/or acknowledged).

The overall project presented here in schematic or summary form is to be "perpetually curated" via new forms of networking, dissemination, and revision. To be developed initially in two volumes, *Knowledge, Spirit, Law* will serve as a "moving and/or shifting anthology" of and toward new forms of expression in humanistic studies. The nominal resemblance to literary travel guides is, therefore, not accidental. *Mutatis mutandis*, this hybrid work will be released in variable forms and revised obsessively to keep pace with the hoped-for revolution in high scholarship—a perhaps "apparitional something else" always just over the horizon.

February 7, 2015

ACKNOWLEDGMENTS

This series of elaborate and somewhat baroque essays was first mapped out and then begun in Ljubljana, Slovenia, in July-August of 2014, while awaiting word on the outcome of then-completed PhD studies in Australia. The author wishes to thank his hosts during that stay for their hospitality (in association with Visa D status)—ZRC-SAZU (Slovenian Academy of Sciences and Arts), Moderna Galerija, and the University of Ljubljana's Faculty of Arts. Foremost in this regard, this book owes its Slovene origins to the kindness of Zdenka Badovinac, Petra Čeferin, Martin Germ, Oto Luthar, Kaja Manndič, Rado Riha, and Martina Tekavec Bembič. Subsequent to that 2014 visit, a series of lectures and multimedia presentations was delivered in Ljubljana, in March-April of 2015, on the subject of Intellectual Property Rights and neoliberal academia. These lectures were sponsored by the Fulbright Specialist Program, US Department of State, in association with the Igor Zabel Association for Culture and Theory and the University of Ljubljana, leading to the Black White Paper, "Tractatus logico-academicus" (to be published in Book Two of *Knowledge, Spirit, Law*). For arranging the Fulbright project, thanks to Or Ettlinger, Peter Gabrijelčič, Carmel Geraghty, Martin Germ, and Urška Jurman. Research and development of Book Two is tentatively scheduled to commence in Venice, Italy, in 2016, via the Giorgio Cini Foundation—"archangels and archons willing." (Notably, apropos of "archangels and archons," in strolling eastward along Bloomsbury Way in London, en route to the past high-literary district and present-day neo-liberal academic district, it is possible to be stopped in one's tracks by the ethereal beauty of the Swedenborg Society's bookshop.) In many respects, the spiritual home for this project is—and remains—Venice-Trieste-Ljubljana (or "Aquileia"). Thus the haunting and haunted image of the James Joyce Café, Trieste, on the cover designed by Chris Piuma—as totemic gesture.

Both the "Agence 'X' Publishing Advisory" and the "Perpetual Petition for the Right of the Author to Have *No* Digital Rights" (Appendix A and B in this volume) were first developed in association with Scholars Minor, an informal network of scholars and artists based in Australasia, Europe, and the USA. Additionally, *Knowledge, Spirit, Law*, as post-doctoral project, is a direct outcome of the author's recent PhD studies in Architecture at Deakin University, Geelong, Victoria, Australia. Thanks are due to David Jones, Flavia Marcello, and John Rollo, as supervisors of the successful thesis by publication, "Visual Agency in Art & Architecture" (2014), and to the esteemed external examiners, Tom Conley (Harvard University), Suzana Milevska (Academy of Fine Arts, Vienna), and Anonymous (unknown academic, Australia).

The author also wishes to thank Ed Keller at the Center for Transformative Media (CTM) at Parsons School of Design, The New School for having been the first to see the dark beauty of this project and Eileen A. Joy of punctum books for guiding the first installment of a long-term study of Intellectual Property Rights and the Moral Rights of Authors into print. Both continue to champion open-access publishing, a model that in many ways stands between for-profit, predatory corporate media (and the excesses of Cognitive Capitalism) and the quixotic, yet admirable attempt by what is left of so-called civil society to re-privilege cultural heritage through not-for-profit mass digitization. Indeed, CTM/punctum is caught in-between the two giants of mass digitization, with and on behalf of all authors, dodging the blows of the competing giants.

Lastly, for invaluable moral, financial, spiritual, and intellectual support for the overall project of *Knowledge, Spirit, Law* (support without which it is impossible to accomplish much of anything), thanks go to friends and colleagues around the planet: Nadine Boljkovac, David Brancaleone, Mark E. Breeze, Christophe Chazalon, Or Ettlinger, Gaia Fidenzio, Anne Godfrey, Thomas Tilluca Han, Isabelle Hayeur, John Murray Herron, Nicholas Keeney, Robin Keeney, Parsa Khalili, David Metzger, Thomas Mical, Marilyn Nahas, Guy Pocock, Maria Rondeau, Ruth Schepper, Eric Schuldenfrei, Juliet Sunara, Judith Taylor, Étienne Sandrin, Verena Tschudin, Oliver Tsuruta, José Vela Castillo, Phil Watson, and Neža Zajc—all of whom, in one way or another, have had an impact on the development of this project, and whom collectively prove that intellectual property is developed socially versus individually.

NOTA BENE

This book is dedicated to Chris Marker for very good reasons. It was Marker's work that was the center of the PhD study, "Visual Agency in Art & Architecture," in the form of the book *Dossier Chris Marker: The Suffering Image* (Cambridge Scholars Publishing, 2012), and it is Marker's *life-work* that suggests one of the best ways to conduct research in the Arts and Humanities is to "wander aimlessly" (not coincidentally, the foundation for the successful Fulbright Specialist Program application in 2013). Thus Marker's return in Book One of *Knowledge, Spirit, Law* in the form of the essay "Film Mysticism and 'The Haunted Wood'" (also an indirect reference to Dante), and thus also his planned return in Book Two in the form of "Marker's Archive," a study of his posthumous and somewhat troubling assimilation to official French cultural patrimony. Marker truly haunts *Knowledge, Spirit, Law*, as he is the modern and contemporary exemplar of the event of literary-artistic catasterism, the elevation to the stars for heroic artists and authors (often as compensation for living in poverty for most of their lives[1]). Thus the Romantic theory of genius and its Other, the socio-cultural or collective basis for valorizing cultural production, return with Marker's posthumous bequest to posterity in 2012. To study Marker is to study Hegelian speculative intellect itself in relation to all of the Greek-Arab problems of Agent Intellect—that very old, unresolved medieval argument regarding where intelligence resides (plus where it comes from and where it returns to).

Regardless, all of the above should confirm that Intellectual Property Rights and the Moral Rights of Authors in the age of Cognitive Capitalism represent the foremost battlefield on which to defend the apparent "uselessness" of the Arts and Humanities.

November 26, 2015

---

[1] The author/artist may, indeed, be stranded today in-between for-profit (corporate) and not-for-profit (cultural-heritage) forms of mass digitization, yet what becomes obvious upon any thorough examination of this situation is that the event of classical catasterism (the socially determined act of becoming immortal for authors/artists or for works) relies upon, and is determined by, the existential rites and rights of the author/artist as rites of passage for works. The diabolical outcome of neo-liberal capitalism's intervention in this age-old, semi-natural phenomenon is that the author/artist is consigned to perpetual precarity, as if the torment or privation that might produce the immortal work is actually necessary and enforced versus elective or incidental. The demonic reification of precarity involved in this implied assumption of omnipotence by Capital is truly frightening, qualifying the judgment that neo-liberal capitalism is a new form of Calvinism. Regarding existential rites of passage for artists, see Lhasa de Sela, "Soon This Space Will Be Too Small," *The Living Road* (Montreal: Audiogramme, 2003).

NOTES ON THE EDITION

The project *Knowledge, Spirit, Law*—as an experiment in "scholarship as work of art"—utilizes a form of "nineteenth-century," Continental (almost-Germanic) capitalization for proper names and key terms that seeks to both qualify cultural phenomenon as authorized or semi-authoritarian and/or to de-familiarize the same, whereas such lexical maneuvers disappear in second-order, adjectival formations. Thus the following mini-glossary to initially orient the reader, with a full topological glossary to appear in Book Two:

High German Romanticism (early nineteenth century); High Marxism (revolutionary-ideological versus literary-critical Marxism); High Modernism (generally post-World War II or mid-century modernist ideology, but prior to 1930 in the case of avant-garde artistic movements); High Post-structuralism (the "literature of despair" of the 1970s and 1980s, as defined in the negative by Michel Houellebecq); High Romanticism (as defined by M.H. Abrams); High Scholasticism (fourteenth-century medieval philosophy and theology); High Structuralism (for example, as practiced by Roland Barthes, Claude Lévi-Strauss, Michel Foucault, and Jacques Lacan); Late Modernity (the late-twentieth century, inclusive of Post-modernity); Modernity (from the Italian Renaissance forward).

Additionally, unorthodox hyphenation is deployed as a means to distance terms from their present-day usage, pushing them backward toward their origin as hybrid or compound terms, and a proleptic slippage in verbs and grammar occurs here and there to de-stabilize the time-senses of orthodox historiography and normative scholarly conventions. While slightly disorienting at times, these semantic and/or syntactical diversions help serve to re-introduce universalizing traits in both textual and artistic endeavors.

The scholarly apparatus (footnotes and references)—while apparently excessive in extent, density, and detail—further seeks to build upon the experimental model and de-stabilize normative discursive exegesis, while the modified open-access form of the edition is consistent with the critique of publication platforms inherent to the overall intentions of the project.

These measures, while in part performative in the context of this project, all support the hypothesis that to escape the circularity and claustrophobia of the Arts and Letters today it is necessary to privilege both archaic or out-moded modalities of discursive and non-discursive expression *in combination with* dynamic principles borrowed from parallel disciplines and practices—"dynamic" in the sense that such principles are common to the Arts and Humanities as age-old humanistic concerns.

Therefore, the resemblance here to the "attenuated chaos" of High Post-structuralism is misleading. *Knowledge, Spirit, Law* seeks as subtending chord the re-universalization of knowledge through the conflation of both effects and means utilized. The resulting complexity is simply the outcome of the developmental model.

December 7, 2015

INTRODUCTION

RADICAL SCHOLARSHIP

I. COMMENTARIES ON COMMENTARIES

The birds are singing in your eyes today / Sweet flowers blossom in your smile / The wind and sun are in the words you say / Where might your lonesome lover be?[1]

Woody Guthrie

As a phenomenology of scholarship, *Knowledge, Spirit, Law* takes the measure of discursive and non-discursive forms of knowledge without resort to an epistemology or theory of language, such as Ludwig Wittgenstein sought in his *Philosophical Investigations*, his post-*Tractatus* attempt to divine how language-games operate when ideality is bracketed and

---

[1] Woody Guthrie, "Birds and Ships" (1947). Guthrie never set these words to music. Instead they were transmitted via his daughter, Nora Guthrie, and the Woody Guthrie Foundation, to the English left-wing folk musician and activist Billy Bragg, who then composed the elegiac song performed and recorded by Natalie Merchant and Bragg (with Wilco) on *Mermaid Avenue* (New York: Elektra, 1998), sessions intentionally designed to transplant the lyrical gifts of Guthrie to a new generation of folk artists.

subjective agency is effectively demoted or neutralized in favor of collective "forms-of-life" and expression.[2] The premise is that subjective agency is the missing ingredient in all theories of instrumental knowledge that return to language to ground discourse and/or system—an irreducible or unavoidable existential return, should anyone wish to attempt to say anything whatsoever about the unsayable. Conjoining high and low, then, or conjoining the ideal and the real in the manner of David Lang's choral work, *The Little Match Girl Passion* (2007), where the high-theological prospects of the libretto for Johann Sebastian Bach's *St. Matthew Passion* (1727) are imported into Hans Christian Andersen's tragic fable "The Little Match Girl" (1845), to exceptional effect, relies on the now-fashionable penchant for seeking the transcendent in the immanent and vice versa (the paradoxical or paralogical act of "planting lotuses in fire").[3] Such a quest

---

[2] Ludwig Wittgenstein, *Philosophical Investigations*, trans. G.E.M. Anscombe (New York: Macmillan, 1953), first developed in semi-incoherent fashion in the so-called Blue and Brown books (lecture notes from 1933-1935). See Ludwig Wittgenstein, *Preliminary Studies for the "Philosophical Investigations," Generally Known as The Blue and Brown Books* (Oxford: Blackwell, 1958). Derek Jarman's low-budget, 1993 film-portrait of Wittgenstein features the seminars at Cambridge University when Wittgenstein was struggling to elaborate his post-*Tractatus* project to the utter dismay and bewilderment of Bertrand Russell. See Derek Jarman, *Wittgenstein* (1993). See also Ray Monk, *Ludwig Wittgenstein: The Duty of Genius* (New York: Free Press, 1990). Monk defended Jarman's film-portrait of Wittgenstein as haunted and neurotic philosopher of language when orthodox hagiography duly collided with artistic theatricality. Monk claimed that Jarman's *Wittgenstein* was, after all, an accurate portrait.

[3] First published in December 1845 in *Dansk Folkekalender (for 1846)*, "The Little Match Girl" has a long history of being assimilated to other media. The somewhat sentimental or mawkish tone of this disarmingly simple tale suggests that its power lies somewhere outside the simple frame of the narrative. Almost Dickensian in spirit, "The Little Match Girl" contains minefields for the moral imagination. So, too, is the purpose of the fantasia (musical or literary), and of both gothic and decadent literatures. As a possible parable for the

has, since time immemorial, served as foundation stone for fusing the arts and humanistic or philosophical studies, generally. Yet this quest or inquisition also advances meta-historically, in apparent reverse chronology, toward the mysterious origin of the arts and allied humanistic concerns that suggests "a secret concordance" only legible from a perspective that collapses normative time-senses and delivers what Wittgenstein sought (but through purely non-objective, non-utilitarian means), natural philosophy thereby falling back into an uneasy relationship with moral philosophy.

Knowledge, Spirit, Law seeks to re-assess and re-configure the resources available today for new-old forms of high scholarship previously advanced under the auspices of pre-modernist, modernist, and post-modernist avant-gardism, but caught somehow in the still-born auspices of neo-liberal capitalism.[4] Thus the anti-capitalist sublime as antidote, plus the relation of disparate forms of anti-modernism to anti-capitalism.

---

redemptive power of the imagination, the importation of aspects of the libretto from Bach's *St. Matthew Passion* (via St. Matthew, Picander, and H.P. Paull) confers wholly other precepts upon "The Little Match Girl," forcing the audience of the "chorale" to make ethical and moral connections (via ethical and moral revelation) between the otherworldly Passion of Christ and the this-worldly nature of human suffering. In this manner, the power of imagination invokes Revelation, exiting the mere existential register for immemorial metaphysical and meta-historical prospects. Comments based on the performance by the Virginia Chorale (Charles Woodward, Conductor) of Bach's Motets BWV 227, 230, and 244, *St. Matthew Passion*, and Lang's *The Little Match Girl Passion (for Chorus)*, February 8, 2015, Sacred Heart Catholic Church, Norfolk, Virginia, USA.

[4] The premise is that all three forms of modernism belong *to* Modernism proper, and that the great missing term is *anti-modernism*. While syllogistic, this eliding of difference returns arguments to the ground at which they might actually accomplish something—Modernism as subset of Modernity. The latter conclusion pushes spectral aspects of anti-modernism into the picture through the retrospective analytic of countering Modernism's claims to have neutralized historical antecedents through the miracle of its virgin birth.

As such, the critical coordinates for proposed new works of this order of intellection in service to nothing are entirely provisional and futural, at once. In many ways the state of humanistic scholarship in Late Modernity has been undermined by pseudo-objective or pseudo-scientific protocols that are, in fact, productive of a stalemate that neutralizes revolutionary praxis *across* the Arts and Humanities. It is the concord or discord between discursive orders and non-discursive orders that tell the tale most succinctly; while it is the transmigration of the tenets of high scholarship to the arts, and the transference of the subjective states of art to scholarship, that might undermine the biases of so-called scientific research in humanistic studies and endeavors. For these reasons, as well, it is the "voice" in such avant-garde works, past and present, that signals what is at stake *through* such works—arguably, subjective states as they exist in or inform collective states.[5] Collective states, here, are configured as the "socio-cultural" register within collective experience, while the "socio-economic" is demoted due to its prevalence as tableau for endless excuses for no progress whatsoever toward ending the stalemate. Incrementalism under present conditions might, in turn, be dismissed as the precise generative cause for the forms of circularity dissected below, insofar as the rapid expansion of the technological supports for neo-liberal capitalism erase any gain via incrementalism and its bias (biological and Darwinian *determinism*).[6] It is for this reason that Thomas Piketty's recent *Capital*

---

[5] This suggests that the primary target of neo-liberal capitalism is subjectivity itself.

[6] Burkeanism always appears and disappears during times of utter socio-economic or socio-political distress, as does (its opposite) Augustinianism. It might be said that one favors teleology and the other eschatology; or, Burkeanism favors the "long march through institutions" and Augustinianism foresees the relegation of such institutions to the scrap heap of History. See, for example, how Augustinianism informed the debates between Aquinas and Bonaventure regarding Agent Intellect in Gavin Keeney, "Not-I/Thou: Agent Intellect and the

in the Twenty-first Century misses entire swathes of so-called labor and cannot account for the most pernicious forms of theft by Capital.[7] This theft now proceeds via immaterial means, and it is immaterial labor that is the ultimate frontier

Immemorial," in Manuel Gausa et al., eds., *Rebel Matters/Radical Patterns* (Genoa: University of Genoa, 2015), 446–451.

[7] Thomas Piketty, *Capital in the Twenty-first Century*, trans. Arthur Goldhammer (Cambridge: Harvard University Press, 2014). In *political* terms, the present failure of the European Union (EU) pact might be seen as the failure of a *socio-economic* union that is, explicitly, not a *socio-cultural* union. Notably, the socio-economic pact, and the intra-state exploitative practices associated with it, attempt to condition and control socio-*cultural* programs within the EU bureaucracy for, solely, socio-economic gains. Thus the EU project, as neo-liberal putsch, has severed productive relations between the economic and cultural regimes of Europe, all the while, through its Brussels-based ministries, attempting to dictate terms to those who actually produce intellectual and cultural capital—including academia, through, for example, the inducements of Horizon 2020 research grants and the Bologna Accords (circa 2010). Thus the Franciscan "anti-capitalist" concept of the "right to have no rights," but from within a Rule ("form-of-life" as larger project and its collective, radical functions/purposes). See Giorgio Agamben, "Highest Poverty and Use," in Giorgio Agamben, *The Highest Poverty: Monastic Rules and Form-of-Life*, trans. Adam Kotsko (Stanford: Stanford University Press, 2013), 123–143. Agamben credits the interpretation of the Franciscan rule as the renunciation of all rights ("the right to have no rights") to Hugh of Digne's *De finibus paupertatis* (*On the Ends of Poverty*): Hugh of Digne, "*De finibus paupertatis* auctore Hugone de Digna," *Archivium Franciscanum Historicum* 5 (1912): 277–290. For a discussion of the "right to have no rights," see Gavin Keeney, "Montanism: Insurrection and Resurrection," in Gavin Keeney, *Not-I/Thou: The Other Subject of Art and Architecture* (Newcastle upon Tyne: Cambridge Scholars Publishing, 2014), 95–110. Hugh of Digne (d. 1285) was a Provençal Franciscan ascetic. Francis of Assisi died in 1226. A mere 59 to 60 years separates their deaths. The Provençal connection is perhaps telltale, as Francis' early days were spent mimicking the Romantic exploits of Provençal troubadours, and (arguably) it is late-medieval "Langue d'Oc" that, in part, animates Franciscan religiosity.

for Capital, its conquest prefigured in the violation of regimes of thought; that is, regimes of speculative praxis previously, for the most part, beyond the reach of mercantile and industrial capitalism. This new form of conquest, labeled here and there as Cognitive Capitalism, clearly requires an equally powerful response at the very level by which the conquest operates.[8] New-old forms of radical scholarship, then, suggest an agenda that must remain ultra-immaterial yet range fully from "star to furrow."

When did high scholarship become commentaries on commentaries—a "commentariat" resembling contemporary media (and its reduction to talking heads)?[9] Why and when

---

[8] Indeed, there is an immaterial aspect to *all* labor that is not reducible to capital. Arguably, this excess is what is now sought by Capital via immaterial means (spectral exploitation). "If capital ever succeeds in quantifying, and subsequently fully commodifying, labour, as it is constantly trying to, it will also squeeze that indeterminate, recalcitrant human freedom from within labour that allows for the generation of value. Marx's brilliant insight into the essence of capitalist crises was precisely this: the greater capitalism's success in turning labour into a commodity, the less the value of each unit of output it generates, the lower the profit rate and, ultimately, the nearer the next recession of the economy as a system. The portrayal of human freedom as an economic category is unique in Marx, making possible a distinctively dramatic and analytically astute interpretation of capitalism's propensity to snatch recession, even depression, from the jaws of growth": Yanis Varoufakis, "How I Became an Erratic Marxist," *The Guardian*, February 18, 2015, http://www.theguardian.com/news/2015/feb/18/yanis-varoufakis-how-i-became-an-erratic-marxist. Article adapted from a lecture originally delivered at the 6th Subversive Festival in Zagreb, Croatia, in 2013. See http://www.subversivefestival.com/.

[9] The exponential explosion of academic conferences, fees and peer-review games included (plus the preference for conferences as proof of "research"), is one example of the increasingly circular nature of academic discourse. Another is the set of rules now managed from above, from within the hierarchical corporate management schemes of universities, for what constitutes "impact" *for* research. Books no longer matter, whereas co-written papers for conferences and highly

did scholars decide to *not* risk their own subjectivity (always more than mere opinions) in the production of texts—bracketing or burying the revolutionary praxis of the speculative? The circularity of textual criticism and the endlessness of commentary is, indeed, a symptom of some larger, mostly unseen or unacknowledged complex that has permeated late-modernist cultural production, no less and no more subservient to capitalist reification than other forms of information and entertainment. "Garbage in, garbage out" has been converted to "Garbage in, product out." Scientific research is an oxymoron, as a result, in the Arts and Humanities. Its premises are borrowed from disciplines that have no relationship to humanistic exegesis or artistic intent—such borrowings simply mirror the productive élan of the sciences. In fact, the protocols of scientific research destroy humanistic concerns, converting them to data, analysis, and repetition—circularity itself. This circularity gives the lie to professed forms of interdisciplinarity and intertextuality, foremost given that the "borrowing" is rarely the speculative gist of a discipline but, instead, the well-worn apparatus or empty rhetorical gesture (emptied of any dynamic content).

Why is the speculative confined to the arts, or—worse still—to cultural studies (the circularity of endless discourse present there mimicking knowledge production based on citation and interpretation of received wisdom)? How have the arts been isolated and rendered toothless since the inception of Modernism, when revolutionary-critical and productive work was one of the key operative elements of the "architecture" of Modernism (if not Modernity)?

The venues for the dissemination of such radical works have been notably narrowed—cinema remains one, while the much-vaunted situational madness of forms of constantly mutating new media (said to be available to one and all) both allows reflexion and disconnects it from most or all larger

networked journals receive the highest marks, a demand-driven campaign for attention that translates into funding and/or promotion.

socio-cultural projects. Yet a *détourned* new-media project (for example, the EZLN campaign noted in Essay Four within this volume) might use these analogues for speculative thought against the grain—against neo-liberalist anomie and the preservation of post-modernist *différance* as means to atomize consciousness and instill the intended—a society of control.[10]

---

[10] For a concise definition of neo-liberalism, see Benjamin Selwyn, "Neoliberalism is Alive and Well," *Le monde diplomatique*, December 2014, http://mondediplo.com/blogs/neoliberalism-is-alive-and-well: "Neoliberal policies have been implemented from 1973 in Pinochet's Chile, in the UK and US under Thatcher and Reagan in the 1980s and then across increasing swathes of the world. These policies include, privatization, the de-regulation of the financial sector, increasing openness to foreign trade and investment, and cuts to public welfare spending. Supporters of neoliberal policies argue that these will increase economic efficiency as state regulation of the economy is replaced by more accurate 'market signals'. These are held to be better at encouraging and allocating investment, which in turn leads to higher economic growth and greater benefits for the economy and population as a whole." Selwyn adds: "Neoliberal policies aim to reduce wages to the bare minimum and to maximize the returns to capital and management. They also aim to demobilise workers' organisations and reduce workers to carriers of labour power—a commodity to be bought and sold on the market for its lowest price. Neoliberalism is about re-shaping society so that there is no input by workers' organisations into democratic or economic decision-making. Crises and austerity may not be intentionally sought by most state leaders and central bank governors, but they do contribute significantly towards pursuing such ends. Consequently, these politicians and leaders of the economy do not strive to put in place new structures or policies that will reduce the recurrence of crisis." And further, according to Selwyn: "The rising levels of inequality associated with neoliberal policies are often decried by critics as weakening social ties and generating social conflict. But this is exactly what neoliberal policies are designed to do—to break apart social organisations such as trade unions, transform worker's into individuals at the mercy of firms' hiring and firing strategies, and transfer resources from workers to owners and managers of capital. In this regard neoliberalism uses crisis and austerity to great effect."

It is the theft of speculative praxis that is most disturbing —its conversion to information, data, and entertainment wellknown and endlessly noted. Post-Marxist diatribes notwithstanding, reification proceeds in many cases by complicity— that is, out of ignorance or out of rote self-interest. The platforms for the dissemination of such "other works" remain the issue, and the hardware and software available increasingly turned against such works, making the advent of the Digital Humanities within academia particularly frightful for revolutionary socio-cultural action, whether *direct* or *indirect*.[11] The appropriations are stunning, as in, for example, "Malevich to

---

[11] See the link between Direct Action in political terms and Direct Cinema via Chris Marker. Marker adopted the term *Direct Cinema* as an antidote to 1950s' French documentary cinema (roughly equivalent to *cinéma-vérité*) around the time of *Le joli mai*, which is curiously the time of his great pseudo-sci-fi film, *La jetée*: Chris Marker and Pierre Lhomme, *Le joli mai: Mai 1962* (1962). *Le joli mai* concerns the mood of the French electorate near the end of the Algerian War. Marker's commentary (the voice-over) has been criticized for being less than objective—more specifically, for being condescending. Notably, the film was also initially censored. "Michel Delahaye says that the people to whom we are introduced [in *Le joli mai*] are all awful, but that this is because Marker's superior attitude portrays them so that we can only judge them thus": Sarah Cooper, *Chris Marker* (Manchester: Manchester University Press, 2008), 40; with reference, also, to Michel Delahaye, "La chasse à l'I," *Cahiers du cinéma* 146 (August 1963): 5 [5–17]. For a summary of *Le joli mai*, plus *La jetée*'s near simultaneous creation out of the dust of the latter film, see Catherine Lupton, *Chris Marker: Memories of the Future* (London: Reaktion Books, 2005), 78–95. Regarding the controversies surrounding this film, via its non-objective, engaged status, see: Cooper, *Chris Marker*, 38–45; Birgit Kämper and Thomas Tode, eds., *Chris Marker: Filmessayist* (Munich: CICIM, 1997), 241–245; and Karel Reisz and Gavin Millar, "Cinéma-vérité and the Documentary Film of Ideas," in Karel Reisz and Gavin Millar, *The Technique of Film Editing*, 2nd edn. (Oxford: Focal Press, 1968), 297–321 (regarding *Le joli mai*, see 303–317). For an analysis of the overall thematic structure of the film ("principles of selection") and the role of the commentary, see the latter.

the Tate" (noted in Essay One in this volume), etc. Generally, the macabre premise is that avant-garde works are worthless until the artist/author is dead (in cases of posthumous success) and out of the way. Appropriation proceeds, mercilessly, via the death of the work itself or the artist/author—the "death of the work" being its belated assimilation.

The mocking of the "care of the self," primarily on the left due to the political implication (but equally on the right), is utterly spellbinding and malicious, at once. Why denigrate those who choose to step back from circular discourses to investigate the articles of subjective agency in close proximity to an idealist inquest into the shattered project of knowledge of the self (knowledge in/for itself)? Sophie Calle et al. (including Bruce Nauman and Bill Viola) might be said to have precipitated in the contemporary visual arts a return to psycho-social navel-gazing on the one hand, while on the other hand, the more severe aspects of hyper-consciousness go unnoted in commentaries that revert to the art-historical or art-critical versions of circular discourse (via academia) or popular commentary (via the art media).[12] The high-idealist prospects must be preserved, regardless, as they lead to, or open onto, other prospects that are, ineluctably, present in all such operations (as proverbial absence, ghost or unholy hole in things).

---

[12] The term *contemporary* in relation to art criticism is relative to contemporary art's relationship to modernist and post-modernist art. *Contemporary* thus confers the status of "not modern and not post-modern" on the work. The term *super-contemporary* has been invented by the art world to signify "now," or that one must be alive to be contemporary, dismissing anyone dead or passé as pre- or not-super-contemporary.

II. PRE-CONSCIOUS MOODS AND BLIND FATE

The pre-conscious or semi-conscious mood (roughly equivalent to, or consistent with Georg Simmel's concept of *Stimmung*) that crosses a work or set of works as series is what gives a work or set of works the ability to synthesize the episodic aspects of its production, Aristotle's point in the *Poetics* (c. 355 BCE); while the mood also conveys an extreme existential crisis, the work becomes strangely universal in an earth-shattering, ethical and moral (non-moralistic) manner. Such is the reason why the libretto of Bach's *St. Matthew Passion* could be mapped onto the fable, "The Little Match Girl," to profound effect in Lang's *The Little Match Girl Passion (for Chorus)*; and such is why in certain artists—for example, Andrei Tarkovsky—all works become one work. In the latter case the mood is sustained across *all works*. This universalizing trait rooted in existential-metaphysical desire is perhaps musical (or, at the least metrical) in its fundamental disposition, proceeding by way of the states or time-senses provided by "musical" composition—perhaps yet another reason for Arthur Schopenhauer's privileging of music, over and against (as antidote to) blind fate. Eros/Thanatos is the structuralist dyad most often used in criticism to signal, discuss, or justify this dance. Shakespeare's universality, in turn, is traceable to themes that permeate his plays (each one a closed book or circuit, operating as sustained mood and Wittgensteinian language-game unto itself), as if they contain an internal weather, with *Cymbeline*, for example, drawn against the often-stormy skies of Arcadian experience. This "weather" is a half-atmospheric, half-linguistic affair that is sustained as subtending chord coming to full self-consciousness in the most poetical moments of the "operatic" apparatus of the play. From such a mood the theatrical *mise-en-scène* emerges, minimalist or not. Dramatist Peter Brook is superb in this former, minimalist regard. Andrei Tarkovsky's acute attention to *mise-en-scène* in cinema is exemplary in this latter, non-minimalist regard, as is Jean-Luc Godard's recourse to "populating" his film-essays with ciphers and enigmatic gestures drawn from parallel disciplines (literature and music) as a way of providing just such a level of reflexion or revelation to the work. Gestures of this order are decidedly not symbolic. They register, instead, an irreality that underwrites reality. *Mise-en-abyme*, in turn, is the inversion of this substantiation of self-consciousness for the work, most often utilized to invert the self-same premises, yet to also signal their absence or presence, anyway, through negation (direct or indirect). Thus we have occurrences and recurrences of anti-aesthetic and neo-iconoclastic movements in art and art criticism, most often during times of crisis. So-called scientific scholarship, on the other hand, versus artistic scholarship, obliterates both *mise-en-scène* and *mise-en-abyme* as formal options for the language-games deployed in the production of knowledge—opting for the clear light (or clear weather) of "pseudo-objectivity." The sunny disposition of natural or analytical philosophy applied to scholarship hides or elides all of the above. It is only in the very origin of this split between natural philosophy and moral philosophy, such as represented in the life-works of Giordano Bruno or Gottfried Wilhelm von Leibniz, that we find both the sunny and stormy disposition played against each other to significant artistic and proto-scientific effect, and arguably this is what resurfaces in the Surrealist excurses of Gaston Bachelard, yet under the rubric of "Surrationalism"—"Surrationalism" surely the same complex that animated Romanticism, the halfway house for malcontents between Neo-classicism and Modernism.

All works of such a caliber are, therefore, *lived*—through sustaining a mood for the duration of the work (through full immersion). The pre-conscious meditation that sustains the work is, then, transferred *to* the work and lives on *in* the work. For these reasons, and in exemplary fashion, art criticism has conferred upon Caravaggio's late paintings a status that approaches an "operatic" structure or whole, conferring upon innumerable paintings a singular mood (shadow of the Kingdom) that resembles what crosses all of the films of Tarkov-

INTRODUCTION :: RADICAL SCHOLARSHIP | 13

sky—that is, recourse to a type of Rule (form-of-life) that might justify one work, several works, or all works by an artist-scholar.[13] Caravaggio's late works share the common theme of the existential threat he lived through and died for via those last paintings—in other words, his always impending arrest, and his flight to Malta and then Sicily. The Rule for the work of art or scholarship, indeed, resembles monastic rules, and the existential plight most often incorporated into such rules is the great subtending chord of the sustained meditation that produces works of this order.[14] So too could Cara-

---

[13] Chris Marker's cinematic portrait of Tarkovsky, *Une journée d'Andrei Arsenevitch* (1999), claims just such a set of dynamic principles for his films by conferring upon them an elemental structure—the appearance and re-appearance of Earth, Air, Fire, and Water.

[14] The Rule sustains the subtending mood of monastic orders. This would, in part, explain the schism between the Conventuals and the Spirituals in the Franciscan Order, a break that occurred just after Francis' death, but a break that was already prefigured in early skirmishes *before* his death. The foremost cause of the schism was the relationship of the order to Holy Poverty, to its preservation through lived experience, versus interpretation and elaboration—that is, the preservation of lived observation for and toward the exceptional Franciscan "right to have no rights." The same might be said for the Early Christians, perhaps justifying the burial of the Gnostic texts in the sands of North Africa as their persecution proceeded from Rome. The absence of a Rule (or, forms-of-life) in the production of works of art (with Lars von Trier's *Dogme 95* manifesto being an extreme example of a Rule *for* cinema) justifies the arch-critical operations of art and textual criticism, while supporting the attendant thematic that artistic and literary works are either episodic or fully synthetic works with a form of self-consciousness that confers upon them qualities of subjectivity or subjective agency—a surplus value that is nonetheless often at odds with the artist-scholar, and most assuredly outliving the artist-scholar. Alain Badiou's statements regarding fidelity to the Event for poets (the event or premonitional aspects of Art, Revolution, and Love) are consistent with this presentiment for the expressive regimes of high art and high scholarship as forms of Being (forms of life) addressed to an "as yet to come" (with Becoming as prefiguration of the inherent multiplicity of an excessive universality

vaggio's last paintings in many instances be called "self-portraits," foremost the very late painting of Francis of Assisi meditating upon a crucifix (the crucifix resting on an open book, and the open book resting on a skull), the gloomy weather of its prevailing mood the exact something else that crosses all of the late paintings.[15]

---

proper to experience itself). The mood, therefore, is the Rule, and the Rule is held in relation to the originary mood by way of dialectical sublimation.

[15] Caravaggio, *St. Francis in Meditation* (c. 1604/06 or c. 1607/10). Caravaggio died in 1610. Regarding Caravaggio's late paintings, see Gavin Keeney, "Nightfall," in Gavin Keeney, *Art as "Night": An Art-theological Treatise* (Newcastle upon Tyne: Cambridge Scholars Publishing, 2010), 3–19. Art historian Roberto Longhi is generally credited with reviving interest in these existential aspects of Caravaggio's late output. Pier Paolo Pasolini appropriately dedicated the screenplay of *Mamma Roma* (1962) to Longhi. The dedication reads: "A Roberto Longhi cui sono debitore della mia 'fulgurazione figurativa'": Pier Paolo Pasolini, *Mamma Roma* (Milan: Rizzoli, 1962), 8.

III. GUIDEBOOKS AS SCHOLARSHIP

> The Universe: His wine cellar; / The atom's heart: His measuring cup. / Intellect is drunk, earth drunk, sky drunk / Heaven perplexed with Him, restlessly seeking, / Love in His heart, hoping at least / for a single whiff of the fragments / of that wine, that clear wine the angels drank / from that immaterial pot, a sip of the dregs, / the rest poured out upon the dust: / one sip, and the Elements whirl in drunken dance / falling now into water, now in blazing fire. / And from that smell of that spilled cup / man rises from the dust and soars to heaven.[16]
>
> Sussan Deyhim/Sa'd Ud Din Mahmūd Shabistarī

How to chart a way out of this claustrophobic mess other than to destroy authorized forms of speculative praxis—"authorized speculative praxis" serving as a faux-glorious oxymoron from which to proceed. Pop scholarship is clearly not an an-

---

[16] Sussan Deyhim, "The Spilled Cup," in Bill Laswell, *Hashisheen: The End of Law*, Audio CD (Brussels: Sub Rosa, 1999). The lyrics for the song are based on Sa'd Ud Din Mahmūd Shabistarī (1288-1340 CE), "The Wine of Rapture," *Gulshan i Rāz* (*The Secret Rose Garden*). *Gulshan i Rāz* reached Europe in 1700 via unidentified travelers and was translated into German c. 1825 and English in 1880. See Sa'd Ud Din Mahmūd Shabistarī, *The Secret Rose Garden*, trans. Florence Lederer (London: J. Murray, 1920), 12. "The whole world is his tavern, / His wine-cup the heart of each atom, / Reason is drunken, angels drunken, soul drunken, / Air drunken, earth drunken, heaven drunken. // The sky, dizzy from the wine-fumes' aroma, / Is staggering to and fro; / The angels, sipping pure wine from goblets, / Pour down the dregs on the world; / From the scent of these dregs man rises to heaven. / Inebriated from the draught, the elements / Fall into water and fire. / Catching the reflection, the frail body becomes a soul, / And the frozen soul by its heat / Thaws and becomes living. / The creature world remains giddy, / For ever straying from house and home" (*The Secret Rose Garden*, 56). Deyhim (presumably the author for this version or transcription of the Sufi poem) has interpolated the middle passage: "Heaven perplexed with Him, restlessly seeking, / Love in His heart, hoping at least / for a single whiff of the fragments."

swer, nor is open-source publishing, which is a form of "authorized speculative praxis," albeit a slightly shady one given that it is formulated as "outside" authorized or predatory neo-liberal academic practices but quietly moves "inside," insomuch as practitioners are generally utilizing the suspect schematics of Open Source from within the academy, pretending to be outsiders, giving their work away with both aplomb and disdain (practiced and feigned disdain) for Intellectual Property Rights and the Moral Rights of Authors.[17]

[17] In academic terms, Open Source started as an institutional alternative to corporate piracy within academic circles, a well-intentioned attempt to circumvent the ownership of platforms (journals and networks) by for-profit interests. Corporate media, in attempting to control distribution, momentarily was confronted by the fact that research is often publicly funded. The universities lost this campaign due to either internal malfeasance by corporate interests that had already situated themselves in the burgeoning bureaucracies of academia or through naiveté, the model being flawed from the beginning due to the very Balkanization of academic regimes—geographically and institutionally. Yet Open Source devolved quickly, after the institutional failure of the model, to become a badge of courage for dissenting academics. As alternative "pre- or part-publication" strategy, Open Source has its merits—that is, to promote a larger *withheld* or "perpetually curated" project. Additionally, the game of losing all control doubled for institutions with the arrival of the Cloud, and Cloud-based instruction and dissemination of work. The Cloud is part of that great apparition called the Digital Humanities. Its arrival marks the last hurrah (with caveats) for independent, non-scalable intellectual work inside of academia. Advocates of the Digital Humanities resemble advocates for late 1990s', early 2000s' post-theory, and the pseudo-avantgarde pretenses are telling. In the case of post-theory and projective practice in architecture, for example, with post-theory arriving late to the discipline (as architecture has a penchant for belated assimilation of de-natured and/or borrowed discourses), the short-lived justifications nonetheless shattered the larger pretenses of architecture as a critical or radical discipline, casting it adrift as hapless operative criticism (Manfredo Tafuri's nemesis). The emergence of post-theory across disciplines is generally attributed to arguments purloined and misread in Terry Eagleton's anti-postmodern jeremiad, *After Theory* (New York: Basic Books, 2003).

There are no clear options to advance the demolition project of circular discourses other than to bring artistic-creative speculation inside of scholarship and, concurrently, to transplant high-discursive practices to the arts, with (hopefully) the two timeless and useless projects meeting in the middle in the timely and useful socio-cultural circumstances specific to, or "native to," socio-economic concerns, thus situating the radical agenda of speculation in service to no singular this-worldly master, plus prefiguring redemption for such works through the absolutely irreducible relationship to subjective states given to the same.

If 100 percent of the world's population spends roughly 33 percent of its time sleeping (not all at the same time, alas), what proportion is spent dreaming? And is dreaming to be reduced to unconscious activity of the brain while asleep, or does it include reverie and, more critically, Revelation?[18] The

See the review by Abdelkader Aoudjit in *Philosophy Now* 55 (May/June 2006): https://philosophynow.org/issues/55/After_Theory_by_Terry_Eagleton. "'Cultural theory,' Eagleton explains, 'has been shamefaced about morality and metaphysics, embarrassed about love, biology, religion and revolution, largely silent about evil, reticent about death and suffering, dogmatic about essences, universals and foundations, and superficial about truth, objectivity and disinterestedness'" (quoted in Aoudjit). Both post-theory and the Digital Humanities, for scholars and humanists, represent a peculiar disembodied form of the Stockholm Syndrome, a hovering spectral nothingness, with the progenitors and apologists for both effectively caught in a carefully crafted wax-works perpetrated by the neo-liberal capitalist putsch. The captive subjects thereby extol the virtues of being held captive in a semi-fictional and macabre world of pseudo-scholarship and patronage (servitude), reversing centuries of escaping such systems of patronage.

[18] One of the more absurd premises of Luc Besson's blood-splattered film *Lucy* (2014) is that humans do not use the majority of their nerve and cerebral resources. Yet how do we know that we do not? Is it not possible that in *sleep* or in reverie (and most certainly in Revelation) we do access such fearful, non-rational capabilities? Might they be transferred to scholarly praxis?

concordances, often invisible, between rationality and irrationality (a false dichotomy anyway) "live" at the nexus of waking and sleeping—in dreaming of or about worlds that do not quite exist. This is escapism, on the one hand, and the utopian project itself, on the other hand. The nexus is the discredited speculative register in systems of knowledge—systems always rooted, one way or another, in dreaming (absence, not-here, over-there, etc.). Reverie and Revelation are forms of time-traveling, and they are productive of guidebooks. Such guidebooks do exist (and have existed), as they are once again called for by the deplorable state of insurrectionary practice in the humanistic discourses of late-modern times. Indeed, "travel" is called for—that is to say, out of this world and toward another. Is scholarship not sometimes a form of lucid dreaming, a faux-objective system for divining pre-conscious or unconscious forces at play in determinist and often noir-ish systems (inclusive of objective scholarship)?[19] Is not radical scholarship similar to the pseudo-science of mundane astrology (the non-determinist kind), which claims to map inscrutable cosmic forces in favor of the individual psyche? And, is this not why radical scholarship annoys empiricists and is reducible for all such epigones of rationality as the functional equivalent of wet dreams, bed-wetting, navel-gazing, and rote narcissism?[20]

Drugs, alcohol, and extreme-existential states (lives) are

---

[19] If yes, this would seem to consecrate Pierre Bourdieu's methodologies for unearthing (making conscious) unconscious mechanisms in socio-cultural production and Wilhelm Dilthey's claims that History itself has an unconscious....

[20] Subsumable under the French term *nombrilisme*, so-called narcissism in scholarship is generally equated with "self-centeredness" versus philosophical self-reflexion. The latter, however, is the foundation for ethics and morality, with extreme forms actually de-centering the subject and inducing what Tristan Tzara and Paul Éluard sought through the poetic states "transindividuelle" and "dé-singularisante," which are, indeed, subject to the subjective state of the poetic subject. See Anne Régent-Susini, *Paul Éluard: Capitale de la douleur* (Rosny: Bréal, 2000).

the foremost "way out" for classic bohemian cultures, past and present. The dream states induced confer upon reality a sense of irreality (commend irreality to so-called reality), and the frightful circumstances of such lives (as lived experience but also retrospective problematic) are often conducive to tragedy, yet on occasion also lead to revelation of an order that approaches religious sublimity.[21] "Chasing the dragon" becomes a path toward dreaming (reverie), against the dictates and protocols of Reason.[22] The escape from circularity, claustrophobia, and paralysis in the Arts and Humanities is no less daunting. Why the avant-garde discourses of past and present need the firepower of unrelated disciplines returns all arguments for and against the avant-garde project to the existential-metaphysical here-and-now with a large or small dose of the here-and-there thrown in as de-stabilizing, homeopathic admixture. For the Arts and Humanities, as singular concern, requires extreme existential-metaphysical states as much as the bohemians required (and still require) the same to escape bourgeois conformity (the *bête noire* for both the decadent and Marxist avant-garde) and intellectual convention, in order to exit imposed variants of Realism (via hedonist decadence or via radical refusal of socio-political orthodoxy).[23]

---

[21] See the life of Francis of Assisi, after the event of the Stigmata. Notably, these grim episodes in the life of the saint have never been dealt with in cinema, both Roberto Rossellini's and Franco Zeffirelli's treatments featuring the early days of Francis. More critically, they have been dealt with, explicitly, within the "cinematic" novel of Nikos Kazantzakis, *God's Pauper: St. Francis of Assisi*, trans. P.A. Bien (London: Faber & Faber, 1975). First published (serialized) in the newspaper, *Eleftheria*, 1954, and, in book form, *Ο φτωχούλης του Θεού* (Athens: Difros, 1955). See Roberto Rossellini, *Francesco, giullare di Dio* (1950), and Franco Zeffirelli, *Fratello Sole, Sorella Luna* (1972). *Francesco, giullare di Dio* was co-written by Federico Fellini.

[22] See Alan Moore's graphic novel (with Eddie Campbell), *From Hell* (London: Knockabout Comics, 1999), first published in serialized form between 1989 and 1996.

[23] For a brief discussion of the Dadaist and Surrealist insurrections in

Where are the guidebooks, past and present? Where are the literary-critical equivalents of Henry David Thoreau's walks, Johann Gottfried Herder's walks? Or Chris Marker's *Petite Planète* series of travel guides? Milton Grundy's provocative and cranky, obsessively revised "anthology guide" to Venice, with its brilliantly imposed and purloined selections from past guides—Ruskin et al.?[24] Such works (texts as sojourns) attack convention from within and without, simultaneously. They sit uneasily in the textual continuum; they fall off of bookshelves and open their pages to passersby as if haunted from within by a language that refuses to be silenced—a language that seeks the outside world (and its putative origin). If America's libraries were full of tears in 1956, it was Allen Ginsberg's "apperception" of other causes hidden in the broken promise of America that allowed him to condemn 1950s' America in such a way, when he was down to "two dollars and twenty-seven cents," invoking Walt Whitman, yes, but also invoking what the Beats later fomented (the 1960s' cultural revolution originating in Beat alienation). In this manner, all books of speculative-radical agency are guidebooks for a mood that is pre-conscious in origin but fused to the formal apparatus of the work. Arguably, the mood of endless commentaries is either contrition or capitulation. Is there a commentary that demolishes this overriding pessimism? Can the commentary comment upon itself (and, perhaps, escape its own deathly closure)?

The verb tenses and time-senses of religious works come close. The syntactical and semantic resources of such often conflict, and the discord is a distended or warped rapport

---

relationship to the nineteenth-century French decadents (in the context of artists and scholars being, on occasion, "failed saints," and saints as being, on occasion, "failed artists and scholars"), see Gavin Keeney, "Critical Introduction: Nervous Systems," in Keeney, *Not-I/Thou*, 1–14.

[24] Milton Grundy, *Venice: The Anthology Guide*, 6th edn. (London: Gilles de la Mare, 2007), first published by Anthony Blond in 1971, with successive editions in 1976, 1980, 1985, and 1998.

with tradition and convention (received wisdom) and an inborn and in-borne rapprochement with Revelation (all nominal times speaking, simultaneously, of one time). From such models (guidebooks nonetheless) the commentary and its analogues trip over their own contentions to servitude (serving commentary). What then of present-day works serving Capital and its invasion of academia? Might such works examine its (Capital's) diktat to produce marketable, or merchandisable wares—popular and erudite, patentable or scalable (given to conversion to data and, thereby, theft)?[25] It would appear the answer is "No." So, what has changed, other than the increasingly extreme and grotesquely irrational measures of Capital, imposed under the imprint of a self-righteous religiosity of its own contrivance, toward dictating all terms for commentary, elaboration, and dissemination of knowledge?

Revolts in scholasticism often proceed by invoking forms of Gnosticism. Indeed, the demiurge today, for academia, is Capital in concert with its twin handmaidens, "metrics" and "data-mining."[26] Deconstruction, for example, and its genera-

---

[25] For those obsessed with data and quantifying such charges, the only way to show that this is true is to open the books of academia—that is, to audit them. Of course, such books are *closed books*, even to the faculties and most of the managerial class of present-day academia. That public universities are increasingly riven by such practices is also a sign that the traditional firewalls between publicly funded research institutions and the machinations of neo-liberal capitalism (historically porous in many cases anyway due to government funding for research) are utterly breached. Only provosts and chancellors are privy to this data, and they are either under confidentiality agreements, unable to speak of such things, or moving in ever-more-rarified circles that benefit the CEOs of universities (recent salary scandals being Exhibit A). It would take a Thomas Piketty to unravel the statistical knot that rules such caprices, while the effects of the same may nonetheless be felt from faculties down to the level of lowly postgraduate students.

[26] In terms of socio-economic systems and models (inclusive of Marxism) and the errors implicit in reducing anything whatsoever to a demonic clockworks, see Varoufakis, "How I became an Erratic Marx-

tive ghosts, was (in its Derridean configuration at the least) a direct outcome of and response to the ruling demiurge in intellectual affairs of mid-to-late, twentieth-century High Structuralism. In all such cases, without question, Gnosticism returns any discipline whatsoever to subjective states voided or suppressed by artificial conventions, arbitrary authority, and misread traditions.[27] The new arrives by way of the old,

---

ist": "Marx's first error—the error of omission was that he failed to give sufficient thought to the impact of his own theorising on the world that he was theorising about. His theory is discursively exceptionally powerful, and Marx had a sense of its power. So how come he showed no concern that his disciples, people with a better grasp of these powerful ideas than the average worker, might use the power bestowed upon them, via Marx's own ideas, in order to abuse other comrades, to build their own power base, to gain positions of influence?" Varoufakis writes further, "Marx's second error, the one I ascribe to commission, was worse. It was his assumption that truth about capitalism could be discovered in the mathematics of his models. This was the worst disservice he could have delivered to his own theoretical system. The man who equipped us with human freedom as a first-order economic concept; the scholar who elevated radical indeterminacy to its rightful place within political economics; he was the same person who ended up toying around with simplistic algebraic models, in which labour units were, naturally, fully quantified, hoping against hope to evince from these equations some additional insights about capitalism. After his death, Marxist economists wasted long careers indulging a similar type of scholastic mechanism. Fully immersed in irrelevant debates on 'the transformation problem' and what to do about it, they eventually became an almost extinct species, as the neoliberal juggernaut crushed all dissent in its path."

[27] Pre-conscious states and the Immemorial are not synonymous in Gnosticism; the former, instead, might be said to lead to the latter. "Life's anteriority to every living (and similarly, the First Self's anteriority to any particular self) corresponds to the most radical forgetting. Forgetting here no longer bears on what one is without knowing it, but rather on what happened before one existed—on the system of autarchic enjoyment constituted by the reciprocal interiority of Father and Son, when there is not yet any me nor any ego such as our own. In the absolute already of Life's autarchic enjoyment lies the Immemorial, the Arch-Ancience that eludes any thought—the always al-

plus—"plus" being what moves toward the present, or the futural, the latter's station unknown but sensed (not unlike a planet orbiting beyond naked or instrumentalized perception, yet part of a system nonetheless). It is all a matter, then, of Odysseus and Ithaca, of Penelope and suitors, of arrival and dissemblance, of night and day. Dreams and the Real conjoin. Scholarship accesses both—night and day, dreams and the Real. All we can ask of it, today, is that it not be complicit in the production and preservation of perpetual nightmares.

February 18, 2015

---

ready forgotten, that which lies in Arch-Forgetting": Michel Henry, *I Am the Truth: Toward a Philosophy of Christianity*, trans. Susan Emanuel (Stanford: Stanford University Press, 2003), 151. An excellent example of the importation of Gnosticism to literary-critical exegesis may be found in the work of Harold Bloom, foremost in his works regarding Romanticism. Regarding the shift from New Criticism to New Historicism, with both Harold Bloom's *Anxiety of Influence: A Theory of Poetry* (Oxford: Oxford University Press, 1973) and Stanley Fish's *Is There a Text in This Class? The Authority of Interpretive Communities* (Cambridge: Harvard University Press, 1980) playing pivotal roles, see Jeffrey J. Williams, "Prodigal Critics," *The Chronicle Review*, December 6, 2009, http://chronicle.com/article/Prodigal-Critics/49307/. Williams tracks the ascendance of the "verbal icon" (New Criticism) through to its being turned inside-out and upside-down and backwards by the anti-objectivist assault (New Historicism) leveled by figures formerly schooled in its very practice—that is, Bloom, Fish, and Stephen Greenblatt. Nikos Kazantzakis paints a macabre portrait of extreme religious states vis-à-vis Gnosticism by way of a visit to a sinister monastery within the Greek Orthodox monasteries of Mount Athos in *Report to Greco*, trans. P.A. Bien (New York: Simon and Schuster, 1965); first published as *Αναφορά στον Γκρέκο* (Athens: Ekdoseis Kōnstantinidē, 1961). Kazantzakis represents an extraordinary example of the tenets of high scholarship transferred to novelistic and memoir form. The sublation occurs by way of the intensely transpersonal voice of the novels and memoirs.

ESSAY ONE

Re-universalizing Knowledge

Said Siddhartha, "There is one thing in particular, O Most Venerable One, that I have admired in your teachings. Everything in your doctrine is utterly clear, is proven; you show the world as a perfect chain, a chain never and nowhere interrupted, an eternal chain forged of causes and effects. Never has this been so clearly beheld, never so irrefutably presented. In truth, it must make the heart of any Brahmin beat faster when, through your teachings, he is able to glimpse the world as a perfect continuum, free of gaps, clear as a crystal, not dependent on gods. Whether this world be good or evil, and life in it sorrow or joy—let us set this question aside, for it is quite possibly not essential. But the oneness of the world, the continuum of all occurrences, the enfolding of all things great and small within a single stream, a single law of causes, of becoming and of death, this shines brightly forth from your sublime doctrine, O Perfect One. But now, according to your very same doctrine, this oneness and logical consistency of all things is nevertheless interrupted at one point; there is a tiny hole through which something strange is flowing into this world of oneness, something new, something that wasn't there before and that cannot be shown and cannot be proven: This is your doctrine of the overcoming of the world, of redemption. With this tiny hole, this tiny gap, the entire eternal unified law of the world is smashed to pieces, rendered invalid. May you forgive me for giving voice to this objection."[1]

Hermann Hesse

I. HIGH SCHOLARSHIP

The problem with names is that, deeply embedded in history, after a certain time and at different rates of speed they begin to show their age. Some systems are canonized and as it were mummified, others begin to rot and stink of an intolerable past, still others give off the musty smell of archives and long-shuttered houses. There then gradually arises a new kind of philosophical ambition, not merely to invent a foolproof new system of correct names, but also somehow to elude the ravages of temporality and to invent remedies to ward off the inevitable historical reification of these historical linguistic systems (the word "reification" is of course itself just another such historical name). The prestidigitation of an operation that might be called name and variations is only one attempt to move so fast as to elude the fatal process; another is the Magritte formula ("ceci n'est pas une pipe") in which, marked as names from the outset, the formula in question is already as it were homeopathically secured against some later denunciation. But of course all such operations are themselves the signals of their own historicity, and condemned, like past fashions, to go into the past without the kind of immortality they desperately sought.[2]

Fredric Jameson

---

[1] Hermann Hesse, *Siddhartha: An Indian Poem*, trans. Susan Bernofsky (1922; repr. New York: Modern Library, 2006), 29.

[2] Fredric Jameson, *The Hegel Variations: On the Phenomenology of Spirit* (London: Verso, 2010), 25–26. "One may argue that in the case of Hegel—as with Beethoven himself—while historicity cannot but be present, there remains a certain distance between the theme or the name and the musical or philosophical operation in such a way that they can be rewritten in the present with a certain effective afterlife, even though they cannot but remain dead. It would be tempting to call this distance the dialectic, were not this last a historical name like everything else, with its own museum waiting for it" (Jameson, *The Hegel Variations*, 26).

In an interview with Jean-Luc Godard regarding his 2014 Cannes-award-winning film, *Adieu au langage*, and regarding the principles operating within the low-tech, 3D production values, there is an oblique discussion of universalist traits of both language and film (film *as* language), traits that have fallen on hard times, if they ever existed at all.[3] This discord between pretensions and actual circumstance suggests that attempts to sublate difference through historicizing measures and methods fall afoul of some irreducible flaw in systems of knowledge *as* forms of expression.[4] Any campaign to sublate all in the one—an idealist venture—in turn invokes all of the problems of ideology and its processes of circular and endless reification. For these reasons Godard asks how high fidelity is not accompanied by its matching term *low fidelity*— or how high-definition cameras are superior to whatever it is they are higher than.

In this manner of speaking it is also possible to establish a datum for discussing scholarship per se, both high and low, and its somewhat parallel construct, high and low culture— asking, then, after the vanishing forms of scholarship that resemble or self-consciously replicate scholasticism, in all of its many forms. For Godard, as filmmaker versus critic, cinema and language share a crisis—perhaps because cinema emerged at the historical moment when older forms of pictorial expression were undergoing a relativization that centered on renascent idealist traits transferred from philosophical inquiry to artistic inquiry. For example, "Monet painting what he did not see," or the reinterpretation of Velázquez as paint-

---

[3] *Adieu au langage* (Wild Bunch, 2014). Directed, written, and edited by Jean-Luc Godard. Camera (color, 3D), Fabrice Aragno; costume designer, Aude Grivas; assistant director, Jean-Paul Battaggia. For the video interview, see Jean-Luc Godard, Sarah Salovaara, *Filmmaker Magazine*, June 13, 2014, http://filmmakermagazine.com/86351-watch-45-minutes-of-jean-luc-godard-on-goodbye-to-language/#.UelmaPQqM0.

[4] For example, experiential-existentialist modalities where abstraction is derived from lived experience and reverts to the same.

ing the spaces between subjects (something Godard says is common to his own later films).[5]

Adieu au langage carries within it the visual double and triple entendres of Godard's contrarian play with language, both at the linguistic level and at the visual or pictorial level—a poetical dissimulation.[6] His belated high regard for Markerian primitive cinematic values (disintegrating imagery, etc.) is consequently shot through with a melancholy streak that invokes high-Romantic compensation (compensatory rites) that valorize the highest standards through the hoariest and least likely means—a combination of low-tech effects and general opacity, a circularity of reference and citation (Descartes, Levinas et al.), and a passion for detail and nuance (dog, stick, and wave), which all resembles a peculiar (truculent) form of cinematic scholarship only apparently thrown together (a common accusation), and only sardonically resembling the mash-up that he valorizes in his usual trenchant remarks about the death of cinema.[7]

---

[5] The relativization in Modernism proceeds via immanence. For example, see art criticism from John Ruskin to Roger Fry....

[6] Godard states that his father requested that the words "On the contrary" be carved on his own gravestone.

[7] "Markerian" refers to the strident protocols of the films and multimedia installations of Chris Marker, a figure often operating in close proximity to Godard while each ignored and/or provoked the other on and off the screen. For comments on Romantic compensation in musical forms, with reference to timeliness or untimeliness, see Jeremy Denk, "Immortal Beloved," a review of Jan Swafford, *Beethoven: Anguish and Triumph* (New York: Houghton Mifflin Harcourt, 2014), *The New York Times*, July 31, 2014, http://www.nytimes.com/2014/08/03/books/review/beethoven-by-jan-swafford.html. "The pianist Leon Fleisher observed that Schubert's consolations always come too late; his beautiful moments have the sense of happening in the past. Generally, Romantic consolations tend to be poisoned by nostalgia and regret. By the modern era, consolation is mostly off the table. But Beethoven's consolations seem to be in the now. They are always on time—maybe not for him, but for us" (Denk). Or, Beethoven's consolations somehow access that time within time known to Early Christian mystics as "the endless ages of ageless ages"—a

phrase embedded in the poetic conceits of present-day Christian liturgy, yet of an apparent a-historical provenance: Second-century Papyrus of Berlin, cited in John A. McGuckin, *Prayer Book of the Early Christians* (Brewster: Paraclete Press, 2011), 174. The Immemorial: "This old, old day of our earth is born again and again every morning. It comes back to the original refrain of its music. If its march were the march of an infinite straight line, if it had not the awful pause of its plunge in the abysmal darkness and its repeated rebirth in the life of the endless beginning, then it would gradually soil and bury truth with its dust and spread ceaseless aching over the earth under its heavy tread. Then every moment would leave its load of weariness behind, and decrepitude would reign supreme on its throne of eternal dirt" (Rabindranath Tagore, *Sādhanā: The Realisation of Life* [London: Macmillan and Co., 1913], 88; from "Part IV: The Problem of the Self," 67–91). And: "Our self has ceaselessly to cast off its age, repeatedly shed its limits in oblivion and death, in order to realise its immortal youth. Its personality must merge in the universal time after time, *in fact pass through it every moment*, ever to refresh its individual life" (Tagore, *Sādhanā*, 87; emphasis added). The paradox is self-evident: Diachronic time must be "eternally" negated by a more primordial, originary time (yet a time that operates in the past and futural tense, at once—noting, in passing, the present, and thereby ennobling life itself). This other (endless, though not circular) sense of temporality and the eternal is, perhaps, the phenomenological essence of Henry David Thoreau's statement that "the Sun is also a morning star," a figure of speech that closes *Walden* (1854). Tagore underscores the "existential" value of these statements in the "Author's Preface" (*Sādhanā*, vii–ix): "To me the verses of the Upanishads and the teachings of the Buddha have ever been things of the spirit, and therefore endowed with boundless vital growth; and I have used them, both in my life and in my preaching, as being instinct with individual meaning for me, as for others, and awaiting for their confirmation, my own special testimony, which must have its value because of its individuality" (viii). Needless to say, the Upanishads are present in homeopathic dilution in both Hegel and Thoreau, though more finely hidden in Hegel than in Thoreau. Arguably, the Eastern Christian world preserved anti-rationalist traditions that were obscured in subsequent developments in the West, foremost in the disputatious tracts of Medieval Scholasticism. See John Anthony McGuckin, *The Book of Mystical Chapters: Meditations on the Soul's Ascent from the Desert Fathers and Other Early Christian*

Under the auspices of such a playful soul (yet one capable of aesthetic brutality) there is a very clear shift in register that portends a return, however deferred or however long deconstructed, to a paradigmatic, associative logic of signifiers—the structuralist élan of cinema or high-discursive operations coming in and out of focus. Such a rebirth (renaissance), while present in Mannian homeopathic form in most works by masters of various disciplines, is in many respects the hallmark of High Scholasticism in its historical sense, while so-called low culture and its analogues are the norm, or the everyday antidote to any call to mastery of the mysteries of Fine Art proper.[8]

Godard's intellectual trickery (his *habitual contrariness*) masks something that has been active in cultural-secular affairs that is actually metaphysical or "mystical"—mystical in the sense of proto-religious, versus the self-hypnosis of the rapt subject facing the abyss of anti-knowledge and finding in the same an echo that matches the emptiness inside his or her own head.[9] The cultural-secular abyss is, on the other hand, the exact referent for Godard's repeated farewells to cinema (now masquerading as a farewell to language, and always a *fare thee well* that is a secret *aubade*—in the sense of T.S. Eliot's "Fare forward, travellers!").[10] The mystical in

---

Contemplatives (Boston: Shambhala, 2002). The texts of this latter book are primarily drawn from an eighteenth-century, multivolume collection prepared by the monks of Mount Athos entitled *Philokalia* (first published in Greek, in Venice, in 1782).

[8] Jameson claims the homeopathic as a means of forestalling criticism, of preemptively *détourning* critics before they even arrive on the scene.

[9] Godard often veers very close to this existentialist stalemate and then swerves elsewhere. The recourse to a light bulb swinging in preternatural darkness in *Notre musique* (2004) is such an example.

[10] Indeed, Godard carefully parses the French-Swiss meaning of "adieu" by stating that the expression has an entirely different meaning in the morning than it does in the evening. Or, it can mean both hello and goodbye, though never simultaneously other than as provocation (the entire point in the case of *Adieu au langage*). See T.S. Eliot, "The Dry Salvages" (1941).

language may be said to animate film, as if the images would otherwise remain mute. Yet this mystical strain (and tension) in language is a peculiar heritage that bridges discursive and non-discursive regimes of/for thought itself—an axiom awaiting its elucidation, perhaps, or an axiom awaiting its annulment in the vaporous (ghostly) region of the paradigmatic.

Images rise like a full Moon at perigee, colossal at first and then settling in to cross the night-sky as temporal apparition of the same—echo again, but iteration and filmic sequence nonetheless. Any goodbye to language is, then, always the secret *aubade* Godard implies. High culture, though much pilloried, quietly raises the question of the re-universalization of knowledge, though, as Fredric Jameson points out in *The Hegel Variations*, each and every form, or each and every historical iteration, anticipates its own tomb.[11]

---

[11] Jameson, *The Hegel Variations*, 26.

II. SPIRIT AND LAW

> The sublime speaks to a few of another unity, much less complete, ruined in a sense, and more "noble."[12]
>
> Jean-François Lyotard

Neo-liberal capitalism's claims on the production of knowledge (books, texts, music, cinema, new media, etc.), and its conversion of such to information, is the first sign that the endgame of nihilism has arrived. With ideology's mythic center exposed as hollow (Friedrich Nietzsche, Jacques Lacan, Slavoj Žižek et al.), the game has, slowly at first (and then exponentially racing forward), shifted to securing the very founts of cultural capital, no longer awaiting the output. The now well-documented assault on academia by neo-liberal capitalism also suggests that the game has become extraordinarily malevolent, as the paradigmatic was always the stratum at which ideology enforced its will (as hegemony) and its protocols were always the production of serfs in service to that willfulness. Books are, therefore, and always have been, targets for the projection of canon (and canon law), while conversely, they have always been the choice venue for portraying what is not seen, or a proto-utopian venture (and/or a proto-dystopian adventure). To convert books to "research," and to convert research to information (data), is to reclaim any possible return to the paradigmatic *in advance*—to forestall, in other words, any and all universalist claims for knowledge. This nihilist remainder is the signature event or moment in the final push to conquer (imprison) Spirit (knowledge and not-knowledge as one thing). Mediatic production incites the obsessive, metrics-driven conversion of intellectual capital to marketable debris, *en masse*—the new dark heresy

---

[12] Jean-François Lyotard, "Aesthetic Reflection," in Jean-François Lyotard, *Lessons on the Analytic of the Sublime: Kant's Critique of Judgment, [Sections] 23-29*, trans. Elizabeth Rottenberg (Stanford: Stanford University Press, 1994), 25 [1–49]. First published as *Leçons sur l'Analytique du sublime* (Paris: Éditions Galilée, 1991).

perpetrated by power in service to Capital and vice versa. The analysis of this hyper-determinism has been done (here and there via anti-capitalist critique) while the conditions of its imposition are constantly shifting. Digital Humanities today is tomorrow's morass of useless information eliding the disposable model imposed (all knowledge relegated to discrete units in a field of malleable disciplines). The outcome is intensification and stratification, the exact opposite of smoothness or liquidity, the morass finely subdivided into tranches closely resembling the practices associated with the production of securities—clearly the introduction of financialization strategies to the management of Intellectual Property Rights.[13]

Thus, while the complexities of naked ideological ambition converge with Capital's voracious appetite to subjugate and extract tribute, knowledge flees elsewhere, into proverbial wildernesses and backwaters. Godard's filmic pretension to de-center subjects (including his own role as filmmaker/ auteur) is a typical maneuver given to re-introducing the spatial metaphors that are all but exhausted in parallel disciplines (Fine Art, Architecture, and the Social Sciences).[14] The center

---

[13] Smoothness and/or so-called liquid cultures are a post-modern condition that quietly supports the re-stratification of life insofar as they mask the true intentions of Capital. See, for example, the books of Zygmunt Bauman, including *Liquid Modernity* (Cambridge: Polity, 2000).

[14] These comments on Godard de-centering Godard primarily involve his role as auteur in the world of French cinema versus his role in his own films, the latter which—given the overall Mannerist sensibility— takes primacy, as "voice," over other aspects. Godard's films are very much self-portraits, and *JLG/JLG: Auto-portrait de décembre* (1994) is, in many respects, one of his finest moments. Regarding the so-called Left Bank School (Alain Resnais, Chris Marker, Agnès Varda, and Alexandre Astruc) and the so-called Right Bank School (Godard, Éric Rohmer, and François Truffaut), a mythic construction in the history of New Wave cinema, see Richard Roud, "The Left Bank," *Sight and Sound: International Film Quarterly* 32.1 (Winter 1962-63): 24– 27. For Roud's later repudiation of his own construction, see Richard Roud, "The Left Bank Revisited," *Sight and Sound: International Film*

that is asked to *not* hold is also the classic empty signifier of various idioms of structuralist and post-structuralist exegesis (and Godard was immersed in literature well before filmmaking). The implosion of systems of representation would, then, seem to be his chief aesthetic concern, while the discursive turns within his works (and his comments on his works) lead toward the exit, or what he refers to in painting as something seen beyond the frame. What this something is, or *where* this something is, connotes the aspect denoted in critical reflexion as subjective agency (and, in Kantian terms, the unassimilated remainder of the aesthetic, which leads to crisis and, according to Jean-François Lyotard, produces the Sublime).[15] Whether Godard realizes it or not, and regardless of whether or not such terms mean anything to him, his late films approach this sublimity that he acknowledges in other art forms. To return it to scholarship and texts, then, is the radical promise of the initiatory rites of Modernity plus its complexly situated antithesis, anti-modernism.

Spirit and Law, then—but Spirit in the ultra-Hegelian (left-Hegelian) sense that demolishes everything in its path to self-consciousness (the merger of subject and object, something always present in Fine Art anyway). If Jameson is right that the dialectic is overrated, one can only then ask what its purpose *was*. To speak in the past tense, in fact, requires that it too be historicized into oblivion.[16] What emerges, as a result,

---

Quarterly 46.3 (Summer 1977): 143–145. For Chris Marker's role in this system of shifting alliances, see Gavin Keeney, "Immemory and the Immemorial," in Gavin Keeney, *Dossier Chris Marker: The Suffering Image* (Newcastle upon Tyne: Cambridge Scholars Publishing, 2012), 77–100.

[15] Lyotard, *Lessons on the Analytic of the Sublime*, passim.

[16] In terms of biographical detail and world-historical forces, plus the propensity of the teleological spirit of so-called Hegelianism to erase individual subjects, see "The Interpretation of Freud," a review by Vivian Gornick of the biography of Sigmund Freud by Adam Phillips, *Becoming Freud: The Making of a Psychoanalyst* (New Haven: Yale University Press, 2014): Vivian Gornick, "The Interpretation of Freud," *The New York Times*, August 8, 2014, http://www.nytimes.com/2014/

is the greater conundrum of world-historical forces which underwrite Jameson's other criticism of "easy Hegelianism"—tele-ology (plus its discontents). Godard notes that cinema emerged at roughly the time that Freud was formulating his own theories of repression—a curious historical moment that might serve to answer to why Monet painted what he could not see. This apparitional aspect of art (mental apparitions versus optical mirage or ghost) is more ancient than art history might permit. For with the apparitional comes the source of *technê*, of the apparatuses of the arts and of the humanities in general.[17] In the latter case the apparatus is entirely

---

08/10/books/review/becoming-freud-by-adam-phillips.html. This book is a published version of the Clark lectures at Trinity College, Cambridge University, delivered by Phillips in Spring 2014. "Adam Phillips explains that what the reader does not need in any biographer's attempt to write 'that impossible thing, a Freudian life of the young Freud, is the always fanciful (i.e., wishful), novelettish setting of scenes, and thumbnail sketches of characters, with their suppositions about what people were thinking and feeling and doing.' What is needed, he believes, is what he supplies: a sketchy chronology of Freud's first 50 years threaded through the step-by-step story, *richly told and richly interpreted*, of how psychoanalysis came to be" (Gornick; emphasis added). Additionally, Gornick states: "In the years between 1900 and 1906 Freud wrote most of his important books: *The Interpretation of Dreams*, *The Psychopathology of Everyday Life*, *Jokes and Their Relation to the Unconscious*, *Three Essays on the Theory of Sexuality*. If he had died in 1906, Phillips posits, the world would still have a completed theory of psychoanalysis. What it would not necessarily have is an analytic movement; which I think might just be fine with Phillips." This last statement suggests that there are aspects of world-historical developments that might be discarded while saving other parts. Such may be one rationale for high scholarship.

[17] See Keeney, *Art as "Night."* The book is divided into two halves: Part One, "Spanish Night," and Part Two, "Universal Night." See especially the essay, "The Apparition of the One," 133–154. The separation of *epistêmê* and *technê* (knowledge and practice) remains a disputed article in Western philosophical systems. See Richard Parry, "Episteme and Techne," *The Stanford Encyclopedia of Philos-*

apparitional. Additionally, the paradigmatic secretly relies on repression or sublimation, and both produce the apparitional that comes to be named Spirit. It is Law that intervenes—Law as subversion of wholly unearthly laws and the imposition of a "cosmic" (all-embracing) determinism. The generation of concepts that inhabit systems is coincidental but also integral to the greater apparatus of History. World-historical moments, in the ultra-Hegelian manner, function or appear via the apparatuses and apparitional states of associative thought—or, as Godard might say, Elsinore is just another castle until it is called Hamlet's castle.

The apparitional, then, is the appearance in all histories (art history, the history of cinema, literary criticism) of the paradigmatic, returning from the wildernesses of language and thought. Law is the formalization and reduction of the same to the same—a very strange recourse to the conversion of nothing to nothing. The nihilist remainder is, as historically determined tragedy, the penultimate antithesis of Spirit (apparitional knowledge). The *ultimate* antithesis is "categorical Death" (the Second Death of Franciscanism, and death in service to nothing)—or, that which will follow any successful outcome of Law converted to absolute nihilism.[18]

---

ophy, Fall 2014, ed. Edward N. Zalta, http://plato.stanford.edu/archives/fall2014/entries/episteme-techne/.

[18] The figure of the Second Death is to be found in "The Canticle of Brother Sun" (c. 1225), in Francis of Assisi and Clare of Assisi, *Francis and Clare: The Complete Works*, trans. Regis J. Armstrong, OFM Cap, Ignatius C. Brady, OFM (New York: Paulist Press, 1982), 37–39. "Blessed are those whom death will find in Your most holy will, for the second death shall do them no harm" (*Francis and Clare*, 39). For a discussion of this potentially catastrophic figure of a Second Death, see Keeney, "Montanism: Insurrection and Resurrection," in Keeney, *Not-I/Thou*, 95–110. Suffice to say, Francis did not invent the concept, but adopted it. "As the first resurrection consists of the conversion of the heart, so the second death consists of unending torment": Saint Fulgentius of Ruspa, *On Forgiveness*, Liber 2, 11, 2–12, 1.3–4, in *Sancti Fulgentii episcopi Ruspensis Opera*, ed. Johannes Fraipont, Corpus Christianorum, Series Latina, 91, 91A (Turnhout: Typographi

I took the M3 bus south from Central Park East (Fifth Avenue) to the New York Public Library (NYPL) at Fifth and Forty-first to read Schopenhauer's *The World as Will and Representation*, looking especially for the justly famous passages on music, expecting dark draughts of so-called pessimism against the anterior sky of some-thing else. The call slip came back marked "Not on shelf" and I was relieved of the responsibility. I ambled over to the Internet stations below the plum-red skies of the palatial Rose Reading Room now rationalized to keep tourists and ne'er-do-wells at bay (now requiring a library card and log-in) and spent some time wasting time.[19]

Given the intensifying determinism of the neo-liberal capitalist project, the only alternative for scholars and artists to contribute to the re-universalization of knowledge is to find the holes in the capitalist machinery and exploit them without mercy, and/or, indeed, to *punch* new holes in things (if necessary).

Brepols Editores Pontificii, 1968), 693–695; cited in Francis of Assisi and Clare of Assisi, *Francis and Clare*, 39n8.

[19] Gavin Keeney and Parsa Khalili, "'Upstream': What is 'in' Formal Agency?" (2010). Unpublished, privately circulated manuscript. "I left walking east toward Tudor City and First Avenue dodging triple-wide strollers, tourists walking three or four abreast, past Grand Central, past rolling luggage, past workmen arc welding air conditioners on the sidewalk, deliverymen wheeling carts of shrink-wrapped bottled water, mounds of decomposing garbage in superheated, supersized black plastic bags, past ranges of newsstands, trash cans and bystanders, crossing the taxi- and car-jammed intersections with and against the light, one eye open for delivery 'artists' on bicycles riding against traffic. In time, I descended, eventually, a set of stairs to the chronically disabled and permanently under-construction UN enclave (sovereign outpost) at Turtle Bay, waiting then to board the M5 bus on First, all the while ignoring a man exposing himself to no one in particular from a window in an apartment high above the urban carnage. When the bus finally arrived, I found that I had $0.00 on my MetroCard" (Keeney and Khalili, "'Upstream'").

Jameson proposes Spirit as the "speculative" par excellence—the very possibility of the union of the subject and the object (of thought).[20] In post-modernist exegesis (almost always formulated as a slightly cynical or only apparent anti-modern-ism), the speculative is the caesura or gap in systems of thought.[21] Yet the speculative only finds its positive form as antithesis to mundane forms or aspects of determinism.

[20] Jameson, *The Hegel Variations*, 4.

[21] On the caesura in post-modern thought, see, for example, Philippe Lacoue-Labarthe, "Caesura of the Speculative," in Philippe Lacoue-Labarthe, *Typography: Mimesis, Philosophy, Politics*, ed. Christopher Fynsk (Stanford: Stanford University Press, 1989). Lacoue-Labarthe singles out Friedrich Hölderlin as an illustration of the power of the caesura: "The meaning of tragedies is most easily understood on the basis of the paradox. Because all power is justly and equally distributed, all that is original appears not, indeed, in its original strength, but properly in its weakness, so that properly the light of life and the appearance belong to the weakness of the whole. Now, in the tragic the sign is, in itself, meaningless, without effect, and yet that which is original is openly manifest. For, properly, the original can appear only in its weakness, but, insofar as the sign in itself is posited as meaningless = 0" (225). Curiously, Jameson claims that the synthesis of subject and object sought by Hegel was acknowledged by Hegel to have occurred in German Romanticism, but primarily in poetry, including the poetry of Hölderlin: Jameson, *The Hegel Variations*, 10 (with reference, at 22, regarding "a kind of Hölderlinian primordial unity," to Dieter Henrich's work on "objective idealism," in *Hegel Im Kontext* [Frankfurt am Main: Suhrkamp, 1971]). For the same reasons, and again to re-trouble the Hegelian dialectic, Alain Badiou cites Hölderlin as the exemplar of "fidelity" to the Event. "Such is the intervenor, such is one who knows that he is required to be faithful: able to frequent the site, to share the fruits of the earth; but also, held by fidelity to the other event [the storm] able to discern fractures, singularities, the on-the-edge-of-the-void which makes the vacillation of the law possible, as dysfunction, its crookedness; but also, protected against the prophetic temptation, against the canonical arrogance; but also, confident in the event, in the name that he bestows upon it": Alain Badiou, "The Event: Intervention and Fidelity," in Alain Badiou, *Being and Event*, trans. Oliver Feltham (London: Continuum,

The tyrant who must have slaves looks upon them as instruments of his purpose. It is the consciousness of his own necessity which makes him crush the will out of them, to make his self-interest absolutely secure. This self-interest cannot brook the least freedom in others, because it is not itself free.[22]

2005), 261. First published as *L'être et l'événement* (Paris: Éditions du Seuil, 1988).

[22] Tagore, *Sādhanā*, 87. A curiously perverse and illogical example of this complex, in a pseudo-benign fashion, was staged in London at the Tate Modern in late 2014 when it launched the first retrospective exhibition of the Russian Suprematist artist Kazimir Malevich in "almost twenty-five years." The prime benefactors for the exhibition were a Ukrainian oligarch (Blavatnik Family Foundation) and a Dutch investment bank (with ties to Russia's Alpha Bank Group). "Alfa Bank Group is known for their multi-year tradition of charitable activities and for the patronage of Russia's historical, cultural and spiritual heritage. It is a part of Alfa Group Consortium, Russia's largest privately owned investment group, founded in 1989, with interests in commercial and investment banking, asset management, insurance, retail trade, [and] many other business areas. The Group typically focuses on value-oriented, longer-term opportunities, primarily in Russia and the CIS, but also invests in other markets within its strategic business objectives": Press Release, *Tate Modern*, 2014, http://www.tate.org.uk/about/press-office/press-releases/malevich. Major works exhibited were borrowed from the Stedelijk Museum, Amsterdam; the State Russian Museum, St. Petersburg; and the State Tretyakov Gallery, Moscow. Malevich died impoverished. Symptomatic of what Benjamin H.D. Buchloh has called "the pseudo-avantgarde culture industry," the exhibition was a crude appropriation of Malevich for contemporary art spectacle. Yet the question arises in such a scenario: Who is using who? A partial answer to this question is that the Tate was using the oligarch, the oligarch was using the Tate, the Dutch bank was using both the Tate and the oligarch, while the spirit of Malevich was, hopefully, laughing at them all. For details, see the Press Release (cited above) regarding "Malevich: Revolutionary of Russian Art," July 16-October 26, 2014, Tate Modern. Admission: Adult £14.50 (without donation, £13.10); Concession: £12.50 (without donation, £11.30); Additional booking fee of £1.75 (£2 via telephone) per transaction applied. Additionally, the Tate Modern offered a

III. AGAINST "NATURE": DARK KNOWLEDGE

> Already, he was dreaming of a refined solitude, a comfortable desert, a motionless ark in which to seek refuge from the unending deluge of human stupidity.[23]
>
> J.-K. Huysmans

The incessantly negative image of the Sublime, arguably first and foremost "sonic" (in an interminably interiorizing sense), rises against "Nature" in the famous Kantian critiques of *what might be known*, and what might be known is always condi-

---

range of "exclusive Malevich prints, geometric inspired homewares, gifts and jewellery," plus a multimedia app for mobile phones (suitable for Android and iOS) for £1.99, downloadable from the Apple App Store or Google Play. The app featured: "Detailed narration and curatorial commentary on 16 key works from the exhibition, accompanied by full-screen colour reproductions and archival images; interviews with 3 contemporary artists, David Batchelor, Atul Dodiya and Borut Vogelnik, whose practices have all been influenced by Malevich; conservation insights from Dr. Maria Kokkori, research fellow at the Art Institute of Chicago; and a timeline of key events from Malevich's life." The latter presumably included the grim details of his last years (see http://www.tate.org.uk/context-comment/apps/malevich-multi media-guide-app). In early 2014, at the Guggenheim New York's opening weekend for "Italian Futurism, 1909-1944: Reconstructing the Universe," protestors from Global Ultra Luxury Faction unfurled banners from the parapet of Frank Lloyd Wright's elegant spiral galleries protesting migrant labor abuses associated with construction of an elite cultural enclave on Abu Dhabi's Saadiyat Island, a complex that includes a new Guggenheim branch, a campus for New York University, and an outlet for the incomparable Louvre. See Matthew Shen Goodman, "Protesting the Guggenheim in Abu Dhabi: An Interview with G.U.L.F.," *Art in America*, February 26, 2014, http://www.artinamericamagazine.com/news-features/interviews/protesting-the-guggenheim-in-abu-dhabi-an-interview-with-gulf/.

[23] J.-K. Huysmans, *Against Nature*, trans. John Howard (Auckland: The Floating Press, 2009), 12. First published as *À rebours* (Paris: G. Charpentier, 1884). Huysmans' point, in part, is to say that if stormy skies and lightning bolts don't cloud your inner horizons (consciousness) from time to time, you are hardly alive.

tioned by a crisis in representation that signals the arrival of *what might not be known*. While the crisis proceeds by way of surplus affects in aesthetic judgment (affects that find their foremost effects in the arts), the negative force of the Sublime nonetheless prefigures another form of knowledge that exceeds rationality: the "what might not be known" being an alternative form of knowledge, or "dark" knowledge, yet a form of knowledge registered only through experience.[24]

It might be said, then, that the arts are *always* "against Nature," when we understand "Nature" as defective construct and Nature as confluence of forces that are named "Nature" at the expense of subjective states (actual, lived experience). Determinism in cultural systems is derived from mundane aspects of the world subjected to the objectivization of experience. Defective forms of cultural determinism build, intentionally or otherwise, upon misunderstood systems of what is merely called Nature. The arts, as inordinate non-objective pursuits allied with humanistic endeavors, only ever succumb to determinism when they fall under the spell of orders and systems imposed from without, yet orders and systems derived from the very ground for the existence of the arts.

Music circles this complex and faux-naturalistic system of determination, but most always, when invoking the Sublime, draws its inspiration from the wildernesses *within* musical expression, the genre-bending appearance of Icelandic artists

---

[24] So-called dark knowledge has an exceptionally long history, beginning in the Western tradition (perhaps) with Pseudo-Dionysius the Areopagite (fifth to sixth century CE). Also known as Negative Theology, it represents (in the case of Pseudo-Dionysius the Areopagite) the importation of pagan themes into Christian exegesis, yet these are themes that are, in fact, universal and belong within Christian theology, providing an immemorial anchor for a just and non-sentimental interpretation of the world as such. Often misunderstood as, or reduced to, Christian Neo-Platonism, Dark Theology has a much more profound provenance in subjective agency proper. It is, therefore, essentially time-less and a-historical. It also proceeds, irreducibly, *by negation*.

as diverse as Sigur Rós or Sólstafir indicating that Nature, indeed, plays a role, even if it is as errant muse, and even if the muse merely establishes a datum from which to ascend to the Sublime and then disappears.[25]

August 15, 2014

[25] Sigur Rós and Sólstafir are both labeled "post-rock" by the music industry in an attempt to market their works. Sólstafir are, additionally, labeled "Viking/Black Metal (early), Post Metal/Rock (later)," a confusing conflation of terms that only confirms that they are utterly unique. For example, see the official music video for "Fjara," from *Svartir Sandar* (2012), directed by Bowen Staines and Gunnar B. Guðbjörnsson, https://www.youtube.com/watch?v=XmGdSOhBx8E. With the release of *Ótta* (2014), Sólstafir might be said to be poised for entry into the pantheon of totally unclassifiable artists, notwithstanding the cowboy-outlaw personae and the backdrop of volcanoes, geysers, and ice sheets.

Essay Two

Estranged Dawns

But now we are delivered from the law, that being dead wherein we were held; that we should serve in newness of spirit, and not in the oldness of the letter.[1]

Romans 7, 6

From painful experience, and bitterness, knowledge grew. / I glide on the wings of death into a red night. / I glide on the wings of death.[2]

Sólstafir

---

[1] Romans has long served as a touchstone for the revolutionary aspects of the Christian dispensation, yet in its historical and messianic sense versus its inward and transpersonal sense. For the latter, one must look to John, plus the various apocryphal books now, in part, restored through the Nag Hammadi Library. In the annals of Christian orthodoxy, it was the suppression of these books (many written before the canonical gospels), plus all forms of Gnosticism, that led to high-Church doctrine and dogma —or, that which instantiates new laws to counter the end of the old laws.
[2] Sólstafir, "Miðdegi," Ótta (Season of Mist, 2014). Lyrics by Aðalbjörn Tryggvason.

I. REVOLUTIONS OF SPIRIT

Vi Veri Veniversum Vivus Vici....[3]

Christopher Marlowe

Revolutions of Spirit almost always start with estranged dawns, and, arguably, they start in the margins of the arts—in literature, music, painting, and poetry. Yet at other times they start in philosophy informed by the arts, as if philosophy is the penultimate art work—the second-to-last art work after life itself. This connotes the well-known Romantic theory of ruins, and of the Phoenix (arising from the ashes of broken worlds).

There is, perhaps, another setting (landscape, strata, discourse) where the true coordinates might be mapped more succinctly, but mapped only in the most abstruse and contentious of forms and figures. Such a setting involves all that has been discussed and belabored in recent philosophical discourse under the title of the "Event,"[4] and for which there is never more than one way to remain faithful to what attempts to dawn through the troubled syrrhesis of times and forces, abstract and quotidian, at once, that leads to the establishment of new worlds.

In music, it is nearly axiomatic that the sonic setting or "landscape" will prevail in such times and that a formidable and somewhat fearful fusion of intimations will emerge from some farflung corner of the planet—say, as of 2014, "Iceland."[5] Or, that

---

[3] "By the power of truth, I, while living, have conquered the universe": Christopher Marlowe, *Doctor Faustus* (c. 1590). This statement was appropriated to particularly potent effect in the film *V for Vendetta* (2006), based on the ten-volume graphic novel by Alan Moore (primarily illustrated by David Lloyd).

[4] Alain Badiou et al....

[5] See, for example, Arthur Schopenhauer's approach to music, or how music functions in cinema—foremost in the cinema of Andrei Tarkovsky or Theo Angelopoulos. For a film utilizing Iceland for very specific antiideological purposes, see Hal Hartley's *No Such Thing* (2001). Iceland also informs the avant-garde music of Björk and the ambient-atmospheric music of Sigur Rós. Parallel dark "Scandinavian" themes emerge in the post-Dogme cinema of Lars von Trier (foremost *Melancholia*) and the

somewhere in the annals of the unacceptable something quite extraordinary will be heard, to sweep through conventional halls and, today, the "ethereum" (the Internet), to more or less stun listeners.[6] It is this "poetics" of soundscapes that covers over the more severe and forbidding aspects noted above as a confluence of abstract and everyday factors, meeting, as it were, in sound—landscapes, nonetheless, which return music to that other ethereum (the originary one), or, subjectivized Time-Space.

In poetry the existentialist and metaphysical golden vein of

---

highly regarded Nordic-noirish television serials of the late 2000s, for example, *The Bridge* and *Borgen*. For a semi-brutal takedown of these pretenses, see Michael Booth, "Dark Lands: The Grim Truth behind the 'Scandinavian Miracle,'" *The Guardian*, January 27, 2014, http://www.theguardian.com/world/2014/jan/27/scandinavian-miracle-brutal-truth-denmark-norway-sweden. For the typical hypocritical neo-liberal reading of the Nordic countries, see "The Next Supermodel," *The Economist*, February 2, 2013, http://www.economist.com/news/leaders/21571136-politicians-both-right-and-left-could-learn-nordic-countries-next-supermodel: "The new Nordic model is not perfect. Public spending as a proportion of GDP in these countries is still higher than this newspaper would like, or indeed than will be sustainable. Their levels of taxation still encourage entrepreneurs to move abroad: London is full of clever young Swedes. Too many people—especially immigrants—live off benefits. The pressures that have forced their governments to cut spending, such as growing global competition, will force more change. The Nordics are bloated compared with Singapore, and they have not focused enough on means-testing benefits."

[6] One of the first major notices for Sólstafir's *Ótta*, even before it was released in early September of 2014, was via the online edition of the left-leaning, French newspaper *Libération*: Sophian Fanen and Gregory Schwartz, "Next musique: Dix albums pour bien finir 2014," *Libération*, August 19, 2014, http://next.liberation.fr/musique/2014/08/19/dix-albums-pour-bien-finir-2014_1076522. Founded in 1995, the band is comprised of Guðmundur Óli Pálmason, Drums; Aðalbjörn Tryggvason, Guitars, Vocals; Svavar Austman, Bass; and Sæþór Maríus Sæþórsson, Guitars. The lyrics for *Ótta* were written by both Pálmason and Tryggvason. The Icelandic term *sólstafir* refers to the "crepuscular rays of dawn." For an interview with Sólstafir discussing the relationship of their music to the landscape of Iceland, see Marzio G. Mian, "Nel Paese delle creature selvagge," in the Italian edition of *Rolling Stone*, October 2014, 140–142.

word and silent or invisible mental image has always produced this confluence of preternatural forms and decidedly physical artifacts (the images, regardless of how de-natured or made strange).[7] For the landscapes of "Iceland" (or of "Ireland") hang in the musical void that signals the continuous re-making of worlds—void as the artistic Imaginary, of course, but also something entirely other than the often-erring prospects of simple and/or elevated *authorized* humanistic inquiry.

---

[7] In Communist-era Yugoslavia, pride of place belongs to Dane Zajc (1929-2005). His bleak, semi-abstract (neo-expressionist) poetry was considered decadent and nihilist, when it was quietly (and secretly) extraordinarily humanistic. The neo-expressionist label is somewhat apt, especially considering what transpired in the early graphic works of Wassily Kandinsky (via *Der Blaue Reiter*) and Emil Nolde (via *Die Brücke*). "Der Blaue Reiter dissolved with the outbreak of World War I in August 1914. Kandinsky, a Russian citizen, was forced to return to his homeland, and [Franz] Marc and another Blaue Reiter artist, August Macke, were killed in action": *Museum of Modern Art*, n.d., http://www.moma.org/explore/collection/ge/styles/blaue_reiter.

II. ABSTRUSE LANDSCAPES

Now I am back home / after a journey through the deep seas. / Aldan was so high, / salinity ate up everything.[8]

Sólstafir

Sonic landscapes are, essentially (and dangerously), "silent" and abstruse landscapes, as literary landscapes are, vocably, "sonic" and abstruse landscapes. The common thread is the still or silent image (the mental image invoked, yet irreducibly internalized).[9]

The "intercalary" markings of works of art, based as they are on de-natured or abstracted phenomenon, readily suggest the fact that formalism at a high level opens the door to completely non-objective and non-formal means to ends. This is the primary feature of any denunciation of formalism and any privileging of the same. These "marks" always indicate what is invisible in the work. And if High Structuralism favored such schemata (at the expense of conventional subjectivity), while late-twentieth-century

---

[8] Sólstafir, "Miðaftann," Ótta. Lyrics by Aðalbjörn Tryggvason.

[9] Chris Marker's use of the still image in the production of his *ciné-essays* and multimedia projects is evocative of this same silent economy of the word-image (image-word), as was his privileging of the power of the Silent Film era—for example, *Silent Movie, Starring Catherine Belkhodja* (1994-1995), created by Chris Marker and first exhibited at the Wexner Center for the Arts, Columbus, Ohio, January 26-April 9, 1995. Production: Wexner Center for the Arts. Installation: metal stand; 5 20" SONY video monitors; 5 Pioneer laser-disc players; computer interface box; 5 video discs with 20-minute sequences (top to bottom: "The Journey," "The Face," "Captions," "The Gesture," "The Waltz"); 18 black-and-white film/video stills; 10 computer-generated film posters (*Bow to the Rain; Breathless; Hastings; Hiroshima mon amour; It's a Mad, Mad, Mad Dog; Owl People; The Quicksands of Time; Rambo Minus One; Remembrance of Things Past; The War That Wasn't*); and soundtrack, "The Perfect Tapeur" (18 solo piano pieces lasting a total of 59 minutes, 32 seconds) and/or 20-minute soundtrack by Michel Krasna, anagram of Chris Marker. Marker often provided the soundtrack, or parts of the soundtrack, for his shorter films and videos under the pseudonym, Michel Krasna. Non-melodic compositions, Michel Krasna's contributions were generally abstract, semi-ambient scores.

High Post-structuralism demolished the pretenses of semi-autonomous structures within cultural production (and reintroduced a de-centered, non-Cartesian subjective agency), it is nevertheless a "rule" of the multiple arts that such crosscurrents animate the work, regardless of whether scholarship and criticism prefers one view or the other, whereas both views are the purview of any proper evaluation of such intercalary systems. It is the movement between them that permits sight of what is ultimately at stake—the experiential nexus where two worlds meet.

Sólstafir's *Ótta* may adopt the old Scandinavian system of dividing the day into eight parts, and their adopted system may reside somewhere between the pre-Christian and the Christian versions (the latter introducing name changes for key portions of the 24-hour cycle to align it with liturgical and administrative laws), yet the appropriation is neither precise nor superficial. Notably, they run this cycle through their eight songs, moving from midnight to midnight, whereas the old ways began with the hour the shepherds awoke to collect their sheep (around 3am), and closed more or less with the disappearance of the sun (around 7pm), never caring too much for the full 24 hours....[10] By realigning these pagan and medieval hours with the present-day

---

[10] Divided into eight parts, the song cycle *Ótta* portrays three hours of the day per song, a division based on Icelandic and monastic tradition. The cycle begins at midnight and concludes at midnight. "Miðdegi" represents 12pm to 3pm. Sólstafir, c. 2014, is alternately described in the music world as "post-Viking black metal" or, more beautifully and uselessly, "post-rock." Sólstafir adopted a conflation of pre-Christian and Christian names for these parts of the day. For example, Nón, present in *Ótta*, is derived from the "Mass Nona (belonging to the *horæ canonicæ*)." See Finn Magnusen, "On the Ancient Scandinavians' Division of the Times of the Day," trans. John M'Caul, *Mémoires de la Société Royale des Antiquaires du Nord* 1 (1839), http://www.cantab.net/users/michael.behrend/repubs/magnusen_day/pages/main.html. The idea for the organization of the songs according to the old ways was suggested by Sæþór Maríus Sæþórsson. See Marcin, "Interview with Guðmundur Óli Pálmason," *Muzyka Islandzka*, September 9, 2014, http://www.muzykailandzka.pl/web/2014/09/16/interview-with-gudmundur-oli-palmamason-from-solstafir/.

means of measuring a day (from midnight to midnight), Sólstafir accidentally or otherwise place their song cycle in a peculiar pre-Christian and post-Christian context. The lyrical values of the songs, while invoking the bleak and beautiful landscapes of Iceland (and their videos claim the same close respect for physical Iceland), are intensely oriented toward the internal dimensions of lived experience.[11] These interior landscapes match the exteriorized images drawn from the natural world but re-abstracted in the abstruse language of landscape as mirror (totemic at times, riven with fissures, broken and bleak, restive and redemptive). If this ancient division of the day also involved markings on the hills and mountains by which to observe the passage of the sun and stars, primarily in association with agricultural practices, and each "farm" might have its own set of such markings, when this structure is embedded into art and/or extracted from art, the result has little to do with origins or utilitarian means. Authorial intention is also, *pace* High Structuralism, quite evidently eclipsed by other factors. The outcome is nonetheless unsettling; for, within this system something else emerges, and that something else is a fairly grave reading of time and its relations within humanistic systems. One senses the Gnostic demiurge at work....There is a suggestion within Sólstafir's *Ótta*, whether intentional or not, that such markings are the beginnings for the imposition of cultural apparatuses that not only mark time but impose arbitrary and punitive law (one outcome of the feudal system, for example) and compromise authentic lived experience; that is, a primary relationship to the world is mapped in the negative, with the distraught, black-metal-influenced lyrics of *Ótta* conveying that hyper-internalized, dialogic sense and non-sense noted above, a map of the battlefield of being locked into time and worlds not quite ever consciously chosen.[12]

---

[11] See, for example, the video *Fjara* (2012), https://www.youtube.com/watch?v=XmGdSOhBx8E. For *Ótta*, see the video *Lágnætti* (2014), https://www.youtube.com/watch?v=GL3LVlDtoUY. In the song cycle, "Lágnætti" represents 12am-3am. Both videos filmed by Bowen Staines and Gunnar B. Guðbjörnsson.

[12] The cover image for the CD and online versions of *Ótta* is telling. It is

III. MORE JOHANNINE PROBLEMS

Even conventional biblical exegesis introduces massive problems with locating and privileging subjective certitude (the locus or nexus of knowledge and self-knowledge). It would seem as if there is, historically, one reading for the public and another for the elite—except, on the external side the elite are the clergy, while on the *internal* side of these documents and readings the elite are those who know how to step outside of the external laws imposed by the apparent elite. Or, such is the beginning of the problems with so-called Johannine exegesis—those speculations drawn from the Book of John, the most cryptic of all the canonical gospels.

In the *Apocryphon of John*, part of the Nag Hammadi codices, the chief literary figure or gesture is the *aeon*, and such would appear to be "time beings," not elective divisions of time per se but expressive age-less beings that sponsor conventional time and space. It is their gaze that produces things....One reading of such austere documents associated with the Coptic Gnostic tradition is that these intensely otherworldly prefigurations of the human condition are coded to appear to be concerned with cosmological occurrences somewhere on the anterior side of lived experience. Yet, when aligned with speculations associated with German Idealism, for example, they become documents of what is perhaps always already occurring *in time*. They would seem to be, then, secret documents aimed at that elite who are trying, at the time of their composition, to step "outside of time"

---

straight out of an Ingmar Bergman film, or, it is highly reminiscent of *The Seventh Seal*. In an interview conducted September 16, 2014, Guðmundur Óli Pálmason tells of its origin: "All the photos on the album are by the Icelandic photographer Ragnar Axelsson (RAX). He's been a favorite of ours for years, I even wrote papers about him when I was studying photography myself[...]. The man on the cover is an old Icelandic farmer whom Rax became a friend of. He shot that photo on the Reynisfjara beach, which was partly his property. He passed away a year or two ago" (Marcin, "Interview with Guðmundur Óli Pálmason"). The photo dates to c. 1999.

(ruled times). As emblematic of the Christic dimension in time (and the import of the Christian dispensation in historical time), such documents would seem, therefore, utterly revolutionary and exceedingly dangerous. As a result, their non-incorporation and suppression by the Church perversely makes sense. That they precede the major innovations of the Church Fathers in the construction of high doctrine and dogma also indicates that the Early Christian experience differed dramatically from everything that followed. Indeed, the great schism between the Eastern and Western churches occurred with the formulation of doctrine that superseded Early Christian experience and in many cases sanctioned it. Factor in Tertullian and Montanism, in association with early Gnosticism, and all that is attempting to make itself known in virtual and real estranged dawns across the arc of Modernity comes into focus (that is, the subjective Real). The subjective Real's untimely radical place in the multiple arts is somewhere between temporality and its antithesis: a-temporality. This places an inordinate emphasis in the arts on the intercalary marks noted above, plus *how* they are to be read/cognized. The austere and abstract renderings of these processes are the indication that what we are almost always dealing with is the universal in the contingent. "Almost always" in such cases, however, because it is the universal exception that animates the highest works of "subjective realism." It is these works that shatter all pretensions to embodied universality—to any possibility of pure immanence (or Utopia here-and-now).

The universal exception is when laws are suspended (or when formalisms collapse) and books might, truly, be thrown on the fire (to keep warm) or buried in urns in the desert (for another day).[13] Such times are when something new arises, or *is born*. It

---

[13] The universal exception is, of course, also the twisted (perverse) foundation for states of emergency. See Agamben's *Homo Sacer* project, passim, on this account. In a strange footnote to the siege of Sarajevo during the relatively recent Bosnian War, it has been noted here and there that Marxist books were favored for feeding the fire because they were very dense and burned for a very long time. The irony, in the case of this particular historical crucible, is spellbinding.

would also seem that it is borne by the gaze....

IV. STARS DOWN TO EARTH (AGAIN)

> Knowledge of Ideal Beauty is Not to be Acquired. It is Born with us. Innate Ideas are in Every Man, Born with him; they are truly Himself.[14]
>
> William Blake

Note that there are always two worlds at play in life, whether one is a believer or non-believer; that is, the existential-metaphysical fuse in experience plays out against a socialized, often parasitical sub-lunar world and a universal, transpersonal world of "angels" and "deities," or, life is animated by desires, dreams, and nightmares mediated by the non-thing otherwise known as Fine Art. These two worlds are endlessly re-configured in quotidian terms, while the play between the two underscores the role of subjectivity as Promethean "gift."[15]

The current "weather" (as of late 2014)—globally—indicates

---

[14] William Blake, "Annotations to Sir Joshua Reynolds's *Discourses*," in William Blake, *The Complete Writings of William Blake: With Variant Readings*, ed. Geoffrey Keynes (Oxford: Oxford University Press, 1966), 459. The "Annotations" were written between 1798 and 1808.

[15] This would seem to be the subtext of the hyper-gnomic *Apocryphon of John*, one of the several leather-bound manuscripts unearthed in Upper Egypt in 1945 and known today as the Nag Hammadi: "The Nag Hammadi codices, ancient manuscripts containing over fifty religious and philosophical texts hidden in an earthenware jar for 1,600 years, were accidentally discovered in upper Egypt in the year 1945. A group of farmers came across an entire collection of books written in Coptic, the very language spoken by Egyptian Christians[...]. This immensely important discovery included a large number of primary Gnostic scriptures. One text in particular received much attention—the Gospel according to Thomas, which was originally called 'the secret words of Jesus written by Thomas'. These texts, scriptures such as the Gospel According to Thomas, the Gospel of Philip, and the Gospel of Truth, were once thought to have been entirely destroyed during the early Christian struggle to define 'orthodoxy.' The discovery and translation of the Nag Hammadi library, completed in the 1970's, has provided momentum to a major reassessment of early Christian history and the nature of Gnosticism" (http://ccdl.libraries.claremont.edu/cdm/landingpage/collection/nha).

waves of possible extinction underway, on a prosaic everyday level, and on a prospective universal level (with consciousness on the verge of being submerged by technology, and humankind in denial of its inordinate impact on the fragile underpinnings for life on Earth).[16] Were we to hear angels weeping, it would not be all that far-fetched. For Humanity itself (or, Humanity proper) is once again in the grips of a massive test, as it were, caught in-between the half-unconscious will to self-immolate (a collective death wish) and the hope to transcend prosaic, utilitarian values, rising to an inherent and higher trans-humanistic calling. There is a sense, then, that "even-ing" in the West, roughly equivalent to the twentieth century and the birth and collapse of Modernism, has passed to the first crepuscular rays of "dawn"—a potential rebirth accompanied by catastrophic shifts in the stewardship of life on Earth.

Theodor W. Adorno mocked astrology in "The Stars Down to Earth,"[17] the Frankfurt School being one venue in which the uni-

---

[16] See Naomi Oreskes and Erik M. Conway, *The Collapse of Western Civilization: A View from the Future* (New York: Columbia University Press, 2014). Note that there would be no Marxism without technology, and that Marxism's emergence is intimately tied to the Industrial Revolution.

[17] Theodor W. Adorno, *The Stars Down to Earth and Other Essays on the Irrational in Culture*, ed. Stephen Crook (London: Routledge, 1994). "The Stars Down to Earth: The Los Angeles Times Astrology Column" first appeared in English in *Telos* 19 (Spring 1974): 13–90. It was written in 1952-53 during a visit by Adorno to the USA and uses the Los Angeles Times astrology column for intellectual cannon or Marxian "canon" fodder. The "Introduction" by Stephen Crook, "Adorno and Authoritarian Irrationalism," 1–45, maps three major theses for the overall collection of essays: "Authoritarian irrationalism is an integral part of enlightened modernity, not to be thought away as historical relic, unintended consequence or marginal other"; "The affinity between modernity and authoritarian irrationalism must be sought in the psychodynamics of modernity, in the characterological bases and outcomes of processes of cultural, economic, political and social modernization"; and, "In their common manipulation of the dependency needs of *typically late-modern personalities* there is a direct continuity between authoritarian irrationalist propaganda and the everyday products of the 'culture industry'" (3; emphasis

versal was only permitted under the auspices of messianic Marxian-materialist rhetoric, a not-unreasonable prejudice against superstition and all that passed then as elective alternative to everyday class warfare. Yet the same protocols survive today in the rhetoric of the Multitude, as formulated by Negri, Hardt et al., in response to the ravages of late-late-modern, global neo-liberal capitalism.[18]

The re-universalization of knowledge (via the arts and otherwise) seems, therefore, a worthy project, yet one caught in the crosshairs of persistent determinist readings of culture and the protocols of the utterly otherworldly and untimely world of Spirit. It is this strange chiasmus that survives ages upon ages. It is also this "strange chiasmus" that animated the arguments between Adorno and Walter Benjamin, Benjamin "salting" his research with Lurianic (Kabalistic) mysticism, the figure of the Hunchback Dwarf in the well-known "Theses on a Philosophy of History," for example, being rightly understood by Giorgio Agamben as "Saint Paul," or, at the least, the specter of theology. Thus, too, Agamben's turn into theology in the last phases of his *Homo Sacer* project, as if the vestiges of theology embedded in secular practices needed to be ferreted out in order to examine an otherworldly, non-positivist economy that sets on edge the nerves of those scholars and exegetes still enamored of pseudo-empirical

added).
[18] See, for example, documents related to the Dark Markets Conference, held in Vienna, Austria, on October 4, 2003: http://darkmarkets.t0.or.at/. Of particular interest is the presentation by Arianna Bove and Erik Empson entitled "The Dark Side of the Multitude": "Control society needs to be subverted rather than limited, and this is not a matter of public dissent but rather of making subversion at once public (in the sense of shared) and invisible, of dispersing through multiple points of attack. Control society is not stopped by a re-assertion of the private, data-protection acts, and civil-rights activism. Ours is not merely a libertarian agenda nor is it an attempt at preserving a constructed category of individual freedom, but it is the very opposition to individuation through forms of socialised disobedience, networked and spread as a form of constitution of new social realities of cooperation as well as exodus" (*Future Nonstop*, n.d., http://future-nonstop.org/c/2300c934c6aec6cbea36f0436b8e5fca).

studies and neo-Darwinian readings of socio-economic and political conditions.

There is the lovely, yet forlorn figure of the wounded centaur, Chiron, in mundane Western astrology.[19] One can find in this grand metaphor the almost-human analogue for subjectivity held in thrall to the time-full landscapes of this-worldly experience, all the while gazing upward toward the "stars." In terms of the movement of the planets and stars in 2014, for example (and indulging astrology momentarily, against Adorno's mocking appraisal), it would appear that deception has been the theme in social and political affairs since early 2014, and as of November 2014 things have begun to clear, somewhat. Mundane astrology (especially Indian and Asian astrology), however, famously reduces humans to fateful automatons, fearfully or fearlessly negotiating the movements of the heavens and the sub-lunary implications (the propitiation of the gods becoming a cottage industry in places)—a situation that brackets subjective agency only insofar as the individual is caught in the mechanisms of the heavens, and must make minute or minor changes to merely survive and/or move forward.

Dreams suggest the same thing, and most all humans dream or, at the least, *attempt* to dream (the actual subconscious version or the proscriptive waking version). How many "houses" burn to the ground in dreams?[20] Or, how many "houses" fall into the sea and are swept away into the abyss of dreams? Such visions are always metaphors, and all metaphors are primarily knots engaging experience and its Other—the universal will to transcend apparent prison-houses of Spirit.

---

[19] Regarding Chiron, as of late November 2014, plus his relationship to Uranus and Saturn, as "bridge," see the Cosmic Intelligence Agency, Melbourne, Australia, http://www.cosmicintelligenceagency.com/2014/11/the-cosmic-mission-the-week-ahead/.

[20] One thinks immediately of Andrei Tarkovsky's films: both *The Mirror* (1975) and *The Sacrifice* (1986), but also *Nostalghia* (1983). Fire plays a role in all three of these wildly mnemonic films.

V. THE LIGHT(E)NING STARE

> It alone [is eternal] since It does not need [anything.] For It is totally perfect. [It] does not [lack] anything such that [anything] would perfect It, [but] It is [al]ways completely perfect in [light].[21]
> *Apocryphon of John*

The gaze produces things....This would seem to be the foremost aspect of the theological-aesthetic complex that is buried in the multiple arts. The word-image and the image-word are often one thing, even if they are also, and often, *different* things. From one perspective they separate; from another they unite. The venerable world of Fine Art circumscribes such mysteries, even if in contemporary terms the entire apparatus is hidden from view (repressed and/or forsaken).

The utility of the arts destroys this vision (the lightening by way of the lightning stare described in the *Apocryphon Iohannis/ Apocryphon of John*).

The Romantic visionary prospects of the arts have come the closest to these immemorial truths. Historically, such intimations fail due to the imperfections of the visionary enterprise; for example, the appropriation of the artistic project by quotidian, prosaic, and mercantile forces; or its demolition in the face of reactionary forces. Not unlike the practice of medicine (of which it is a subdivision), the Gnostic dispensation cannot be bought or sold.

---

[21] *Apocryphon of John* (Fourth Century AD), Nag Hammadi Codex II, 1 & Nag Hammadi Codex IV, 1, trans. Michael Waldstein and Frederik Wisse, ed. Lance Owens, http://www.gnosis.org/naghamm/apocjn-long.html: "It cannot be [limi]ted because there is nothing [before It] to limit It. [It is] inscrut[able because there] is no one who exists before It [to scrutinize It.] [It is im]measurable because there is nothing [which exists before It to measure] It. [It is] in[visible because there is] no one to see [It. It is an eternity existing] eternally. [It is ineffable because] there is no one able to comprehend It in order to sp[eak about It.] It is [un]nameable because [there is no one before It] to name [It.] It is [the immeasurable light,] which is pure, [holy, and unpolluted. It is in]effable [being perfect i]n incorruptibility. (It does) [not] (exist) in per[fection], blessed[ness, or] divini[ty] but It is [far] superior (to these)."

Its assimilation to commerce destroys it.[22]

Knowledge, in this regard, as artistic practice or as commodity, is curiously caught in processes of continual or perpetual relativization—bound to time while attempting to escape time.

The antidote, and the contravening position for the arts, is for the Event to move, migrate, vanish, re-appear, and otherwise evade capture. The battlefield of the so-called artworld slowly turns to desert, time after time, with key works "buried in urns," awaiting rediscovery.

> O man, take care! / What does the deep midnight declare? / "I was asleep – / From a deep dream I woke and swear: / The world is deep / Deeper than day had been aware. / Deep is its woe; / Joy – deeper yet than agony: / Woe implores: Go! / But all joy wants eternity – / Wants deep, wants deep eternity."[23]

If Nietzsche demolished German pietism (the etiolated spirituality of the Northern church versus the artistic movement associated with the Early German Romantics), it was turning the concept of *ressentiment* on its head that seems to have accomplished the necessary corrective—an inversion that emptied religious sentiment of its de-spiritualized and re-naturalized "demons of poverty" (that is, admonitions plus the "sale" of the

---

[22] A curious aside in contemporary literature on the apocrypha notes: "Within the academy more narrowly its value largely has to do with intellectual production and prestige, including concerns about tenure and promotion—salvation, if you will, of a rather different sort": Karen L. King, *The Secret Revelation of John* (Cambridge: Harvard University Press, 2006), 23. "And he said to him, 'Cursed be any one who should exchange these things for a gift, whether for food or drink or clothing or anything else of this kind'" (*Apocryphon of John*).

[23] Friedrich Nietzsche, "Zarathustra's Roundelay" (or, "The Midnight Song"), from *Thus Spoke Zarathustra* (1883), in *The Portable Nietzsche*, ed. and trans. Walter Kaufman (New York: Penguin, 1976), 436. The poem first appears in chapter 59 of *Thus Spoke Zarathustra*, "The Second Dance-Song," and was incorporated into Gustav Mahler's Third Symphony as an ode to Nature minus its Promethean urges.

nineteenth-century functional equivalent of indulgences by the Church-State) while setting in motion the terrifying Will to Power and the poeticized, yet revolutionary aubade to the Eternal Return of the Same. This is a problematic, however, that has as many topological knots in it (plus holes) as any overwrought critique of morality (that is, the penchant for formulating a higher morality through amorality being a weak derivative of escaping the dominion of mere quotidian and ecclesiastical and/or ontotheological laws—Martin Heidegger's *bête noire*). The Nietzschean supermen to follow (for example, George Bernard Shaw) would succumb to much the same fate—"fate" being, as fauxmetaphysical entity or law, that very psychic specter created by the Gnostic demiurge to counter the absolute freedom of Spirit, with the supposed "fable" of Gnosticism almost perfectly serving any dreams whatsoever for or against Power proper. If fate is the Spirit of Gravity, Nietzsche would nonetheless perplex thousands by nodding in its direction, even as he reached for the proverbial escape hatch, through Zarathustra, that ends with a Schopenhauerian-inspired plunge into the abyssal (and, as many have said, madness).

The secret escape hatch was and remains the fact that historical time eventually implodes, typically under duress, and the circles (cycles) become spirals (vortices), which then become ladders. Aubade and estranged dawn are more or less synonymous in the multiple arts—foremost when the arts are suffused with a proper respect for the demons of poverty (representational poverty without the reactionary plunge into iconoclasm). Returning to a proper economy of the image means effectively the same thing as working out a genealogy of morals for the arts.

January 5, 2015

Essay Three

The Film-essay

I. *FILM SOCIALISME*

So the most beautiful aesthetics—the most desperate, too, since they are generally doomed to stalemate or madness—will be those aesthetics that, in order to open themselves completely to the dimension of the visual, want us to close our eyes before the image, so as no longer see it but only to look at it, and no longer forget what Blanchot called "the *other* night," the night of Orpheus. Such aesthetics are always singular, strip themselves bare in not-knowledge, and never hesitate to call *vision* that which no waking person can see.[1]

Georges Didi-Huberman

At the time of its release in 2010, it was reported that *Film Socialisme* was Jean-Luc Godard's last film.[2] Yet it was fol-

---

[1] Georges Didi-Huberman, *Confronting Images: Questioning the Ends of a Certain History of Art*, trans. John Goodman (University Park: Pennsylvania University Press, 2005), 157. First published as *Devant l'image: Questions posée aux fins d'une histoire de l'art* (Paris: Éditions de Minuit, 1990).

[2] Jean-Luc Godard, *Film socialisme*, DVD (New York: Kino Lorber,

lowed by *Adieu au langage* in 2014, and, in retrospect, serves as an extended prelude to that new "last" film.

The avant-garde pretensions of *Film Socialisme* are mocked by various detractors, even if all of the various annoyances Godard assembles have been used before, by others and in his own work.[3] Foremost in this mélange of affects is the disjointed syntax of so-called narrativity. In fact, when weighed against other avant-gardist filmmakers who eschew narrative (for example, Tarkovsky or von Trier), Godard is not so much guilty of elliptical and gnomic utterances as the conflation of affects that resemble literary exegesis. The primary address for these high-handed and high-minded asides is abstract thought, and one is left with no other solution than to go through the film slowly, freezing frames and studying what resides therein. In this way, *Film Socialisme* is, indeed, a film-essay (*ciné-essay*), but not in the sense that critics wish to assign it to a Markerian regard for self-conscious discursive means at odds or in accord with the casually assembled, intuitive visual side that connotes pre-conscious forms of knowledge.[4]

Inc., 2012). Since at least *Éloge de l'amour* (2001), film critics have been calling each new film by Godard a "swan song." Regarding this latest, yet rolling anticipation for Godard's last film, see Amy Taubin, "Wiping the Slate Clean: *Film Socialisme*," *Film Comment*, September-October 2010, http://www.filmcomment.com/article/film-socialisme-review.

[3] For example: "Mr. Godard's more pious partisans may object, but like many other great figures of 20th-century culture—Picasso as well as Pound, John Cage along with Andy Warhol—his genius is inseparable from a certain carefully cultivated charlatanism. And his desire to give offense or to be able to feign surprise when someone takes it has long guaranteed his permanent membership in the priesthood of the avant-garde" (A.O. Scott, "On a Mediterranean Cruise Ship Steered by a Godardian Crew: *Film Socialisme*," *The New York Times*, June 2, 2011, http://www.movies.nytimes.com/2011/06/03/movies/film-socialisme-by-jean-luc-godard-review.html.

[4] See Chris Marker's role in Groupe Medvedkine versus Godard's Groupe Vertov, c. 1968. These groups were formed in the late 1960s

Godard's work has advanced to the gates of visual exegesis at the expense of discursive content, with the abstract

during the last battles in France between Marxist-Leninist factions of the Old Left and Maoist factions within the New Left. They generally crossed paths only when Direct Action was called for or during skirmishes within the bureaucratic machinations of the French Communist Party. Godard was associated with the Maoist faction, post-1968, while Marker kept his distance from party politics and remained a high-Romantic Marxist. Marker took a rather dim view of the fratricidal warfare of the New Left (primarily on the far Left), a position that came to a fairly conclusive end with *Le fond de l'air est rouge* (1977), foremost with its histrionic opening sequence by way of Luciano Berio's interpretation of "Musica notturna delle strade di Madrid," by Luigi Boccherini. Originally constructed from film archives, Super-8 films, posters, audio tapes, and newsreels, and originally a television broadcast in four parts (the original version of *Le fond de l'air est rouge* was four hours long), its English version, *A Grin without a Cat* (1993) was cut to 180 minutes. Marker states: "There are in fact *two* three-hour versions. One was made for England's Channel 4 in 1988, minus whatever was too bluntly 'French-oriented' (that's what was shown in the U.S.). The other one was meant for France, shortened simply because four hours was really too long and many elements (especially at the end), which were crystal clear at the time I made it, had become so obscured in people's memories years later that I'd need an extra hour just to explain them. In both cases the process was one of shortening, never modifying, so when it was released last year I was a bit sorry to read in most U.S. reviews the words 're-edit' or 'new cut,' which implies rewriting History. The thing remains what it originally was, simply shorter for the comfort of the viewer (with brief updating of text at the end)." Cited in Catherine Lupton et al., "Total Recall: Film, Video and Multimedia Works by Chris Marker," *Film Comment* 39.4 (July-August 2003): 49. For a summary of the various versions of *Le fond de l'air est rouge*, see Catherine Lupton, *Chris Marker: Memories of the Future* (London: Reaktion Books, 2005). The title *A Grin without a Cat* originated with the special edition of the film produced for British television in 1988. For an extended discussion of the 1988 version of the film, see Lupton, *Chris Marker*, 109–112, 140–147. The three-hour English and French versions followed in 1993 to encompass the collapse of the Soviet Union.

linguistic aspects noted above presented as fragments of broken worlds—broken conversations and abandoned texts. The sense that lost causes animate his films is also a red herring instigated by the auteur, as his "historicizing" sensibility never fully accomplishes anything other than to summon ghosts, ghosts that reside in the literary, cinematic, and philosophical traditions he draws on. For example, the presence of the Hermetic motto, "Clarum per obscurious," in *Film Socialisme*, suggests its opposite—"Obscurum per obscurious," said to be the basis for intellectual parlor-tricks. These tricks, while mainly rhetorical games, are yet the foundation for the filmic version of high scholarship. Thus, we are indeed charged with *reading* Godard's films. One may let them wash over the eyes and ears, reveling in the cacophony of references and the visual splendor of HD video, but it is obvious that Godard has other intentions for his late films, and that the obscurities that annoy critics are the beginning of a voyage out of film into the socio-cultural vacuum of Late Modernity. The lost causes invoked are the lost causes of Modernity, not Modernism proper, the latter which, for Godard, has utterly failed. The arc of cinema across the timeframe of Modernism reaches its peculiar apotheosis with all that has not failed within Modernity, and all that hides within but pre-dates Modernity.

Film Socialisme, subtitled *A Symphony in Three Movements*, reaches upward toward the stars when it crosses into "Nos Humanités," the third section that includes "Des Légends," "Des Histoires," etc. Some would consider this the most self-reflexive, if not pretentious section reminiscent of the eight-part *Histoire(s) du cinéma*, 1988-1998. These parts are the most fragmented of all the shards that comprise the film. It is no accident that this is also the passage where the most gnomic images or statements are surrendered to the eyes and ears of viewers. "[It is in the desert] where we must go [to] find them" is an example of already peculiar syntax rendered ultra-peculiar through re-organization to prefigure the following remark as to why all images are ultimately obscure and sepulchral: Such reside in the desert, therefore, "to safeguard all the images of language and [provide means to] make use of them."[5] Doubly troubling when parsed in this way, the statement is circular. "Here," at this point in the film, we are in "Égypte," a mnemonic zone that seems almost like a detour from "Haifa," the destination for the cruise ship that occupied the first third of the film.

In the opening credits of *Film Socialisme* Godard offers us, as readers, some modest help. Under the intertitle "Textos" we find "W. Benjamin, J. Derrida, H. Arendt, J. Giraudoux, L. Aragon, H. Bergson [et al.]," while on "page two" of this now-classic technique (Brechtian sign boards resembling primitive PowerPoint slides) we find "F. Braudel, P. Ricoeur, A. Malraux, W. Goethe [et al.]" The red-and-black intertitles are semi-sublime moments (red-and-black arrows) in an otherwise hurried review of the ravages of Modernism on the perpetual eve of its collapse. It is Fernand Braudel who figures mightily in this mix of allusions and compacts with past senses of timespeech (a figure that might be Godardian in the extreme, as it connotes the linguistic farewell he has been assembling since *Éloge de l'amour*, 2001, and will finalize with *Adieu au langage*).[6] Notably, Braudel's main work on the cultural history of the Mediterranean region was written from memory in a German concentration camp.[7]

Where is this time-speech? As in the statement above regarding burying secrets in the desert, and their recovery, the approach to zero, mentioned repeatedly in the first third of

---

[5] For a discussion of these sepulchral traits and the pre-conscious, see Gavin Keeney, "Séance 'C.M.'," *Senses of Cinema* 64, September 2012, http://sensesofcinema.com/2012/feature-articles/seance-c-m/. Also published in Gavin Keeney, *Dossier Chris Marker: The Suffering Image* (Newcastle upon Tyne: Cambridge Scholars Publishing, 2012), 223–232.

[6] Jean-Luc Godard, *Éloge de l'amour* (*In Praise of Love*), DVD (New York: New Yorker Video, 2003).

[7] That is, the first draft of *La Méditerranée et le monde méditerranéen à l'époque de Philippe II* (Paris: Colin, 1949).

Film Socialisme, amidst the socio-political kitsch of the cruise-ship sequence, registers the presence of abstract thought in cinema as "zero," beyond which is the negative (negative numbers, if you accept the mathematical principles or premise of the locution), yet a "negative" that is the secreted positive of the filmic conventions upturned. The negative as positive, then, as in avant-garde photography, and the positive as negative, as in the socio-cultural maelstrom Godard is examining.

II. THE *CINÉ-ESSAY*

> Thus then also in the of now time [a] remnant according to [the] election of grace has become; but if by grace, [and] no more from works, then—grace no more becomes grace.[8]
> Saint Paul

When Theodor W. Adorno's comments on the virtues of the essay form are applied to cinema, the main criterion of similitude and/or dissimilitude is the "containment of time"—or, how the film begins and ends, and how that necessary closure either opens, or not, onto *other* times.[9] This seems common to all progenitors of the film-essay and to all latter-day proponents of its sometimes epistolary, but almost always literary-critical modalities.[10]

---

[8] Giorgio Agamben, "Appendix: Interlinear Translation of Pauline Texts," in Giorgio Agamben, *The Time that Remains: A Commentary on the Letter to the Romans*, trans. Patricia Dailey (Stanford: Stanford University Press, 2005), 161. First published as *Tempo che resta: Un commento all Lettera ai Romani* (Turin: Bollati Boringhieri, 2000).

[9] Theodor W. Adorno, "The Essay as Form," in *Notes to Literature*, ed. Rolf Tiedemann, trans. Shierry Weber Nicholsen, Vol. 1 (New York: Columbia University Press, 1991), 3–23.

[10] Arguably, at least in Film Studies, the contemporary film-essay form dates to Alexandre Astruc's essay, "La caméra-stylo" (1948). In *Histoire(s) du cinéma*, Godard attributes the idea of the camera as pen to Jean-Paul Sartre, who then suggested it to Astruc. See Alexandre Astruc, "The Birth of a New Avant-Garde: La Caméra-stylo," in Peter Graham, ed., *The New Wave: Critical Landmarks* (Garden City: Doubleday, 1968), 17–23. First published in *Écran français* 144 (March 30, 1948) and considered one of the major influences on the development of Chris Marker's approach to the film-essay. See also Jean-Luc Godard, *Godard on Godard: Critical Writings*, ed. Jean Narboni and Tom Milne (New York: Viking, 1972), a translation of essays selected from *La gazette du cinéma* and *Les cahiers du cinéma*, and Richard Brody, *Everything is Cinema: The Working Life of Jean-Luc Godard* (New York: Metropolitan Books/Henry Holt & Co., 2008). For Godard's omnivorous reading habits prior to making films, plus his apparent "fear" of the complexities and discipline of

Are not all avant-garde films quietly, or noisily, *ciné-essays*? It is the transferability of these traits that is the determinate feature of works that invoke the speculative while they also privilege either the visual or the linguistic (the latter not always co-equivalent with high discursivity). The essay proper, while notably discursive, also indulges the mnemonic resources of "images buried in deserts," left there to attain a certain patina, and words assembled in such a manner draw on the patent firepower of their "imageability" (the seemingly archaic provenance of pre-conscious strata in thought).

Godard uses diegetic sound in an equally disjointed manner, the flapping wind in the cruise-ship section of *Film Socialisme* signaling both the ever-present background noise of the given world but also the convenient annoyance he requires to further fracture things. There is no Romanticism in his appropriation of the natural world, for his work seems to be fully consistent with the subjectivization of that milieu for other, "ambient" purposes. Neither is it Post-Romantic. The lake in *JLG/JLG: Autoportrait de décembre* (1994) and *Adieu au langage* function as visual-sonic metaphors, to a certain degree erasing other things or prominently displacing other things—in the case of *JLG/JLG*, Godard himself.[11] In the same manner of speaking, Godard's shadowy appearance in his auto-portrait produced for television is similar to Tacita Dean's maneuvering around the actual Michael Hamburger and favoring his house and garden in Suffolk, England, in her 2007 portrait of the renowned translator of Hölderlin, Brecht, Rilke, and Grass.[12]

---

literature proper, see Brody, *Everything is Cinema*, 18. These reading practices are on full display in *Histoire(s) du cinéma*. The point is that Godard expropriates from literature what he requires and re-deploys such fragments as aphorisms and/or epigraphs to support the larger suppositions of the work.

[11] Jean-Luc Godard, *JLG/JLG: Auto-portrait de décembre*, DVD (Neuilly-sur-Seine: Gaumont Vidéo, 2010).

[12] Tacita Dean's 28-minute, 16mm color anamorphic film *Michael Hamburger* (2007) is "a film about the Berlin born British poet and

The obscurity Godard laces his works with pushes the art work as form of scholarship to the edge of things, deeply embedding the visual-sonic landscape in an existentialist milieu that contains the primordial chord that runs through the grave and forbidding works of many of his chosen antecedents and exemplars (dead or alive). One might name this chord the Death Drive, were it not that Sigmund Freud has already commanded that term. In fact, the disintegrating aspects of the image and the tortuous, deconstructed narratives of Godard's films appear to be inhabited by a will to dissolve into pure idea, versus Nature as such. They seem Platonic. The discord is utterly contingent; for one senses that the containment of time (the inner time of the film) is what wishes to vanish/end. Yet vanish into what type of thin air? Where does the time of film go when it is extinguished/ended? The easy answer is that it returns to a constructive milieu or archive to be re-constructed, quoted, re-assembled, and re-deployed once more in service to an immemorial source for its incommensurate resources.

translator Michael Hamburger, which evolved from a commission for an exhibition about the writer, W.G. Sebald. Dean chose to film Michael Hamburger, whom Sebald meets in a chapter of his book, *The Rings of Saturn*, and focuses on him exclusively in relation to the subject of apples—'fruit to outlast our days'—which Hamburger cultivated in his Suffolk orchard" (Press Release, Marian Goodman Gallery, New York, New York, http://www.mariangoodman.com/exhibitions/2009-04-02_tacita-dean/). "Tacita Dean," Marian Goodman Gallery, April 2–29, 2009, was an exhibition that included *Fernweh* ("a longing to travel"), "large scale overpainted photographs" (a technique long exploited by Gerhard Richter, but here "gravure")— for example, *Urdolmen* and *Hünengrab* (2008), and *Riesenbett* (2009), boulders floating in a "sea" of black paint. "Unlike the large photographs of ancient trees, which Dean has worked with before, the images of the stones are isolated by dark matte backgrounds making them otherworldly—detached from and of history [at once]— and imposing in their solemnity" (Press Release, Marian Goodman Gallery).

If one listens with a "third ear" to the ambient music of Brian Eno, for example, originating in the early 1970s, including its incorporation into the work of David Bowie (*Low*, 1977) and U2 (initially in *The Unforgettable Fire*, 1984, and *The Joshua Tree*, 1987), the impression is that the distortion, dissonance, and atmospheric effects are derived from an *internal* landscape versus an external landscape, yet an internal landscape that produces the sonic landscape that reverberates with that very exterior landscape that it is, perhaps, nonetheless abstracted from. Thus Guy Debord's sentiment: "At night we walk in circles and are consumed by fire...."[13] There is a Gnostic remainder somewhere in the shadowy undercurrents of cinema and ambient music.

And there is a two-way street that may never have actually been a one-way street. The range of effects in electronica, trance, and such that is derived from these early experiments by Eno and confreres, while dependent on an array of synthesizers, quite often is incorporated into more conventional musical forms (such as the sampling of Thievery Corporation) to provide new or belated cachet. In the case of recent work by Nick Cave and The Bad Seeds (*Push the Sky Away*, 2013), the ambient-atmospheric wall or wave replaces the previous clarity of layered musical expression, imparting a breakthrough to new performative and expressive forms. (The departure of guitarist Mick Harvey in 2009 does not completely explain this shift.) Notably, the lyrics on many of the new songs, though not all, recede behind the music (at least in the studio version) and the piano work of Nick Cave becomes less overtly lyrical and submerged within the totality of the sonic tableau. Yet, in the case of Nick Cave and The Bad Seeds, this atmospheric aspect was always present in the occasional outbursts by Warren Ellis, a violin virtuoso reminis-

---

[13] Guy Debord's last film, *In girum imus nocte et consumimur igni* (1978). For an English translation of the voice-over from this film, see Bureau of Public Secrets, http://www.bopsecrets.org/SI/debord.films/ingirum.htm.

cent of Paganini, and in the subtle guitar effects of Blixa Bargeld (metal slides, etc.), in Ellis' case an excess that was further exemplified in his work with Dirty Three, and in the case of Bargeld, a predilection for industrial sounds (with the West Berlin band, Einstürzende Neubauten, meaning, "Collapsing New Buildings") that he never quite left but returned to when he did leave The Bad Seeds. Yet now Ellis has switched to electric guitar (with loops) on *Push the Sky Away* and Bargeld is long gone. (The mix of the songs on *Push the Sky Away* vary depending on performance. In many cases the live or official video mix for key songs reverts to the lyrical form versus the ambient studio form, suggesting the mélange is indeterminate or unsettled.) Former Talking Heads' front man David Byrne's experiments with "wiring" buildings for sound and then interacting with the environment also suggests that the sometimes quixotic quest for the origins of music in Nature or the Real is more myth than reality, which prompts all the usual questions regarding whether or not what inhabits Nature and the Real is the same web of ethereal forces that lives inside our heads. The elusive Thing-in-Itself of Immanuel Kant's *Critiques* is knowable, after all, in the short circuit known as the aesthetic-sublime.

Thus avant-garde music and avant-garde cinema intersect, and Godard's maniacal collecting (of images, sounds, literary *bons mots*, and such) supports his high-discursive project, which does, indeed, resemble the literary project he abandoned in the 1950s, cinema providing, arguably, an easier road. That is, the *redemption of the multiple arts via the diremption of the fictive whole* (or, per avant-garde inquests, the quest for the universal in the shattered tableaux of the contingent).

III. *HISTOIRE(S) DU CINÉMA*

> It is the activity of the intellect that constitutes complete human happiness. / Such a life as this however will be higher than the human level: not in virtue of his humanity will a man achieve it, but in virtue of something within him that is divine.[14]
>
> Aristotle

Godard's critical project for cinema (its aporistic redemption) proceeds by way of an often-excruciating examination of its spectral *dynamis*—its semi-conscious embedded agency or power.[15] This comes to expression in Godard's eight-episode, 266-minute *Histoire(s) du cinéma* foremost due to the explicit discursive nature of that ten-year project (1988-1998).[16]

If Godard identifies sex and death (Eros and Thanatos) as

---

[14] Aristotle, *Nicomachean Ethics*, trans. H. Rackham (Cambridge: Harvard University Press, 1934), Book X, VII, 7–8 (617).

[15] The term *dynamis* is used by Giorgio Agamben to signify the signature of a work, in the sense that the "archaeology" of discursive practices he performs requires the erasure of surface in favor of retrieving what is buried in a work. In the last phases of his *Homo Sacer* project, and consistent with the theological themes he closes with, the archaeology of knowledge he undertakes involves the transference of a form of "biblical exegesis" to secular practices, which only ever hide their relation to ancient magico-religious practices. Indeed, Agamben's recent excavations of such unconscious precepts develops from Foucault and the latter's unfinished work on the emergence of the bio-political as the locus of the most pernicious practices imaginable under the auspices of power for the sake of power—arguably, the very issue now laid bare in late-modern, neo-liberal capitalist exploitation of knowledge proper.

[16] Jean-Luc Godard, *Histoire(s) du cinéma*, DVD (St. Charles: Olive Films, 2011). For an inventory of the cinematic and literary references utilized in the film, see Céline Scemama-Heard, *Histoire(s) du cinéma de Jean-Luc Godard: La force faible d'un art* (Paris: L'Harmattan, Paris, 2006). See also Jean-Luc Godard, *Histoire(s) du cinéma*, 4 vols. (Paris: Gallimard/Gaumont, 1998), and Jean-Luc Godard, *Jean-Luc Godard par Jean-Luc Godard*, ed. Alain Bergala (Paris: Éditions des Cahiers du Cinéma, 1998).

two great themes in early-to-high Hollywood cinema (generally the years between World War I and World War II), and then resorts to the mordantly dark joke that Germany "took France from behind" at the outbreak of World War II (a grotesquerie stated and re-staged repeatedly by interweaving images of gratuitous sex and violence as imagistic-linguistic romp), the purpose is not an overt insult to either High Hollywood or Third Republic France, but, instead, a means to set up the debatable inference that cinema's first redemption came by way of newsreels and films (Chaplin et al.) able to document or mock the absurdities of the Nazi atrocities perpetrated from the ancient ground of the reptilian cortex—the inhuman origin of the bio-political game that dances over the surface of history, and the only starting point for assigning to film history the role of humanity's "epiphenomenal" conscience (that is, should film ever connote and/or reach the abstract power of the classical term *humanitas*[17]). Godard makes of cinema, then, a new *danse macabre*. In doing so, he is also establishing a rogue regime, spectral agency, given to film itself (albeit a dangerous liaison with truth), plus, as redemptive chord, a regime of abstract agency *outside* of film proper (reminiscent of medieval arguments regarding Agent Intellect), and to which the supposed autonomy of film (the infamous "art with no future") might relate. In this way moral perspectives return, even if Godard is only comfortable presenting them in an aporistic, fragmented, self-consciously avant-garde manner. Yet the Socratic method is not real, for Godard prefers sophistry laced with occasional, perhaps accidental and generally sardonic instances of apperception—all such instances of transcendental apperception nonetheless explicitly exiting the regimes of visuality he deconstructs. This

---

[17] A term distinguished historically by the interrelated and loquacious concerns of a modified Medieval Trivium, "poetry, grammar, rhetoric, history, and moral philosophy..."—or, the *Studia humanitatis* of Renaissance humanism. See Paul Oskar Kristeller, *Renaissance Thought II: Papers on Humanism and the Arts* (New York: Harper Torchbooks, 1965), 178.

great stress placed on visuality (*visualitas*) is, after all, the only credible reason one might find for Godard's exceptional penchant for using sophistry as bludgeon. Captive within his own regimes of fragmented signification, Godard is nonetheless wise enough (throughout these late films) to understand what is at stake in utilizing the "kingdom of shadows" to speak truth to arbitrary power, including the arbitrary power of cinema.[18]

[18] See Gavin Keeney, "Anamnesis," in Keeney, *Dossier Chris Marker*, 7–76. "In this manner, the 'Markerian' kingdom of shadows (images) is a rite of passage. And if that kingdom is a land of colorless shades, an under-world that leads to an over-world, it is a land haunted by the luminous debris of ideological shards that have, as remnants of false consciousness or ideologies past, *fallen even further*, so to speak, betraying true consciousness of the whole anyway through negation, a perhaps lost continent within the worlds-within-worlds model he embraces, but forever present nonetheless *in memory*": Keeney, *Dossier Chris Marker*, 25. See also Jacques Rancière, "Documentary Fiction: Marker and the Fiction of Memory," in Jacques Rancière, *Film Fables*, trans. Emiliano Battista (Oxford: Berg, 2006), 157–170. First published as *La fable cinématographique*, Collection "La librarie du XXe siècle" (Paris: Éditions du Seuil, 2001): "In *The Last Bolshevik*, Marker tells the cinematographic history of cinema's double relationship to Sovietism. He suggests that it is possible to tell the history of the Soviet century through the fates of Soviet filmmakers, through the films they made, those they didn't make, and those they were obliged to make, because all of these attest to the common destiny of cinema and Sovietism. But there is also a more profound reason: the art of cinema is the metaphor, indeed the very cipher, for an idea of the century and of history that found its political incarnation in Sovietism. Marker's project, in its own way, mirrors Godard's in *Histoire(s) du cinéma*, where Godard proposes to read the history of our century not by looking at its history, but by looking at the stories, or some of the stories, of the cinema, since cinema is not only contemporaneous with the century, but an integral part of its very 'idea'" (166–167). Rancière notes that the difference between Godard and Marker, in cinema, is that with Marker the word takes precedence over the image: "Of course, Godard's method and Marker's are quite different. Godard produces another form of the 'poem of the poem' by using the resources of videographic writing to

Visuality has its own troubled history in the multiple arts, with John Ruskin registering its discordant relationship to the "ideal as the Real" at the near-end of classicism and neo-classicism in the pictorial arts.[19] Godard's version of cinema

render the power of the blackboard and the power of pictorial montage identical on the screen. He sends the machine devoted to information into shock with his method of saturating images or zigzagging through them; he superimposes in the same 'audio-visual' unit an image from one film, an image from a second film, the music from a third, a voice from a fourth, and words from a fifth; he complicates this intertwining further by using images from painting and by punctuating the whole thing with a commentary in the present. Each of his images and conjunctions of images is a treasure hunt: they open onto multiple paths and create virtual space of indefinite connections and resonances. Marker favors a dialectical approach instead. He composes a series of images (interviews, archival documents, clips from the classics of Soviet cinema and from propaganda films, scenes from the opera, virtual images, etc.) that he arranges, always in strict adherence to the cinematographic principles of montage, in order to define very specific moments in the relationship between the cinematographic 'kingdom of shadows' and the 'shadows of the [utopian] kingdom.' While Godard gives us a smooth plane, Marker creates a memory we can scan. And yet he falls prey, like Godard but even more so, to an obvious paradox: he feels compelled to punctuate all these 'images that speak for themselves,' as well as the interlacing of series of images that make cinema into a meta-language and into a 'poem of the poem,' with an imperious voice-over commentary that tells us what it is that they 'say'" (167). The term *The kingdom of shadows* (*Le royaume des ombres*) comes from the first half of Marker's *Le tombeau d'Alexandre* (1993), a two-part portrait of Russian filmmaker Alexandre Medvedkine that was produced by La Sept/Arte, for French public television. Hi-8 video (transferred to film), black and white, and color, 120 minutes (Part 1, "Le royaume des ombres," 58 minutes; Part 2, "Les ombres du royaume," 62 minutes).

[19] This Hegelian privileging of the ideal in the Real is a hallmark of Ruskin's socio-cultural bias (socio-political work), despite his often-stated antipathy to German Idealism. These remarks on Ruskin and *visualitas* come from Gavin Keeney, "Pure Visuality," privately circulated manuscript (2010), a conflation of field notes, short poems, and comments surveying multiple events and readings in 2009, inclusive

(through his own works) therefore resembles what Ruskin called "grotesque idealism": "The imagination, when at play is curiously like bad children, and likes to play with fire; in its entirely serious moods it dwells by preference on beautiful and sacred images, but in its mocking or playful moods it is apt to jest, sometimes waywardly, sometimes slightly and wickedly, with death and sin; hence an enormous mass of grotesque art, some most noble and useful."[20]

Yet Godard is in good company: "If by words,—how do you know their meanings? Here is a short piece of precious word revelation, for instance. 'God is love.'...All the words and sounds ever uttered, all the revelations of cloud, or flame, or crystal, are utterly powerless. They cannot tell you, in the smallest point, what love means. Only the broken mirror can."[21]

---

of: browsing John Ruskin's *The Poetry of Architecture* (1837) and *Modern Painters* (1885); seeing "Tacita Dean" at the Marian Goodman Gallery, New York, New York, USA (April 2–29, 2009); hearing Slavoj Žižek at Jack Tilton Gallery, New York, New York, USA ("Architectural Parallax: Spandrels and Other Phenomena of Class Struggle," April 23, 2009); witnessing "Titian, Tintoretto, Veronese: Rivals in Renaissance Venice" at the Museum of Fine Arts, Boston, Massachusetts, USA (March 15–August 16, 2009); reading and abstracting Janet Harbord's *Chris Marker: La Jetée* (London: Afterall Books, 2009); reading and mapping John Ruskin's *The Relation Between Michael Angelo and Tintoret: Seventh of the Course of Lectures on Sculpture Delivered at Oxford, 1870-71* (London: Smith, Elder and Co., 1872); and attending, as critic, "The Politics of the Envelope," Princeton Envelope Group (PEG), ARC 504, Princeton School of Architecture, Princeton, New Jersey, USA (May 8, 2009) and Degree Project Reviews, Division of Architecture & Design, Rhode Island School of Design, Providence, Rhode Island, USA (Woods Gerry Gallery, May 16, 2009).

[20] John Ruskin, "Of the True Ideal: Thirdly, Grotesque," in John Ruskin, *Modern Painters*, Vol. 3 (New York: John W. Lovell Co., 1885), 112–113 [112–128].

[21] John Ruskin, "Part IX: Of Ideas of Relation: – II. Of Invention Spiritual, Chapter I. – The Dark Mirror," in John Ruskin, *Modern Painters*, Vol. 5 (New York: John W. Lovell Co., 1885), 220 [213–221].

Thus the grotesque (as it also appears in *The Stones of Venice*), and an appalled Ruskin—though thrilled at the same time by "appalling" and "eventful" truths. This "colossal grasp" of the sacred leads toward Chapter I, Part IX (Vol. 5), the concluding volume of *Modern Painters*—that is, toward "the dark mirror." What is this "dark mirror," despite its biblical allusion? Is it not pure visuality, the same that haunts the quest for non-ideological utopian projects, arguably the purpose of art itself? "A mirror dark, distorted, broken"—here one finds shades of the self-same radical orthodoxy embraced by G.K. Chesterton, and, its antidote, an eschatological something (non-diachronic, non-teleological), or the proverbial "redemptive whatever" Ruskin assigns to the arts and consigns the arts to (as seeing). For Chesterton, "It's not that the world could be better or worse. It is better *and* worse, fully fallen and perfectly redeemable. We are to go at it with 'a fiercer delight and a fiercer discontent', and rather than deny optimism and pessimism, which is where his logic seemed to be leading us, we are to seek both of them in their extreme, irrational forms. One needs to be 'a fanatical pessimist and a fanatical optimist.'"[22]

Ruskin, not unlike Godard, is notably split in half by his relationship to Fine Art: "If Ruskin is eventually alone (and *desertion before disconfirmation* informs much of his performance), he is not, in any case, unified in his loneliness. Rather, solipsistically antiphonal, with only himself as company, he is, as if severed by a double axe, either halved or doubled, with his consciousness, like a double tiered labyrinth that is his penultimate Theatre of Blindness, in attempted dialogic discourse with itself, which is, perhaps, Ruskin's ultimate point of failure/success."[23]

There are extraordinarily elegiac moments in *Histoire(s) du cinéma*, foremost those passages that invoke the multiple

---

[22] Michael Wood, "A Preference for Torquemada," *London Review of Books* 31.7 (April 9, 2009): 8 [8–10].

[23] Jay Fellows, "Preface," in Jay Fellows, *Ruskin's Maze: Mastery and Madness in His Art* (Princeton: Princeton University Press, 1981), xv–xvi; emphasis added.

arts. In the section dealing with the emergence of post-war Italian neo-realist cinema, focusing primarily on Roberto Rossellini's *Roma città aperta* (1945), Godard suggests that Italy was capable of producing this seminal shift in European cinema due to its vast and deep literary traditions (Dante et al.).[24] "Things are there, why manipulate them?" is the operative question for privileging Rossellini, Pasolini, Fellini, and the Visconti Brothers. Indeed, some of the more savage interludes, here and there, throughout *Histoire(s) du cinéma*, are scenes from Pier Paolo Pasolini's *Il Vangelo Secondo Matteo* (1964) intercut with some of the most brutal aspects of cinema's obsession with sex and violence. Godard uses Pasolini's almost apocalyptic portrayal of an accusatory Sermon on the Mount to counter cinema's dark side (an abject revivification of magico-religious themes identified by Aby Warburg in, for example, Baroque art). The further recourse to the concept of "shapes that think" (*Denkbild*) notably unsettles the passive nature of this history of projective geometry (Renaissance perspective) transferred to visual exegesis, for titillation or not.[25]

In "Part 5: The Coin of the Absolute,"[26] Godard returns to themes broached in previous sections and, while discussing French New Wave cinema, in "Part 6: A New Wave," proposes the somewhat severe judgment that the image is "in the order of redemption" (via Henri Langlois).[27] In "Part 8: The

[24] *Histoire(s) du cinéma*, Chapter 3(a), "Le monnaie de l'absolu" (1998), 27 minutes.

[25] Godard pushes the theoretical origins for cinema backward as far as the Napoleonic Wars, with a French officer pacing his prison cell in Russia while fashioning through internal conversation with himself the geometric principles for the projection of images. Regarding *Denkbild*, see David Foster, "'Thought-images' and Critical-lyricisms: The *Denkbild* and Chris Marker's *Le tombeau d'Alexandre*," *Image [&] Narrative* 10.3 (2009): http://www.kravanja.eu/pdf_files/ChrisMarker1.pdf.

[26] *Histoire(s) du cinéma*, Chapter 3(a), "La monnaie de l'absolu."

[27] *Histoire(s) du cinéma*, Chapter 3(b), "Une vague nouvelle" (1998), 27 minutes. "Parce qu'oublié déjà / interdit encore / invisible toujours / tel était notre cinéma / et cela m'est resté / et Langlois nous le

Signs Among Us,"[28] we are told that the image that denies emptiness is emptiness itself looking back at us." Shapes that think (filmic images) are, earlier on, first discussed by way of the paintings of Édouard Manet, all of whose female subjects seem to be saying, "I know what you are thinking" (which is to say, the subject of the painting, with Manet, begins to think *and* speak, no longer mute). For Godard corrects an interlocutor at one point who claims cinema for the twentieth century by saying that it was developed in the twentieth century, but it belongs *in spirit* to the nineteenth century.

Yet "Part 4: Fatal Beauty"[29] seems to be where things lost to cinema return with vengeance, passion, and tenderness, intertwined in a Holy Trinity of the sort that requires the intervention of poetic language and the literary virtues that appear to concern Godard above all else. Sabine Azéma serves notice on cinema (reading passages from art historian Jacques Élie Faure) regarding its putative origins, just as later in the film, "Part 7: The Control of the Universe,"[30] cinema

confirma / c'est le mot exact / que l'image / est d'abord de l'ordre de la redemption / attention, celle du reel": Godard, *Histoire(s) du cinéma*, 148–149. He adds elsewhere: "Careful, though: the redemption of the real." Regarding Godard and Henri Langlois, founder of the Cinémathèque Française, see Michael Temple, "Big Rhythm and the Power of Metamorphosis: Some Models and Precursors for *Histoire(s) du cinéma*," in Michael Temple and James S. Williams, eds., *The Cinema Alone: Essays on the Work of Jean-Luc Godard, 1985-2000* (Amsterdam: Amsterdam University Press, 2000), 81-82 [77–96].

[28] *Histoire(s) du cinéma*, Chapter 4(b), "Les signes parmi nous" (1998), 38 minutes.

[29] *Histoire(s) du cinéma*, Chapter 2(b), "Fatale beauté" (1997), 28 minutes.

[30] *Histoire(s) du cinéma*, Chapter 4(a), "Le contrôle d'univers," (1998), 27 minutes. "Le cinéma ne pleure pas sur nous, il ne nous réconforte pas, puisqu'il est avec nous, puisqu'il est nous-mêmes....Il est encore là quand nous sommes vieux, que nous regardons fixement du côté de la nuit qui vient, il est là quand nous sommes morts...": see "Contrôle de l'univers," *Histoire(s) du cinéma*, Jean-Luc Lacuve, ed., *Le Ciné-club de Caen*, 2005 (with reference to Marie Anne Lanavère, ed., *Le site de l'Encyclopédie Nouveaux Médias*, Centre Georges

seems to speak from the crypt, in a grisly voice, in defense of itself against charges of apostasy.³¹ This extended "reading" by Azéma regards "homecoming"....Who is ventriloquizing/ anathematizing cinema versus memory? It is Godard. Who is later defending cinema "from the crypt"? It is Godard. Godard/Azéma's soliloquy invokes universal time, arguably what is caught in the throes of the compressed or contained time of cinema. The voice in "The Control of the Universe" invokes contingency. Elsewhere Godard tells us that the only proper cinematic question is "where to begin and end a shot." This, as well, denotes the internal time of the work of art and the art work as form of scholarship (here the film-essay), an aspect of art described to great effect by Giorgio Agamben apropos of the sestina.³² Again, to distend, paraphrase, and rearrange

Pompidou, http://www.newmedia-art.org/sommaire/francais/sommaire. htm), http://www.cineclubdecaen.com/realisat/godard/histoiresducin ema4a.htm.

³¹ For the "contrasting temporalities" of Faure's *Histoire de l'art: L'esprit des formes* (Paris: G. Crès, 1927), for example, and why Godard may prefer such "phenomenological" treatments of art versus dialectical or rationalist-positivist forms of art history, see Temple, "Big Rhythm and the Power of Metamorphosis," 86–95. He could as easily have used Henri Focillon, except that Faure has a certain grade-school pedigree that Godard favors over the more erudite and austere Focillon. This is, of course, a populist affectation. The other main art-historical figure often drawn upon by Godard, including in *Histoire(s) du cinéma*, is André Malraux, especially his *La voix du silence* (1947-1949). The common ground is the *longue durée* of Braudel et al., versus the episodic penchant of contemporary historical and art-historical exegesis and cultural criticism. In many respects, Godard is combining Romantic historiography as practiced by Jules Michelet with the exquisite story-telling powers of the Annales School (Braudel et al.). The outcome is that he addresses Big History through micro-history, his method for examining the history of cinema fragmenting into a kaleidoscopic telling of the conflicting histories of precise cinematic moments. The deconstructivist play with the intertitle "Histoire(s) du cinéma" signals this intent, as does the parenthetical 's' of the title of the project.

³² Agamben, *The Time that Remains*. See also, Giorgio Agamben,

the rhetorical resources of Godard's more gnomic diatribes (eloquent or otherwise, via intercessionary or in person), "art [to create its despair] creates the nonperishable with perishable things." This is so, such that "the space formed might outlast time." Therefore, cinema is "neither an art nor a technique." It is a mystery: "O homecoming / O universal time [where nothing was mute / to the child's mute eyes / and everything was a new creation]."[33]

Godard's *Histoire(s) du cinéma* connects—backward—to Marcel Proust through Faure. (At one point we do see Proust on his deathbed.) For Faure's "florid" aesthetics resemble those of the first volume of *À la recherche du temps perdu*, which have been shown to be Ruskinian, and which Proust sought to kill off. Yet Godard, as avant-gardist, must hide the

---

"The Time that is Left," *Epoché* 7.1 (Fall 2002): 1–14. See especially Agamben's explication of the concept of "chronogenetic time," derived from the linguist Gustave Guillaume, or, "a time which includes its own genesis" (4–5), with reference to Gustave Guillaume, *Temps et verbe: Théorie des aspects, des modes, et des temps. Suivi de L'architectonique du temps dans les langues classiques* (Paris: Champion, 1970). "In every representation of time, in every discourse by means of which we try to define and to represent time, another time is involved, which cannot be exhausted in them. It is as if man, insofar as he is a thinking and speaking being, produces an additional time, which prevents him from perfectly coinciding with chronological time, with the time of which he can make images and representations. Yet this time is not another time, not a supplementary time that could be added from outside to chronological time. It is, rather, a time within time—not ulterior, but interior—which measures only my disconnection with it, the impossibility of coinciding with my representation of time—but for the same reason, it also opens up the possibility of grasping and accomplishing it": Agamben, *The Time that Remains*, 5. Regarding Guillaume's system of psychomechanics, see Walter Hirtle, *Language in the Mind: An Introduction to Guillaume's Theory* (Montreal: McGill-Queen's University Press, 2007). Regarding verb tenses, see especially in Hirtle, "Chapter 10: The System of the Verb," and "Chapter 14: Concord, Discord, and the Incidence of Verb to Subject."

[33] *Histoire(s) du cinéma*, Chapter 2(b), "Fatale beauté" (1997).

trail. If cinema belongs in spirit to the nineteenth century, Ruskin's austere aesthetics plus his valorization of the ideal in the Real acts to ground Godard's more speculative flights regarding the redemptive value of cinema (the redemption of the Real). What its second redemption might look like, after its confrontation with the killing fields of World War II, and then Bosnia, is an open question. It would seem, however, that with *Notre musique* (2004),[34] and all films following that exquisite and explicit forensic report on the state of all things cinematic, Godard assumed a Markerian posture that resembles the cyclical and semi-apocalyptic pronouncement of the end of cinema per se as the end of the world. Godard's overriding synchronic, structuralist vision of history has absorbed cinema; history and the history of cinema are now inseparable and synonymous. What Chris Marker saw, however, was the emergence of a generation of new film-essayists (some exceedingly young) pushing once again against the dictates of the market ("the coin of the realm") and producing short films that essentially reveal the "deep grammar" of cinema.[35] Made for the most part outside of the film industry, such films were neither documentary per se nor indicative of a penchant for classic *nombrilisme* or narcissism—though many appeared as such. But is not Godard guilty of feigning the self-same self-reflexivity? These new forays into video are, indeed, often highly self-reflective films; yet they detail in being so the inner resources *of* film. By extolling their virtues through mimicry, both Marker and Godard shifted the expectation for the death of cinema forward several generations at a minimum.

January 16, 2015

[34] Jean-Luc Godard, *Notre musique*, DVD (New York: Wellspring Media, 2005).
[35] Marker's production under the name "Kosinki" for YouTube is instructive. See, for example, *Leïla attaque* (c. 2006). Uploaded November 23, 2007. Video, 1 minute 9 seconds. Marker uploaded at least 11 short videos to YouTube between the years 2006 and 2011.

Essay Four

Film Mysticism and "The Haunted Wood"

I. *FILM MYSTICISME*

Car ce n'est pas à des anges que Dieu a soumis le monde à venir....[1]

Chris Marker

In terms of the speculative-intellectual pursuits of cinema, especially via the film-essay (but also via the film-fairytale), there is an unauthorized and heretical film buried within *all* cinema—it is called *Film mysticisme*. It functions as morality tale, but it is (quietly) a high-moral critique of the Imaginary itself as it comes to reside within cinema. Occasionally portions of this film escape the Saturnian pull of dark silence and appear in the world. Marker and Godard have facilitated many such sightings.

---

[1] Epigraph from Chris Mayor [Chris Marker], "Les vivants et les morts," *Esprit* 122 (May 1946): 768 [768–785], with reference to Hebrews 11:5. Marker published this text under the pseudonym "Chris Mayor." It is one of two articles by Marker from 1946 preceding the adoption of the nom de plume "Chris Marker," in *Esprit*, in 1947.

A rumored, "lost" 8mm film said to have been made by Marker around 1946, if it ever truly existed (and if it did not, its role in his obscure early work becomes doubly interesting, as apocrypha), concerned the apocalyptic dimension within mid-century cinema, as cinema became indissolubly intertwined with history. This lost film, *La fin du monde, vu par l'ange Gabriel*,[2] is indicative of a surrealist vein that runs through his work from the late 1940s, and from *La jetée* (1962) to *Owls at Noon Prelude: The Hollow Men* (2005).[3] The

---

[2] The title of the film is a reference to Blaise Cendrars' ciné-roman *La fin du monde, filmée par l'ange N-D* (Paris: Éditions de la Sirène, 1919). The novel was originally written as a screenplay but later published as a novel with illustrations by Fernand Léger. The rumor is attributed to Alain Resnais. In characteristic self-effacing fashion, Marker mentions in 1962 his experiments with 8mm films prior to his apprenticeship with Resnais, and their collaborative project *Les statues meurent aussi* (1950–1953), saying they were "little bits of 8mm that were rather awful," while also mentioning Resnais' experiments with 16mm, "which one day should be the concern of cinémathèques": cited in Jean-Louis Pays, "Extract from an Interview with Chris Marker by Jean-Louis Pays...," in Anatole Dauman, *Anatole Dauman: Pictures of a Producer*, ed. Jacques Gerber, trans. Paul Willemen (London: British Film Institute, 1992), 93 [90–93]. Resnais described Marker's *La fin du monde* as "mostly blurry and sometimes unidentifiable images shot in a devastated Berlin at the end of the war." See Nora M. Alter, *Chris Marker* (Urbana: University of Illinois Press, 2006), 8. Resnais' comments may be found in Alain Resnais, "Rendez-vous des amis," in Birgit Kämper and Thomas Tode, eds., *Chris Marker: Filmessayist* (Munich: Institut Français de Munich, 1997), 207.

[3] *Owls at Noon Prelude: The Hollow Men* (2005). Installation/video: Two-channel, eight-screen CD-ROM-based video [text composed in Javascript], color, 19-minute loop with sound. Created by Chris Marker for the Museum of Modern Art, New York, New York, USA. "This nineteen-minute piece takes its starting point and its title from Eliot's 1925 poem 'The Hollow Men,' which reflected on the European wasteland that resulted from the first World War. Marker's meditation mixes his thoughts on the poem with images of wounded veterans and achingly beautiful women, evoking the hopelessness of those who lived through Europe's near suicide. As this war comes

film's possible non-existence hardly matters when other works attest to a similar exploration of the proverbial Night of the World. There are innumerable "intertexts" as well (or those written works of Marker's that are often cinematic-literary events), and which one might surmise influenced later films and installations.[4]

---

back to haunt us in both the Balkans and the Middle East, Marker combs a vast beach of images to create an echo chamber in which the viewer can either remember or witness for the first time the reality of a civilization's self-slaughter" (*Museum of Modern Art*, http://www.moma.org/calendar/exhibitions/115?locale=en). See Adrian Martin, Raymond Bellour, and Chris Marker, *Owls at Noon Prelude: The Hollow Men*, ed. Robert Leonard, Ben Wilson (Brisbane: Institute of Modern Art, 2008), published following the exhibition "Owls at Noon Prelude: The Hollow Men," Institute of Modern Art, Brisbane, Australia, 2007. Includes the essays: Adrian Martin, "Crossing Marker," 5–11, and Raymond Bellour, "Marker's Gesture," trans. Adrian Martin, 13–19. The balance of the book is a portfolio of images (*découpage intégral*) from the video *Owls at Noon Prelude: The Hollow Men*, plus select photograms or stills. See also Keith Sanborn, "Shades without Colour," *Artforum* 43.10 (Summer 2005): 79 (a review of "Owls at Noon Prelude: The Hollow Men" at the Museum of Modern Art, New York, New York, which includes an image of the installation—photo by Elizabeth Felicella).

[4] Additionally, there is Chris Marker, "Till the End of Time," *Esprit* 129 (January 1947): 145–151, dated "Octobre 1945" ("A vivid, disquieting short story," according to Catherine Lupton, *Chris Marker: Memories of the Future* [London: Reaktion Books, 2005], 27). "Set after the war in an unspecified location, 'Till the end of time' hallucinates the dissolution of the world in the mind of a shopkeeper who becomes transfixed by the mouth and voice of a mysterious woman after she has taken shelter in his shop during a rainstorm. With its descriptive economy and abrupt shifts of viewpoint, the story anticipates the cinematic construction of *Le Coeur net*": Lupton, *Chris Marker*, 27–28. Also broadcast on December 30, 1949, as *Jusqu'à la fin des temps* (a 17-minute "essai radiophonique"), by the postwar, public radio station Paris-Inter (precursor to France Inter). This short story was translated into English after Marker's death and is included in the catalogue for the Marker retrospective at Whitechapel Gallery, London, England. See Chris Darke, Magnus Af Petersens, and Habda

Thus, the occasional apocalyptic visions of Godard and Marker (film-essays or otherwise) point to that dimension within cinema that most interests both, *as auteurs*. The resources of the filmic imagination closely resemble the deeply buried, immemorial processes of thought and enunciation (language and mimesis). In many ways the visual arts (inclusive of cinema) are means for conversing with the self-same. It is axiomatic that the Revelation of John is an event that occurs on an inner plane, as vision, but it is less agreed upon that its historical value may be founded on the same schism in language and representation that tore Ruskin and Warburg in two, as above, and which accounts in part for the metaphysical-existential torsion of Godard's *Histoire(s) du cinéma*. More cannot be said on such a subject directly, a fairly consistent aspect of art and high scholarship, other than to privilege the dynamic aspects of such a vision in works of literary, textual, and visual merit.[5] Suffice to say that there is a trinitarian something working through Apocalypse, Death, and Resurrection. This trinitarian something is also present in cinema,

---

Rashid, eds., *Chris Marker: A Grin Without a Cat* (London: Whitechapel Gallery, 2014). Published to accompany the exhibition "Chris Marker" held at the Whitechapel Gallery, London, April 16–June 22, 2014 and Lunds Konsthall, Lund, Sweden, February 6–March 29, 2015.

[5] "In a sense, fear is the daughter of God, redeemed on Good Friday night. She's not beautiful, mocked, cursed and disowned by all. But don't get it wrong: she watches over all mortal agony, she intercedes for mankind. For there's a rule and an exception. Culture is the rule, and art is the exception....Nobody speaks the exception. It isn't spoken, it's written...It's composed...It's painted...It's filmed...Or it's lived, and then it's the art of living....": Jean-Luc Godard, *Je vous salue, Sarajevo* (1993). Godard's two-minute film was included in the exhibition "The Image in Question: War – Media – Art" at the Carpenter Center, Harvard University, October 21–December 23, 2010. The exhibition was curated by Harun Farocki and Antje Ehmann. *Je vous salue, Sarajevo* is included in the DVD set, Jean-Luc Godard and Anne-Marie Miéville, *Four Short Films: De l'origine du XXIe siècle* (2000); *The Old Place* (1999); *Liberté et patrie* (2002); and *Je vous salue, Sarajevo* (1993), DVD (Munich: ECM, 2006).

but only when cinema is conscious of the mysterious origins of its own internalizing time-images. These images are, indeed, projected outward. Yet these images return to the threshold of thought, where they have a more archaic purpose to contain and give life to moods, premonitions, ideas, thoughts, and whimsy. The Holy Trinity of Apocalypse, Death, and Resurrection in cinema belongs to the regime of cinema only insofar as cinema escapes final closure. The analogous relation to history is, therefore, that the trinity of Apocalypse, Death, and Resurrection proceeds on the world-historical stage as externalized event, on the one hand, while its secret address is (quietly versus noisily) elsewhere—*in Spirit*.

The film-essay, as avant-garde "text," engages linguistic reserves that are clearly of a pre-conscious order (utilizing what Gustave Guillaume calls time-images and scrambling tenses accordingly and according to rules that apply from within the parameters of the work underway). It is within such a strata within filmmaking that both visual and discursive knowledge, as complex, resumes its quest for the nonperishable in the perishable. *Verb tenses betray (speak of) the mystery of the time-image active within thought proper (an immemorial reserve).* The entire event of history and its mirror, historiography, is predicated on tectonic shifts in verb tenses, as is the strife to be observed in biblical exegesis and elsewhere when comparing teleological time and eschatological time. This is Godard's cinema as mystery (or, cinema as Passion Play). Re-mapping many of his most gnomic statements, as above, reveals what is at play in his own pre-filmic pre-consciousness.

Thus, care of Chris Marker, a preliminary report on the second coming of cinema after its reputed death c. 2000:

> When I announced in the French newspaper *Libération*... the emergence of a new new wave of which *Half-Price* would be the *Breathless*, many were kind enough to go and see the object in question, and had no regrets afterwards, but a few curious minds came back to ask me, ra-

ther sensibly, what I precisely meant by that.

Of course, there is neither Belmondo nor Jean Seberg, neither crime nor pursuit, nor even *The Herald Tribune*, and in order to explain that I hadn't been heavy on the vodka that day, I must go back to a moment in my life. The very moment I saw *Breathless* for the first time. As it is not a comparison "movie to movie" I had in mind, but a comparison "moment to moment." I can still see us on the sidewalk of the avenue Mac-Mahon, it was the end of the day, Agnès Varda was there, with Paul Paviot, and when later we compared our memories, what had struck us was to hear ourselves talking faster and louder than usual, as if something had just happened to us like a kind of urgency, a message to send out immediately. The message approximately was "whatever it is, this we've just seen, we had never seen it before on a screen." Since then I had admired many magnificent, moving, innovating movies, but that physical sense of freshness and urgency, I had never felt that again until *Half-Price*. I had seen, we all have seen many children in movies, sometimes full of genius, and filmed by geniuses. But even geniuses can't forget to be adults and to film children, in a way, from a high angle. During the glorious period of militant cinema, I had explained one day to my workmen comrades that the real movies about their condition, they would have to manage to make them themselves, because the real movies about penguins could only be convincing the day that a penguin would be able to use a camera. This animal metaphor had had some success, and I found it again in quite a number of commentaries about that period. And here we are: thanks to DV cameras, penguins have seized power, and that "wildlife" aspect of Isild's movie—my friends know that coming from me this is a huge compliment—allows us to see what we had never seen before, children the way they are by themselves, when there is no adult gaze, however benevolent, however subtle, to modify what is filmed. Thus another danger: that others may cry "but it's so easy, you only have to put a camera into their paws, and you will get as much as you wish of the childhood you were seeking, raw childhood...." Those people should really make the effort of imagining the work, the amount of work by which a young lady still living in the echo of her childhood found the talent and the energy to reconstruct, with other children, in set-up chosen places, according to a rhythm and a style of her own, not by chance or luck, moments of a lifetime still close enough for her to transmit through them the vibration of captured reality, and already distant enough for her to be able to realize its complexity. This is neither a reality show that the Le Besco kid is offering us, nor that other moronic thing that was called "cinéma-vérité," this is a real director's work, and this is the birth, whether one likes the word or not, of an artist.[6]

---

[6] This letter was sent to *Libération* by Chris Marker in March 2003. See "Les pingouins ont pris le pouvoir," *Libération*, February 11, 2004, http://next.liberation.fr/cinema/2004/02/11/les-pingouins-ont-pris-le-pouvoir-par-chris-marker_468585. Translation courtesy of http://demitarif.lefilm.free.fr/english.htm. *Demi-tarif* was the 2003 directorial debut of actress Isild Le Besco. Marker's 1-minute, 9-second *Leïla attaque* (c. 2006) was intended as an introductory short for a feature-length film by Le Besco. Le Besco is the daughter of actress Catherine Belkhodja. Not coincidentally, Belkhodja starred in Marker's *Level Five* (1996) and his multimedia installation project, *Silent Movie, Starring Catherine Belkhodja* (1994–1995). See also Scott Foundas, "Wildlife: Isild Le Besco," *Film Comment*, January/February 2011, http://www.filmcomment.com/article/wildlife.

II. CODA

Some possible answers to this problem of the redemption of cinema come by way of Marker's *Level Five* (1996),[7] yet problematic answers—"problematic" in the sense that this film was generally poorly received by critics and only confounded a proper reading of its intentions due to it being a type of fairytale.[8] Additionally, its apparent extolling the virtues of the World Wide Web as repository for collective memory only misled viewers and the critical response was essentially an argument over the forms of digital media invoked versus their mnemonic power of persuasion or dissuasion.

At one point we hear Laura (Catherine Belkhodja) in typical Markerian soliloquy asking if the angels do not tap us on the forehead a second or so before birth such that we forget everything (the premise being that we already know everything prior to birth—everything that will befall us and, presumable, *why* such will befall us). She then asks if they do not

[7] Chris Marker, *Level Five*, DVD (New York: Icarus Films, 2014).

[8] For a full description of the technical aspects of the film (computer programs utilized, incorporations, etc.), see Kämper and Tode, eds., *Chris Marker*, 371. For a detailed discussion of this film, see Lupton, *Chris Marker*, 200–205. For various reviews, see Françoise Audé, "*Level Five*: La migraine du temps," *Positif* 433 (March 1997): 76–78; Thierry Jousse, "*Level Five* de Chris Marker: Mr and Mrs Memory," *Cahiers du cinéma* 510 (February 1997): 60–62; Raymond Bellour, "*Level Five*," in Raymond Bellour, *L'entre-images 2: Mots, images* (Paris: P.O.L., 1999), 227–233; Christa Blümlinger, "The Imaginary in the Documentary Image: Chris Marker's *Level Five*," *Image [&] Narrative* 11.1 (2010), http://www.imageandnarrative.be/index.php/imagenarrative/article/view/51/32; Catherine Lupton, "Terminal Replay: Resnais Revisited in Chris Marker's *Level Five*," *Screen* 44.1 (Spring 2003): 58–70; and Allan Francovich, "The Mind's Eye: Chris Marker's *Level Five*," *Vertigo* 1.7 (Autumn 1997): 35–37. Francovich's review is followed by a rare interview with the director by "Dolores Walfisch," originating in the *Berkeley Lantern* (November 1996). This "interview" is considered a fabrication, and is generally accepted as Marker interviewing Marker.

tap us again on the forehead before death, and we forget everything once again. The proximity of this philosophical affectation to the Eternal Return and to Platonic anamnesis is obvious (and Marker at least mentions Plato, to orient us, if he does not mention Nietzsche). Yet *Level Five* ostensibly concerns the tragedy of Okinawa, as precursor to Hiroshima and Nagasaki, because the Japanese military sacrificed Okinawa (with 150,000 civilian casualties, one-third of the archipelago's population, many by mass suicide). The enormity of the tragedy covers the enormity of the questions posed via the computer game Laura has inherited from her deceased lover. What "Level Five" within the game entails is entirely unclear.[9] But Laura asks at one point whether or not we have to be dead to reach it. The computer game is unfinished, and half of the pretense of the film is that Laura has been charged with completing it through additional research into the Okinawa debacle by entering into conversation with masked interlocutors on O.W.L. (Optional World Link, a digital platform and forum resembling both The Well, from San Francisco, and the early days of the Internet, and Marker's own *Ouvroir*, a digital museum in cyberspace designed with Max Moswitzer in conjunction with the 2008 exhibition, "Chris Marker: A Farewell to Movies," at the Museum of Design in

---

[9] Christophe Chazalon states (within an essay contained in the booklet accompanying the DVD issued by Icarus Films in 2014) that "Level Five" is when all of the information in the game is complete and accurate, thus implying that Level Five is equal to the truth. Yet Marker suggests, elsewhere, that such is impossible and Level Five seems to imply a zone in memory where everything becomes, instead, luminous, or, as in *Immemory*, completely subjectivized. Raymond Bellour writes as to the significance of *Level Five*, that "[it is] the last of his 'cinema films' strictly speaking, [and] for that very reason the one in which we see the best way to inscribe the mutations which cinema has undergone—in a career that is singular out of all others, and within which cinema has always been submitted to paradoxical pressures": Raymond Bellour, "Chris Marker and *Level Five*," trans. Adrian Martin, *Screening the Past*, 2009, http://www.screeningthepast.com/2013/12/chris-marker-and-level-five/.

Zurich, Switzerland). Thus *Level Five*, *Immemory*, and *Ouvroir* cross the ground of *fin-de-siècle* pessimism regarding the future of cinema, and, indeed, Marker is found making grave statements about cinema in the run up to the new *Year Zero* (2000).[10]

If cinema resides in the interstices, so to speak, of this "game" (Level Five or any other virtual enterprise of the same order), if the various programmatic codes and permutations of the events of Okinawa serve to schematize cinema as maelstrom of imagery (historical, mnemonic, iterative, and *possibly* recombinative), Marker is addressing the inherent anti-schema of the unmakeable *Film mysticisme*; or, of hyperconsciously altering events and *not* forgetting them, at once —in a similar manner to the Zone in *Sans soleil*, origin for many of his later experiments with disintegrated imagery.

The fact that *Level Five* is roughly contiguous with the creation of *Immemory One* (1995–1997) is not coincidental. (That *Silent Movie* also falls within this time frame is also instructive.) Marker embarked on a trip through the possible purposes and technical proficiencies of new media as early as the 1980s. Yet by the late 2000s he was back at the origin— the very-still photographic image. This circularity is emblematic of the redemptive path for cinema in Markerian terms, yet also spirals outward toward much larger and much more

---

[10] "From *Wings* to *Star Wars*, I will have seen many things fly over the world's screens. Perhaps cinema has given all it can give, perhaps it must leave room to something else. Jean Prevost writes somewhere that death is not so grave, that it consists only in rejoining all that one has loved and lost. The death of cinema would be only that of an immense memory. It is an honourable destiny": Chris Marker, *Immemory One* (Paris: Éditions du Centre Georges Pompidou/Les Films de l'Astrophore, 1998). See Raymond Bellour, "The Book, Back and Forth," in Laurent Roth and Raymond Bellour, *Qu'est-ce qu'une madeleine? À propos du CD-ROM "Immemory" de Chris Marker*, ed. Christine van Assche, trans. Brian Holmes (Brussels: Yves Gevaert Éditeur; Paris: Éditions du Centre Georges Pompidou, 1997), 149 [65–107, 109–154]. Catalogue for the exhibition, "Immemory," Centre Pompidou, Paris, June 4–September 29, 1997.

ominous "universalizing" terms. For what he seems to extol in the work of Isild Le Besco and others is its profound and proleptic "innocence."[11]

Paratactically, the hyper-conscious tenses of *Level Five* are configured as traces of the Immemorial and of immortality proper (the Markerian term *Immemory* connoting the same). In a preternatural or hyper-natural sense we do have to be "dead" to be immortal (to speak across time). It is for this reason that Marker still speaks through his works today, following his death in July 2012. Indeed, the paratactical exuberance of his works is matched, if not countered, by the grave and somber reflections given to anamnesis (a formidable return to memory of things forgotten and/or things forsaken). This returns the immortal élan or *spirit* of cinema, literature, and the multiple arts to the proverbial and utterly contingent figure of the Other—yet the Other who lives. In this Other who lives, time moves forward, and in this respect for the Other, the "other always to come" is immemorialized (set free). The prospective resources of *Film mysticisme* overlap time forgotten, time lost, time regained, and time redeemed. To regain and redeem are not synonymous. The former connotes "to [temporally] recover," whereas the latter connotes "to [end and] start again." Marker's hyperbolic extravagances within *Level Five* place the immemorial resources of the arts of memory on the side of, or in the hands of, the angels, while the primary non-visual gestures within the film-

---

[11] In part: "We possess the wherewithal—and this is something new —for intimate, solitary filmmaking. The process of making films in communion with oneself, the way a painter works or a writer, need not now be solely experimental. My comrade Astruc's notion of the camera as a pen was only a metaphor. In his day, the humblest cinematographic product required a lab, a cutting room and plenty of money....Nowadays, a young filmmaker needs only an idea and a small amount of equipment to prove himself. He needn't kowtow to producers, TV stations, or committees." Chris Marker, *"Level Five"* [interview with Dolores Walfisch], *Berkeley Lantern* (November 1996); cited in Alter, *Chris Marker*, 146–147.

fable reveal that to reach this immemorial threshold in things ("Level Five") requires crossing through fire and the strange liquidity of memory. The world seems to end, then, by both fire *and* water.

Thus we have—finally—the ideal in the Real, again, but without destroying either (making the One subservient to the Many, or the Many subservient to the One). The avant-garde and antinomial quest for pure immanence, while normally favoring the contingent, might through the redemptive power of memory and its analogues preserve the curious and instructive measures of the multiple arts in service to thought as conception (or, those regions in thought that are purely generative). The film-essay seems, upon examination, to contain this exact prolepsis—a nuanced foreshadowing, but also an eclipse, of some things for other things.

III. NOTES ON "ZAPPING ZONE"

> Marker's storehouse of images produces a new cosmos of over determined meanings. In this sense, the filmmaker's game with the documentary film genre becomes more of an ironic analysis of the documentary's latent tendencies to monumentalize. Marker's approach is more like a kind of evolution than a lofty sublimity, like folding Japanese origami paper, or new digital photo processes, such as the zapping, windowing, linking, and morphing that actually dominate Marker's more recent works ("Zapping Zone," 1990, *Level Five*, 1997, "Immemory," 1997).[12]
>
> Michael Wetzel

There are five antinomies that animate Marker's work across various media and platforms: (1) Here and There; (2) Image and Word (non-discursive agency versus discursive knowledge); (3) Politics and Life (Power and its Other); (4) Self and Other (Not-self); and (5) Art and Culture (knowledge or experience versus ideology). These antinomies are in many respects the "signature" aspects of his work, or dynamic principles that have no true content as such, or have *shifting* content, based on the context in which they are embedded. To excavate them is to also reveal their universality and formal or austere purposes in the production of works of art (whether filmic, literary, or pictorial). While present-day formalism tends to focus on non-discursive aspects of artistic production, in Marker's world it is actually a highly evocative means to no particular end that invokes the dynamic field of visual agency proper, or *visualitas*—as defined prior to the emergence of High Modernism in the Arts and Letters, *pace* Thomas Carlyle (and, perhaps, Ruskin), and as present in homeopathic form in Marcel Proust, Proust but one reference for the translation of the same toward modern literature, *from its pre-modernist past*, and literary criticism's shift toward structuralist brinks-

---

[12] Michael Wetzel, "Acousmêtrie: On the Relationship between Voice and Image in the Films of Chris Marker," *Media Art Net*, 2004, http://www.medienkunstnetz.de/themes/art_and_cinematography/marker/1/.

manship (plus so-called New Criticism). Marker, arguably, has inherited this more austere, grave, and *formative* aspect of formalism through Russian progenitors (in film, Sergei Eisenstein and Dziga Vertov), while it is his inherent literary-critical intelligence that safeguards this older, more speculative form of artistic praxis that contains or focuses its own subterranean/furtive sublimity (feigned closure) while opening, nonetheless, onto the infinite.

The multimedia works from the 1990s forward are, as a result, testing grounds for many of these "structural" (dyadic) presentiments, but only insofar as they cut across various projects, returning to Marker's earliest forays into film while retaining the late-1940s' imprint of his first literary-philosophical undertakings under the spell of left-wing Catholic praxis (personalism) and his alliances with the radical collective Peuple et Culture and the existentialist-inspired journal *Esprit*. The entire course of Marker's investigation of the image, then, almost always circles back to the seminal moment (the mid-to-late 1940s) of the twin essays by André Bazin and Emmanuel Levinas regarding the ontology of the photographic image and its implied limit (what it indexes as limit). If *Lettre de Sibérie* was the first place/instance where Marker's "three rays of intelligence" (sonic, pictorial, and narratological) converged, from "eye to ear" (*and back and forth*), in a symphonic-filmic poem as high-Romantic "literary work of art," all of the subsequent works might be related to this thematic, which is always half-apocalyptic and always in reference in some way to Bazin's recourse to the foremost singular image *of* the suffering image, the Shroud of Turin (as touchstone for the production of images drawn nominally from a metaphysical-immemorial reserve that transcends the media utilized and the existential factors invoked). Never to be defined or pinned down, Marker would first deny the truth-telling apparatuses of documentary film (in the late 1950s) and then undermine its antithesis or Other, the film-essay or film-poem. Circumventing what he was, in fact (and in part), helping to produce (that is, French New Wave cinema), he would then exit (or denounce) "auteur-driven" film and return to collaborative and semi-collaborative works in the 1960s (after *La jetée*, with few exceptions), until exhausting that vein (the semi-anonymous, overtly political film), and then producing his second semi-solo masterwork, *Sans soleil* (1982), where the "Zone" first appeared and where EMS Spectre was first broached as a means for pushing filmic images back into a realm where they hovered on the horizon of legibility and disintegration, between historical/narrative value and formal value (or "no" discernible value whatsoever). This fruitful vortex, in turn, led to the earliest projects with digitizing his archive and the beginning of the highly experimental new-media installations.

In this manner, "Zapping Zone" is a pre-eminent moment in Marker's experimentation across multiple platforms (digital and otherwise), plus the cannibalizing or "plagiarizing" of his own work.[13] As "Zapping Zone" went through various incar-

[13] "Zapping Zone: Proposals for an Imaginary Television" (1990). Created between 1989 and 1990 for the exhibition "Passages de l'image," Centre Georges Pompidou, Paris, France, incorporating video work from 1985 forward, and expanded and re-configured for subsequent exhibitions between 1994 and 2009. "Zapping Zone" was initially compromised of 14 color-video monitors, 13 laser-disc players, 13 loud speakers, 13 video-disc recorders, 7 computers, 7 computer programs, 4 light boxes (with 20 slides each), 11 color photos (10 black-and-white photos), and 7 photomontages. Initially composed of some 20 zones (with two interactive zones), subsequent iterations included the removal of some material and the addition of newly completed short films and videos. Pompidou documents of the floor layout ("Disposition Paris Centre Pompidou, exposition 'Air de Paris'"), plus shipping specifications ("Liste de colisage [dix caisses]"), for the "Air de Paris" version of "Zapping Zone," show a total of 20 computer stations supplemented by 10 digital-photographic collages and four light boxes. "Zapping Zone, Chris Marker, 1990, coll. Centre Pompidou AM 1990-160," Nouveaux Médias Archive, Centre Georges Pompidou, Paris, France. See the exhibition catalogue, *Passages de l'image*, ed. Raymond Bellour, Catherine David, and Christine van Assche (Paris: Éditions du Centre Georges Pompidou, 1990). Regarding "Zapping Zone," see Raymond Bellour, "Éloge en

nations after its initial installation at the Pompidou, it also stands as the essential artistic vortex *out* of which, and *into* which, much of Marker's later digital experiments will emerge and/or vanish.[14]

The origins of "Zapping Zone" reside somewhere around 1985; that is, its first versions. The release of the Apple IIGS computer, in 1986, with its enhanced graphics capabilities and sound synthesizers, was also instrumental in Marker's move away from the projection toward the monitor. The IIGS' demise in 1992 prompted the homage that occurred with the subsequent 1997-1998 iterations, culminating in the 2009 version of "Zapping Zone" for the Pompidou's "Air de Paris" exhibition, while also prompting a belated reply to Steve Jobs via YouTube—a somewhat sardonic, short animated video entitled *iDead* (2011).[15]

"Zapping Zone was initially called *Logiciel/Catacombes* (*Software/Catacombs*). It involved putting images onto the computer reminiscent of the subterranean tunnels in *La jetée* or those in Fellini's *Roma*, consequently leading back to *Sans*

Si Mineur," in *Passages de l'image*, 169–171. English translations of these essays appeared in the Spanish edition of the catalogue, *Passages de l'image* (Barcelona: Centre Cultural de la Fundació Caixa de Pensions, 1991).

[14] It is important to distinguish between the various iterations of key Marker new-media projects, such as "Immemory One" and "Zapping Zone," as they subsequently traveled and/or re-appeared in published form, re-formatted and otherwise altered. Criticism of the CD-ROM platform, both for the installation "Immemory" and its two published editions, is, therefore, of limited value. While both projects nominally started as exhibitions at the Centre Pompidou, and each had a very specific *mise-en-scène* in which they appeared (in the case of "Immemory One," an accompanying mural of Guillaume-en-Égypte, and in the case of "Zapping Zone," a series of wall-mounted photos, etc., as above, plus the original "Tatlin-esque" stand that supported the various television monitors), the beginning, middle, and end for each project is utterly indeterminate.

[15] Chris Marker, *iDead* (2011). Video (2 minutes 27 seconds). Posted to YouTube under the pseudonym "Kosinki."

soleil and memories of Tarkovsky."[16] The subject of the "Zone," in its "Markerian" dimensions as a place for reducing images to their most primitive or—perhaps—innocent stage, is first broached in *Sans soleil*. The reference is to Tarkovsky's *Stalker*, with its own version of the "Zone."[17]

"The Zone is preeminently a universe of haunted memories, new obsessions brought about by 'the world of technology', against which we would be helpless if we didn't have the strength to seize the techniques to generate—as a way of resisting—an increasing amount of metamorphoses."[18] The collages included in "Zapping Zone" are in many respects Marker's removal of the digital image from the vortex of the machine and the placing of that image in the semi-conventional setting of the art gallery as *still image* of re-synthesized images, etc. The *mise-en-abyme* aspects of this are self-evident.

> Zapping Zone is thus a space enabling to zap in the zone. Zapping means moving between zones. Some twenty monitors crammed together, a few individual sound entries and computers. Altogether they form a mass which is compact and discrete—in the linguistic sense. It is both a

---

[16] Raymond Bellour, in Christine van Assche et al., eds., *Collection New Media Installations: La collection du Centre Pompidou Musée National d'Art Moderne* (Paris: Éditions du Centre Pompidou, 2006), 197 (regarding "Zapping Zone," see 197–201).

[17] See Michael Sand, ed., *Aperture 145, Surface and Illusion: Ten Portfolios* (Autumn 1996), for comments on Marker and Wim Wenders in this regard. See Jan-Christopher Horak, "Chris Marker's Reality Bytes," in the same volume, 60–65, for remarks regarding still photography and moving images, human memory, transformation of real geographical places into subjective visions, the camera as a tool for the objective documentation of reality bytes, and consciously constructed aesthetic subjectivity. With reference to Charles Baudelaire's comments in 1859, "If photography is allowed to stand in for art...."

[18] Raymond Bellour, "Eulogy in B Minor," in *Passages de l'image* (1991), 190.

rattling chaos and a calculated arrangement, a dump and the dream of an oeuvre originated in the waste disposal of History and its utopias. More simply *Zapping Zone* is a small supermarket, a mini department store cleverly disorganized where if you cannot find whatever you need at least you can see some of your desires displayed.[19]

Close viewing of the various elements of "Zapping Zone" reveal the mesmeric aspects of the project.[20] Summaries,

[19] Bellour, "Eulogy in B Minor," 190.

[20] The first iteration of "Zapping Zone," Centre Pompidou, 1990, included the following components, divided into 13 zones: "Zone Frisco" (*Junkopia*, 6 minutes, 1981); "Zone Christo" (*From Chris to Christo*, S-VHS video, 24 minutes, music by Dmitri Shostakovich, 1985); "Zone Matta" (*Matta '85*, S-VHS video, 12 minutes, 1985); "Zone Tarkovski" (*Tarkovski '86*, S-VHS video, 26 minutes, 1985); "Zone Éclats" (video, 21 minutes 51 seconds); "Zone Bestiare" (S-VHS video, 9 minutes 4 seconds); "Zone Spectre" (EMS-spectre video, 27 minutes); "Zone Tokyo" (*Tokyo Days*, video, with Arielle Dombasle, 24 minutes, 1986); "Zone Berlin" (*Berliner Ballade*, Hi-8 video, 20 minutes 35 seconds, 1990); "Zone Photos" (*Photo Browse*, 301 computer-animated photographs, 17 minutes 20 seconds, 1990); "Zone Clip" (*Getting Away With It*, 4 minutes 17 seconds, 1990); "Zone TV" (*Détour Ceauşescu*, video, 8 minutes 2 seconds, 1990); and "Zone Séquences" (20 minutes 45 seconds). "Zone Bestiare" included: *Chat écoutant la musique* (2 minutes 47 seconds, 1990); *An Owl is an Owl is an Owl* (3 minutes 18 seconds, 1990); and *Zoo Pièce* (2 minutes 42 seconds, 1990). "Zone Séquences" included clips from: *Le fond de l'air est rouge* (3 minutes 57 seconds; and 1 minute); *Sans soleil* (3 minutes 32 seconds; and 3 minutes 3 seconds); *La solitude du chanteur de fond* (2 minutes 57 seconds); *Le joli mai* (2 minutes 39 seconds); *La sixième face du Pentagone* (1 minute 37 seconds); and *L'héritage de la chouette* (1 minute 52 seconds). "Zone Éclats" included: *Cocteau* (47 seconds); *2084* (3 minutes 40 seconds); *KFX* (38 seconds, 15 frames); *Statues 1* (1 minute 23 seconds); *Taps* (32 seconds); *Statues 2* (52 seconds); *Kat Klip* (54 seconds); *Alexandra* (1 minute 40 seconds); *Vertov* (1 minute 52 seconds); *Arielle* (26 seconds); *Chouettes* (33 seconds); *Zeroins* (2 minutes 47 seconds); *Moonfeet* (1 minute 5 seconds); and *Flyin' Fractals* (3 minutes 41 seconds). By the time of "Air de Paris," Centre Pompidou, 2009,

while useful, hardly do justice to the full effect of a darkened room full of simultaneously screened vignettes, plus the mixing (and blurring) of their soundtracks. The effect is to enter a haunted wood....[21] Nonetheless, both summary and full immersion suggest that everything Marker was dealing with in cinema was transferred to (and further elaborated upon in) new-media installations, thereby justifying his constantly shifting intentions and means toward suggesting, but never quite saying that such media (cinema and video) have the potential for invoking intelligences that are strangely "ex officio"—that is, *of, but also somehow beyond* cinema and video.[22]

"Zapping Zone" had expanded to 20 zones (plus 10 collages, four lightboxes, and one Maneki Neko): "Zone Frisco"; "Zone Matta"; "Zone Photos"; "Zone Christo"; "Zone Tokyo"; "Zone Bestiare"; "Zone Berlin"; "Zone Séquences"; "Zone Clip"; "Zone Bosniaque"; "Zone Tarkovski"; "Zone Spectre"; "Zone TV"; plus "Zone Show"; "Zone Collages"; "Zone HyperStudio"; "Zone Slide Show"; "Zone Vidéo"; "Zone Graphs"; and "Zone Éléphant." The latter seven, new zones were presented on Apple IIGS computer stations as homage, by Marker, to the by-then-defunct computer system. "Zone Show" was placed at the entrance to the gallery, as an introduction/program guide to the installation, and utilized a television monitor. Technical specifications, layout of the exhibition, etc., plus images of the "Air de Paris" installation at Arts Santa Mònica, Barcelona, Spain, are to be found in "Zapping Zone (Proposals for an Imaginary Television): Chris Marker, 1990." The various monitors were set upon pedestals, dispensing with the iconic, pyramidal metal stand (the "Tatlin-esque" version, with antennae) of the 1990 installation. For an image of this earlier installation (1990-1991), see *Passages de l'image* (1991), 190.

[21] A restored "Zapping Zone" was included in the 2014 Marker retrospective held at Whitechapel Gallery, London, England.

[22] "Zapping Zone" media viewed courtesy of Sylvie Douala-Bell, at Nouveaux Médias, Centre Georges Pompidou, Paris, France, June 25, 2012. The 13 DVDs, prepared for the "Air de Paris" exhibition, and now in the Pompidou archive, are: "Zone TV"; "Zone Spectre"; "Zone Tarkovski"; "Zone Bosniaque"; "Zone Clip"; "Zone Berlin"; "Zone Séquences"; "Zone Tokyo"; "Zone Bestiaire"; "Zone Christo"; "Zone Photos"; "Zone Frisco"; and "Zone Matta." See "3/ Liste des DVDs," in "Zapping Zone (Proposals for an Imaginary Television):

"Zone Spectre" is emblematic. Subtitled "Formes aléatoires," it is composed of lights, apparitions, principalities, and/or "angels," generated with EMS Spectre.[23] The synthesizer generates two fields: One (the middle ground), spinning like a top (formed along two axes, X, Y), and a second (the apparent background), composed of a geometrical pattern of abstract cubic units (à la Gustav Klimt and such). This two-fold dynamic structure, of course, floats in a third space, which is the ether of the digital void (the synthesizer's virtual void), a possible encapsulation of an unknown field that resides in all works of art, and a field that forms the basis of all theories for "framing" a work.

"Zone Séquences" (1994 version), a highly focused section from the subsequently withdrawn 13-part, 1989 television series *L'héritage de la chouette*, consists of a sustained view of the slightly upturned faces of an audience in a theater watching film images drift across a screen (with narrative references to Plato's cave), but with Marker's camera mostly watching the audience watching the images, and the images drifting (flickering/reflecting) across the faces of the audience as screen. See *Level Five* and *2084* for the human/digital interface (skin as screen) this invokes, as Marker's camera is interested in the expressions on the faces of the people sitting in the theater, in the same manner that his camera has repeatedly focused on the faces of people sitting in the subway or marching through the streets of Paris or elsewhere. The face becomes, as such, a screen/mask, and the images are projected/reflected onto the face both literally and expressively, both by Marker and/or by the subject in terms of their response.[24]

Chris Marker, 1990," 6.

[23] See *Sans soleil* for the early use of this analogue video synthesizer from the early 1970s.

[24] See Susan Sontag, "In Plato's Cave," in Susan Sontag, *On Photography* (New York: Dell Publishing Co., Inc., 1977) , 3–24: "Humankind lingers unregeneratly in Plato's cave, still reveling, its age-old habit, in mere images of the truth" (3). See also Jean-Louis Schefer's mus-

"Zone Bestiare" (1994 version), ultimately an oblique, yet elegant homage to Guillaume-en-Égypte (Marker's cat, correspondent, alter ego, and "familiar") and his various confreres, with the central moment being (and forever remaining) *Chat écoutant la musique*[25]—a very short film of Guillaume catnapping on the keyboard of a Yamaha DX7 electric piano, in Marker's studio presumably, "listening" to a recording of an *étude* (the piano sonata "Pajaro triste"/"Sad Bird," no less) by Spanish composer Federico Mompou—is stunningly simple in its presentiments for elegiac time. LED light levels rise and fall as Guillaume opens and closes his eyes. "He was fond of Ravel (any cat is) but he had a special crush on Mompou. That day (a beautiful sunny day, I remember) I placed Volume I of the complete 'Mompou by Mompou' on the CD player to please him...."[26] As counterpoint, *An Owl is an Owl is an Owl* is a repetitive, surrealistic, digitized voice poem read by two voices (perhaps male and female) to an owl.[27]

ings on cinema as a gigantic body (a giant "leaning across a white screen") and the spectator's place within this "giant anatomy"—"a body infinitely larger than our own (and not just because the eye that momentarily projects images of it is like a lighthouse)." "I don't think that we're seated in Plato's cave; we are, for an unthinkable eternity, suspended between a giant body and the object of its gaze. So I am, not seated, but suspended beneath a sheaf of light. This sheaf is animated. The easy anteriority of its movement in the animation of the film's objects is visible as a scissor effect, or as if the rays hit upon legs, and from time to time crossed them, uncrossed them": Jean-Louis Schefer, "Cinema," in Jean-Louis Schefer, *The Enigmatic Body: Essays on the Arts by Jean-Louis Schefer*, ed. and trans. Paul Smith (Cambridge: Cambridge University Press, 1995), 130–131 [108–138]. See also, Jean-Louis Schefer, "On *La jetée*," in the same volume.

[25] *Chat écoutant la musique* is an exceptional, short film that also formed the "Entr'acte" for *Le tombeau d'Alexandre*. It was subsequently added as an extra to DVD releases of *Chats perchés* (2004).

[26] Chris Marker, "*Bestiare* (1985-90)," *Electronic Arts Intermix*, n.d., http://www.eai.org/title.htm?id=2373.

[27] Marker has processed the soundtrack in such a way that it renders the voices nearly inhuman.

Perhaps "Zone Tarkovski" speaks for the entire operation —for video as cinema. It features an excerpt from Marker's documentation of *Offret* (*The Sacrifice*), but acutely focuses on Tarkovsky filming, in his usual painstaking manner, Leonardo's *Adoration of the Magi*, tracing the tree upward through the foliage by way of his signature, excessively long tracking shot, but this time by moving "inside" of a painting, *by way of scanning its surface*, as he did, as well, in the closing sequence of *Andrei Rublev*. There is no narrative or commentary added by Marker other than the on-site dialogue and occasional diegetic sound from the set/soundtrack, extracted, in part, from Tarkovsky's *Offret* proper (a sonic montage, by Marker, nonetheless, of voice, wind and fire, by appropriation). Filming the final conflagration from Tarkovsky's last film, plus on-site deliberations (focusing on the construction and orchestration of the sequence, or the *final, extraordinarily long* Tarkovskian tracking shot), Marker brings it to a close with "post-production" scenes he filmed in a Paris hospital, with Tarkovsky editing the film (intercut with passages from the film itself), and the penultimate "ending" for this ending; that is, scenes of the Maestro watching the final edit of *Offret* for the first time from his hospital bed in Paris, in January 1986 or so. *Offret* was subsequently released in May 1986, in Europe, and November 1986, in the United States. Tarkovsky died on December 29, 1986, in Paris. *Offret* was the last of seven acknowledged masterpieces. Elsewhere, by way of a detour through an anecdote about a séance, Marker notes that, yes, Tarkovsky made seven masterpieces; but he also made *only seven films*....[28]

February 5, 2015

---

[28] Marker tells the story of the séance in Chris Marker, *Une journée d'Andrei Arsenevitch*.

Essay Five

Circular Discourses

I. "LUCID NOSTALGIA" AND MONISM

> In the underground, unlike the world of bourgeois intellectuals, the word is not what is most valued. It is relegated to a secondary position. It was when we got to the indigenous communities that language hit us, like a catapult. Then you realize that you lack the words to express many things, and that obliges you to work on language. To return time and again to words, to put them together and take them apart.[1]
>
> Subcomandante Marcos

What better place to enter circular discourses than through the centuries-long arguments over the unitary protocols of the Enlightenment (roughly equivalent to philosophical monism), and what better example of the discord generated through such examples of cultural production than an examination of complaints by scholars against attempts to raise the

---

[1] Subcomandante Marcos, in Gabriel García Márquez, Roberto Pombo, and Subcomandante Marcos, "The Punch Card and the Hourglass: Interview with Subcomandante Marcos," *New Left Review* 9 (May-June 2001): 77. First published in *Revista Cambio*, Bogotá, Columbia, March 26, 2001.

Enlightenment's origins to the meta-historical level of "the socio-cultural" and demote the importance of "the socio-economic" (the bias of nineteenth-century pragmatism and utilitarianism, Saint-Simonian and Marxian historical-materialist schools, and—*tout court*—the celebrated Annales inquisition of the late twentieth century), albeit a pattern that has also played out in recent revisionist histories of the French Revolution (François Furet et al.), the French Revolution being an event which is, of course, always more or less situated within the vague historical contours of the Enlightenment, even if the Jacobin period remains unassimilable to most such synoptic projects.

Alternatively, in pushing the origins of Modernity back to either the Renaissance or the French Revolution, and by privileging one or another ideological formation to account for the apparently non-spontaneous efflorescence, scholars and historians embed their own subjective prejudices and preconscious biases into the historical record, the more blatant examples of this being the projection of ideological formations that are part of their privileges as scholars (through patronage) onto previously existing or imaginary formations of the same type. For Erwin Panofsky to push the origins of the Renaissance, in turn, back toward Provençal poets and wandering medieval scribes is instructive of his own position in arguments concerning iconography versus iconology, the latter most closely resembling what is generally subsumed under the rubric of "the socio-cultural," the former hovering somewhere between visual-cultural exegesis and art-historical mindreading.

In the reaction to Jonathan I. Israel's recently completed trilogy on the Enlightenment (*Radical Enlightenment, Enlightenment Contested*, and *Democratic Enlightenment*)[2] we find

---

[2] Jonathan I. Israel, *Radical Enlightenment: Philosophy and the Making of Modernity, 1650-1750* (Oxford: Oxford University Press, 2001); Jonathan I. Israel, *Enlightenment Contested: Philosophy, Modernity, and the Emancipation of Man, 1670-1752* (Oxford: Oxford University Press, 2006); and Jonathan I. Israel, *Democratic Enlightenment: Phi-*

every manner of excuse for dismissing the hyper-logical formations that inform his work. Yet within that admirable, if not misguided project (insofar as it seems afraid of its own shadow at times) there emerges a host of figurative gestures that serve to demolish the pretexts of the circular discourse he is entering into in an attempt to liberate what he calls the Radical Enlightenment, even if the historiographic apparatus of his inquiry resembles those that came before (Cassirer et al.). This monumental treatment of the Enlightenment, according to critics, indulges all manner of sleight of hand, foremost pushing the origins of the Enlightenment back further than most scholars might allow. The major grievance is his privileging of Spinoza, or his attributing all manifestations of the Enlightenment to a radical version that always returns to Spinoza and his philosophical project for the presentation and preservation of a this-worldly monism (bracketing all previous forms of scission originating in, arguably, religion and/or deism, and most emphatically Cartesianism).

What is at the heart of Israel's project is the projection of the intellectual currents of the Enlightenment toward a generally frustrated radical origin, the French Revolution being the one event that seemed, for him, to permit such to emerge from the shadows and alter historical time-space (and the socio-economic "metrics" of such a historical time-space). This resembles the project assumed by others in analyzing the French Revolution (including the reactionary side) toward attributing the outbreak to Swabian idealists or a *transmontane illuminati*, conspiracy theories most often traceable to the twin peaks of reaction, on the left and the right, against anything resembling a cultural or collective unconscious that might actually know what "it" is doing (even if we do not know what "it" is doing). Israel steps into the breach by way of key moments he never explores, such as the literature of libertinage or the ahistorical prospects of Romanticism (pre-

losophy, Revolution, and Human Rights, 1750-1790 (Oxford: Oxford University Press, 2011).

Kantian and post-Kantian). As rationalist, his survey wishes to wish away anything irrationalist, as he is also generally averse to any and all post-structuralist or post-modernist interpretations given to the same type of sweeping overview, reductivist or otherwise.[3]

This same fear of the irrational is present in the historical works of Isaiah Berlin, traversing especially his sorties on Romanticism.[4] Floundering about in the historical record (acknowledging its necessity, but also noting its inability to account for the uprising/insurrection of Romanticism), Berlin

---

[3] This reductivist purview would somehow seem, according to the rules of circular discourses, to permit the following slap: "Whatever our final judgment about either the foundations or the superstructure of *Radical Enlightenment*, *Enlightenment Contested*, and *Democratic Enlightenment*, they certainly comprise no ordinary building. If there really is a touch of Romanticism in Israel's temperament and outlook, then perhaps one parallel for the trilogy might be seen in those soaring nineteenth-century edifices, which sought to recapture the lost glories of medieval architecture, in stylized fashion, such as they never quite were in reality (Neo-Gothic, Romanesque Revival). That would imply that Israel's conception of 'Radical Enlightenment' stands in about the same relationship to the real world of eighteenth-century thought, as the Houses of Parliament and the *Schloss Neuschwanstein* do to the Middle Ages. That may sound unkind—still, no one has ever denied that the Palace of Westminster and that castle in Bavaria are certainly something to see" (the key term here, in order to denounce Israel's project, is *real world*): Jonathan Kent Wright, "Review: Jonathan Israel, *Democratic Enlightenment*," *H-France Forum* 9.1 (Winter 2014), http://www.h-france.net/forum/forum vol9/Israel1.pdf. This 25-page jeremiad (posing as a review) is actually an assault on Israel's project, which seeks, through its vitriol, to condition any further volumes he may produce beyond the trilogy in defense of his thesis. Ironically, the review serves to hypostasize circular and near-endless commentaries and, far from attempting to cut off Israel, proposes to extend the debate, ad nauseam, concerning the origins and the singularity of the historic event of the Enlightenment.

[4] Isaiah Berlin, *The Roots of Romanticism* (Princeton: Princeton University Press, 1999).

dismantles French Rationalism (Rousseau included) to find Germany and Protestant Pietism as source and place of the revolt. Tracking Johann Gottfried von Herder (ignored in Paris by the French cultural elite), Berlin ransacks nonetheless the precursors to High German Romanticism (and German Idealism), focusing on Johann Georg Hamann and little-known literary moments en route to Immanuel Kant. David Hume is noted (a vast influence on Kant), while Voltaire and the Encyclopedists are dismissed as sophists. What remains unsaid (or only inferred) is that it is, after all, the pursuit of Truth (metaphysical "fire") that moves all forms and variants of Romanticism, from the elegiac to the pathetic to the monstrous (the divine, inhuman), and that such is the actual place (non-place) Berlin fails to locate and/or access in the historical record, because it is simply never to be found there as such (there is no "it" or point of purchase without the primordial fold/division).

Notably encountering Kant, friend of Hamann (a deranged, Northern mystic in Berlin's estimation), the facts of Romanticism dissolve away, into a rarified space-time (the rational-irrational a priori) always at stake in insurrectional/titanic turns toward what might be known and what remains obscure (what might be known without quite knowing "it")—skepticism plus something else.

When Berlin discusses and dismantles eighteenth-century French rationalism (neo-classicism) we hear but do not see the paintings of Jacques-Louis David, perhaps referencing, in passing, the (unseen and unmentioned) paintings of Nicolas Poussin. "Just as mathematics deals in perfect circles, so the sculptor and the painter must deal in ideal forms."[5] For Berlin, such first appeared in the arts and, then, pervaded ethics and politics.[6] What is meretricious in painting is the severe (rational) geometric *parti* underlying pictorial works (the devastating "interior"), or that which is not lost on the Romantics,

[5] Berlin, *The Roots of Romanticism*, 28.
[6] Berlin, *The Roots of Romanticism*, 25.

most surely, in fact, the main "pictorial" point (perspectival and *otherwise*) with Kant's vast and spellbinding three Critiques.

Berlin indulges a type of scholarship (a form similar in spirit to the Annales School's forensic focus on "physical remains") wherein a masterful mélange of historical material is amassed to determine the outcome of the inquest. In itself "rational," it is also given to a type of art-historical, picturesque journalism that verges on gossip (Gérard de Nerval's lobster, Novalis' blue flower, etc.). To amass tales, quips, and judgments is to concede defeat in advance, insofar as criticism is wholly otherwise, and it is criticism that lies at the vanishing point of all romanticisms—criticism of two worlds, and why they are not one world. Philosophical monism may have failed Romanticism, yet it is quietly the point of Romanticism to figure out why it failed/fails.

Since Hayden White and Michel de Certeau, historians have been summarily warned to watch their own biases—to perhaps *enjoy* watching their own biases, as symptoms, toward hyper-self-consciousness, but to be respectful nonetheless for the fact that history proceeds via biases. For this reason White promoted Jules Michelet, as pre-eminent historian of the French Revolution. If Michelet's Romanticism was his primary bias, connecting re-revolutionary, mid-nineteenth-century France back to Joan of Arc, one must (if in agreement with White) finally discard any pretense to an authorized formalization of history (any meta-history that is more true than any other form), or, finally discard any bias for a preferred methodology or vantage point. The arguments for and against Realism in literature and film are typically of the same circularity. Yet the escape route is often the same as well—that is, "a poetical" escape route, even if that is never quite so accurate in describing what actually transpires in figures such as Michelet, Dostoevsky, Proust, Bachelard, Éluard, Dreyer, Marker, Godard, or Pasolini.

Notably, Israel's *Democratic Enlightenment* is accused of embodying the academic crime of "lucid nostalgia" (a pejorative in the Jamesonian sense),[7] an accusation that might be a compliment under the right conditions, except that the time-sense is backward (and any post-structuralist reading of the same would actually convert it to a paradoxical "futural" time-sense, making of nostalgia a presentiment of things to come versus a longing for things past—or, redemption, in the utterly "socio-cultural" manner that converts lost causes, through paratactical maneuvers, to future causes, at once lost and found *through* so-called nostalgia, burying them in texts, if necessary, to be found later). The realist perspective would be to further hypostasize the general clamor for lost causes as a broken promise, pushing the entire affair into the here-and-now, as ideo-grammatical trifle for Romantics unwilling to admit defeat. The moral and/or ethical tenor of all such arguments circling nostalgia as reactionary fiction for a phantom past, futural presentiment of a time to come, or defeat in the face of noir-ish coefficients generative of anomie and class struggle are all suggestive of the eventual outcome for such deferred and preferred events—the chronically, non-chronological belated return of something half forgotten in the ideo-grammatical register of the arts. This is the reason why Israel's trilogy serves a purpose that he appears or pretends to be only half conscious of, or worse, in denial of. The Radical Enlightenment he seeks is a classic synchronic event: it resides nowhere (and not because it is past). This "nowhere" is the ideo-grammatical register in the socio-cultural that empirical histories cannot reach. And it is the register that animates and hollows out literary and artistic production toward the re-presentation of the not-lost cause.

Israel's best maneuvers are the ones that he does not make, or is unwilling to make overtly. Yet they are present in homeopathic dilution (per Thomas Mann) in his work, as illustrated by the criticisms that work generates. If the literature of libertinage makes an appearance and then vanishes without trace, what would he make of the French Decadents to come,

---

[7] Wright, "Review: Jonathan Israel, *Democratic Enlightenment.*"

of Dada and Hugo Ball or Tristan Tzara, of Surrealism and Georges Bataille and Paul Éluard? The Radical Enlightenment escapes his books, and his hypostasization of "Spinoza" (a lost cause) returns in the post-structuralist period, with Deleuze and others (or, those looking for transcendence in contingency, as in Deleuze's late quest for a figurative and ghostly version of "pure immanence").

In fact, Israel's inquest into the death of the Radical Enlightenment (as he is paying forward this presentiment for lost causes) would run into very rough sledding when and if he crosses over into the twentieth century. For as early as the first outbreaks of revolutionary activity in Russia he would find monism in the form of pan-sophism, later to be locked in deathly embrace with pan-Slavism. But then the edifice will collapse and only short occasions, however hidden in artistic movements, will re-occur until the late-twentieth century and neo-liberal capitalism slams the door on any presentiments whatsoever for an enlightened monism and the evocation of universals. Indeed, he states:

> A process was set in train in the late eighteenth century, a democratic enlightenment based on liberty, equality, and the "general good", which was then arrested by kings, aristocracy, and Robespierre's Counter-Enlightenment and driven back, but which resumed after a fashion in the post-Second World War era. Many scholars argue that at the end of the eighteenth century the hopes of the enlighteners were blighted by the contradictions within the Enlightenment. Another way of looking at the Radical Enlightenment's defeat is to see it as a temporary and partial setback. In 1789, it seemed to be possible to drive a powerful wedge between the conservatism of ignorance and the conservatism of landownership and money so that the two no longer mutually reinforced each other. It did not happen. But in response to today's fundamentalism, anti-secularism, Neo-Burkeanism, Postmodernism, and blatant unwillingness to clamp down on powerful vested inter-

ests, it is at least conceivable that the universalism and social democracy of radical thought might advance again and this time drive the wedge home harder.[8]

---

[8] Israel, *Democratic Enlightenment*, 951; cited in Wright, "Review: Jonathan Israel, *Democratic Enlightenment*." "Many scholars argue that at the end of the eighteenth century the hopes of the enlighteners were blighted by the contradictions within the Enlightenment..." seems to invoke the Frankfurt School and later versions of taking the Enlightenment to task for crimes implicit to liberalism proper—for example, indifference, intolerance, and obeisance to rote materialism, positivism, and utility as foundation for politics and/or ideological management of the socio-cultural.

II. MNEMONICS VERSUS MEMES

Arguably, mnemonics (as conscious memory system) and memes (as pre-conscious figures of thought) are at odds. The former involves specific content, whereas the latter connotes fearful indeterminancy or malevolent manipulation.[9] Yet mnemonics are also quite often a case of indeterminate content of a hopeful versus fearful form. The concomitant recourse to a type of formalism that remains vague and ameliorative is the premise for artistic mnemonics, whereas the recourse to a programmatic dark or noir-ish predeterminism is the chief qualification for discussing memes. Notably, the meme is the figure that best describes the malevolent aspects of media in the late-modern period, or a penchant for vague signifiers that rattles anything resembling clarity.

If clarity is an element of classical mnemonics (for example, the memory theatre),[10] present-day post-modernist mnemonics invokes the spectral, though not the frightful spectral, even if the hopeful is often the frightful for reaction on the left and/or the right. For this reason the EZLN fabricated the

[9] The term *meme* was coined by Richard Dawkins in *The Selfish Gene* (Oxford: Oxford University Press, 1976), but is by no means an original conception regarding the spread and mutation of ideas and/or vague fashions (intellectual or otherwise). The biology of Dawkins model underscores the determinist aspects of the phenomenon, as well as its semi-unconscious or unconscious proliferation. Its more pernicious aspects suggest that it is an element of the programmatic DNA of cultural systems, easily manipulated and easily turned toward brainwashing. "We need a name for the new replicator, a noun that conveys the idea of a unit of cultural transmission, or a unit of *imitation*. 'Mimeme' comes from a suitable Greek root, but I want a monosyllable that sounds a bit like 'gene'. I hope my classicist friends will forgive me if I abbreviate mimeme to *meme*. If it is any consolation, it could alternatively be thought of as being related to 'memory', or to the French word *même*. It should be pronounced to rhyme with 'cream'": Dawkins, *The Selfish Gene*, 192.

[10] For example, see Frances A. Yates, *The Art of Memory* (Chicago: University of Chicago Press, 1966).

myth of Subcomandante Marcos, a hologram later to be destroyed in May 2014 in a memorable press conference held in the mountains of Chiapas, home base for the Marxist insurgency fighting for indigenous rights in south-east Mexico. Constructed for the media, "Marcos" was, indeed, a fabrication that played directly into the mythic stature of revolutionaries—from Robin Hood, to Che Guevara, to, perhaps, Alan Moore's V. Manufactured for the press, "Marcos" operated as a hopeful meme within leftist circles and a frightful meme within rightist and neo-liberal circles.[11] Yet his rhetorical gifts were explicitly mnemonic, as if the meme were constructed to undermine the very nature of the frightful games of modern media and its penchant for sensation at all costs. Foremost, as gesture toward mnemonics, Marcos was given to "literary prose," his pronouncements of a type that invoked a tableau within revolutionary praxis that was neither Marxian nor identifiable as vaguely liberationist.[12] Importantly, Marcos

[11] "In the monotony of a political order now virtually without significant conflict of ideas, any ruffling of the ideological consensus is liable to attract considerable—even disproportionate—media attention: a paradox to be welcomed, as involuntarily widening the reverberations of dissent": "A Movement of Movements," Editors' Introduction to García Márquez, Pombo, and Marcos, "The Punch Card and the Hourglass." With extraordinary flair, Marcos explains that the purpose of the EZLN militants is very different from other guerrilla movements, "because its proposal is to cease being an army." He adds: "A soldier is an absurd person who has to resort to arms in order to convince others, and in that sense the movement has no future if its future is military. If the EZLN perpetuates itself as an armed military structure, it is headed for failure. Failure as an alternative set of ideas, an alternative attitude to the world" (García Márquez, Pombo, and Marcos, "The Punch Card and the Hourglass," 70). "You cannot reconstruct the world or society, nor rebuild national states now in ruins, on the basis of a quarrel over who will impose their hegemony on society" (García Márquez, Pombo, and Marcos, "The Punch Card and the Hourglass," 71).

[12] See especially the "Press Release" from May 2014 when Subcomandante Marcos announced his own demise and then immediately returned as Subcomandante Galeano: Subcomandante Ga-

always batted aside attempts to enlist the EZLN in global politics, always returning to the *terroir* of Chiapas for grounding, even if he spoke of global neo-liberal capitalism as the primary enemy.[13] If the actor playing Marcos was the son of bourgeois parents, as the myth goes, and if he was once allied with Jesuit liberation theology, as his purported studies as a student suggest, the circularity of Marxian critique collapsed when entering the charmed circles of his pronouncements and writings. The 2001 interview with Gabriel García Márquez is instructive.[14] Literature is invoked as the antidote to newspapers and media. The somewhat privileged upbringing (that is, of the actor-protagonist, at the least), a formation of character via the mnemonic resources of literature, nonetheless fails to account for the powerful meme unleashed in the West. This, in turn, signals that the construction of the myth of Marcos also, paradoxically, invoked what is ultra-mythic and transpersonal beyond the construction of the singular myth, or, what is real beyond the prosaic definitions of what the real contends via socio-economic measures. Though these measures are absolutely integral to the EZLN cause, the hologram of Marcos lives in the socio-cultural spectrum, and its auto-destruction in 2014 speaks to the very issue of its usefulness and uselessness—its timeliness and its universality.

In one memorable communiqué, dated January 16, 1994 and published one year later in *La Jornada* on January 18, 1995, Marcos describes sitting in a library, which no doubt is utterly imaginary (and thus, spectral), when a book falls off

leano, "Between Shadow and Light," *Roar Magazine*, May 2014, http://roarmag.org/2014/05/subcomandante-galeano-between-light-shadow/.

[13] For example, his mostly polite December 2002 letter to the Basque ETA, in response for an invitation to collaborate, effectively but emphatically telling them to get lost: Subcomandante Insurgente Marcos, "Carta del Subcomandante Marcos a ETA," *Rebelion*, 2002, http://www.rebelion.org/hemeroteca/spain/021212marcos.htm.

[14] García Márquez, Pombo, and Marcos, "The Punch Card and the Hourglass," 69–79.

the shelves and opens to a passage in Jorge Luis Borges' famous short story, "The Library of Babel":

> That dawn was, like others, empty of people. The Library began its complicated ceremony of exposition. The heavy bookcases began a movement much like a disorganized dance. The books changed places and the pages, and in the transfer one of them fell and exposed an undamaged page. I did not pick it up, moving dancing shelves in order to get near enough to read it....
>
> "The Library exists ab aeterno. From that truth whose immediate corollary is the eternal future of the world, no one can reasonably doubt. Humanity, the imperfect librarian, can be a work of luck or of malevolent demiurge; the universe with its elegant dosage of cupboards full of enigmatic tomes, indefatigable ladders for the traveler and latrine for the sedentary user, can only be a work of a god.
>
> The imps affirm that the babble is normal in the Library and that the reasonable (even a humble and pure coherence) is almost a miraculous exception.
>
> The Library is limitless and temporary. If an eternal voyager traverses it in any direction, he would prove that at the end of the centuries the same volumes are repeated in the same disorder (which, once repeated, would be an order: an Order). My loneliness becomes joyful with that elegant hope."[15]

---

[15] Subcomandante Marcos, "The Library of Aguascalientes," *La Jornada*, January 18, 1995, 15; with reference to Jorge Luis Borges, "La biblioteca de Babel" (written in Mar de Plata, 1941). The section concerning the Library is in a postscript that dwarfs the actual letter addressed to the authorities who are in the process of trying to buy off the insurgents via "peace agreements." It opens with: "He remembers a previous morning and a cold interior. One night of tanks, planes and helicopters, I was in the library of Aguascalientes. Alone, surrounded by books and a cold rain which forced the use of the ski mask, not to hide from anyone's eyes, but to hide from the cold. I sat

Does not Marcos step straight into the indeterminancy of texts proper by invoking Borges? Is there not an invocation of the "Man of the Book" and/or the "Crimson Hexagon"— insane expectations from the pages of "The Library of Babel" that doubly mock utopian and messianic expectations? Does he not signal madness as sanity (apropos of, or as antidote to, official insanity)? In such a scenario the doubly mocked is the *hoped-for*. For to doubly mock something is to mock your own mocking of that something, returning to an uneasy yet reconstituted admiration for the mocked.

> The Library of Aguascalientes is the beginning and the end of the spiral and it does not have a defined entrance nor exit. I mean to say that in the gigantic spiral which Tacho described in order to explain the architectural origin of Aguascalientes, the Library is in the beginning and the end. The safe-house which "kept the greatest secrets of the organization," is at the other end and beginning of the whirl. I run my eyes over the gigantic spiral in which the construction is aligned and I imagine that from a special satellite one can appreciate the spiral that "calls from the jungle."[16]

The hyperbolic discourse ends in the jungle. The Zapatistas set up innumerable "Aguascalientes" across Chiapas, commemorating a real city where a real revolution once took

---

in one of the few chairs which was still intact, and contemplated the abandonment of the place." The image of the revolutionary huddled against the cold in an old library is a masterful mnemonic device, true or otherwise, used to counter the governor general and his bodyguards huddled in the governor's palace plotting to threaten and/or cajole the Zapatistas into submission. Translated by Cecilia Rodriguez, National Commission for Democracy in Mexico, *Flag Blackened*, n.d., http://flag.blackened.net/revolt/mexico/ezln/marcos_library_jan95.html.

[16] Marcos, "The Library of Aguascalientes."

place....[17] The library and its books return to their origin—the insurrectionary power of language.

> My gaze runs from the safe-house to the Library, which now gives out a phosphorescent blue and a continuous, hoarse noise. The Library, tells what can be thought, and by day, is inhabited by children. They don't come there because of the books. They say, according to what Eva told me, that there are multi-colored balloons there. Apparently no one finds them, because the children end up painting color pictures. Lately, helicopters and planes are abundant, not just in the skies of Aguascalientes, but also in the flat pictures of the children. The purple, reds and greens are much too abundant in the pictures for my liking. Yellow seems to limit itself to the sun which, these days, is covered by the grey of the sky. At night, the Library shelters and agitates transgressors of the law and professionals of violence (like the one who writes this). They gaze at the shelves filled with books looking for something which is missing, and which they're sure was once there. The Library was the only thing, in all Aguascalientes, considered the property of the Democratic National Convention, and it sometimes has books. The caravaneers made efforts to give it electricity, bookshelves, books, tables, chairs and an old computer which has the virtue of never being used. The rest of Aguascalientes has remained abandoned since that 9th day of August 1994. Every once in a while, Mister, Bruce, and Saqueo will make an effort to sew the canvas for the parties, which are less every time.
>
> Now the Library remains in silence, the phosphorescence is concentrated in one point, in its center, and it turns emerald green. I move carefully to one of the windows. The green light was blinding and it took some time

---

[17] Acknowledging the first Zapatista uprising of 1914 and the Convention of Aguascalientes.

to get used to looking at it. In it I saw.

All of a sudden, the blue sails of Aguascalientes caught a favorable wind. I turned toward the command post but it remained empty. The sea thrust its waves against the keel and the creaking of the chains of the anchor could be heard above the wind. I climbed on starboard and took the rudder in order to free it from the labyrinth of the spiral. Was it leaving or arriving?

The emerald of the library went out.[18]

Marcos closes this magical-realist report with "Vale once again. The Supmarine from the high seas." He has floated off to sea, having opened his letter with, "From the mountains of the Mexican Southeast." *Circularity implodes in the collision of metaphors.* "The blue sails of Aguascalientes caught a favorable wind...."

In a 2001 interview with Gabriel García Márquez and Roberto Pombo, Subcomandante Marcos is asked why he wears two watches:

Your attire is a little strange: a threadbare scarf tied at the neck and a cap that's falling apart. But you are also carrying a torch, which you don't need here, a communications device which looks very sophisticated, and a watch on each wrist. Are they symbols? What does all this mean?[19]

His answer is paradoxical but also devastatingly tautological (in the futural sense), serving to demolish discursive circularity:

The torch is because we have been put into a lightless pit and the radio is for my image consultants to dictate my

[18] Marcos, "The Library of Aguascalientes."
[19] García Márquez, Pombo, and Marcos, "The Punch Card and the Hourglass," 75. Regarding the overt symbolism or iconography of the Zapatistas, see Sandra Escalona Urenda, *A Cultural Analysis of the Visual Signs in the Zapatistas Websites*, Master's thesis, Department of Art and Cultural Studies, University of Jyväskylä, Finland, 2012.

answers to questions from journalists. No. More seriously: this is a walkie-talkie which allows me to communicate with security and with our people in the jungle in case there is a problem. We have received several death threats. The scarf was red and was new when we took San Cristóbal de las Casas seven years ago. And the cap is the one I had when I arrived in the Lacandón jungle eighteen years ago. I arrived in that jungle with one watch and the other dates from when the ceasefire began. *When the two times coincide* it will mean that Zapatismo is finished as an army and that another stage, another watch and another time has started.[20]

Time implodes between two watches (two versions of reality, productive of a third). This is not Hegelian dialectics, however. The images are irreconcilable, shipwrecked instantiations of historical or diachronic time. Their synthesis is the impossible other time of literary exegesis. For a revolution to proceed by such auspices requires that it traverse the sociocultural strata within cultural production. Marcos erased himself when the meme "Marcos" was no longer useful. The rewards of this venture were ameliorative. The therapeutics of the imagined revolution extend beyond the frame of the picture and the portrait. The Zapatista regard for language is extraordinary. The Zapatista recourse to taking language apart, as noted in the above epigraph, suggests that one tires of language when it becomes circular. Revolutionary language resembles, therefore, the quest for an originary language, the ur-language of the Earth—in this case "Chiapas." The socio-economic register was the starting point. The rights of the indigenous people of Mexico to cultivate their land was supplanted by the universal and inalienable rights to cultivate their linguistic *terroir*. The existentialist *gravitas* of this double plight is the foundation for the Zapatista uprising.

---

[20] García Márquez, Pombo, and Marcos, "The Punch Card and the Hourglass," 75; emphasis added.

Language circles such rights. Yet the polished discourses of polite society betray these rights. The circularity of high scholarship and elevated discourses are often a disgrace to such "indigenous rights." Thus, the circle closes and the hermeneutic game ends. But, as above, the Library of Aguascalientes is locked into a spiral, not the hexagons of Borges. The difference in geometry is significant; for one is locked in an icy embrace with time and the other is the prefiguration of a vortex—the great gyres of Yeatsian time.

Language, when it spirals, moves "upward" or "downward." Upward or downward are relative terms, justifiable by ideology and by ideological lock-step or imaginative praxis toward liberation. Borges drew a figure of icy closure and populated it by presentiments of doubly ironical escape. Marcos draws a Figure Eight in the sands of his hourglass, because he never knows what might happen next.

Literary exegesis trumps historical exegesis, except when historical exegesis is also literary exegesis. Back to Michelet. As a result, what matters most is one's intentions. Historical exegesis when it becomes literary becomes, indeed, a vortex. As literary-historical praxis, all things are possible. At such a point—now, then, or never—strange things start to happen. Ghosts reappear out of nowhere. Governments fall like dominos. People awaken from sleep smiling, instead of angry.... Such are the projective clichés of semiosis under the spell of Revolution as Revelation.

A last word might be "Enough." Historical exegesis tires from its own weight and circular discourses produce grey and tired tomes that resemble their authors' pallor. Entombed in libraries they moulder further, not unlike their deceased authors enshrined in granite. But enough is never enough in this regard. Language insists on being torn apart and reborn. Scholarship suffers only when it refuses to acquiesce to this truth that may only be glimpsed from below, as Subcomandante Marcos might say.

January 28, 2015

Essay Six

Verb Tenses and Time-senses

I. THE IDEO-GRAMMATICAL

So all originals exist in faith, faith in God and in the Future as artistic, scientific and religious beginnings which will come to their own beginning as to a second end or a second coming of the future.[1]

Kasimir Malevich

If the ideo-grammatical is the key to the passage of moods and pre-conscious states toward expression in words (the construction of critical discourses), the issue of time-senses becomes central to any deconstruction of rationality as it confronts its *bête noire*, irrationality. To speak in all time-senses at once (is/was/will be) confers on works of artistic and scholarly merit an elliptical manner of speaking that elides any one time-sense through favoring all, all at once.

Revelation in artistic disciplines and discursive speculation in scholarly disciplines might, then, converge by way of a

---

[1] Kasimir Malevich, "The Philosophy of the Kaleidoscope," in Kasimir Malevich, *The World as Non-objectivity: Unpublished Writings 1922-25*, ed. Troels Andersen, trans. Xenia Glowacki-Prus and Edmund T. Little (Copenhagen: Borgen, 1976), 13 [11–33].

configuration of verbal tenses that undermine the distribution of time-senses that govern Western rationality, portending, in turn, through distension and apparent discord, the futural time that marks all such projects that point toward the magical egress in circular thought that, indeed, converges in a dimension given solely to the work at hand—the point of the exegetical labors or the justification of the irreducible artistic mélange, as all scholarship is forward-looking in some sense, and all artistic endeavors are a synoptic view of decidedly preternatural "landscapes" that float just over the horizon of the so-called Real, "landscapes" where past, present, and future exist in an elective versus actual simultaneity. The unverifiable premise that every avant-garde project (by definition) seeks to condition both the present and the future, while some, being so out of joint with their own times, register their presence only in a vague sensibility that connotes a futural tense (and, therefore, the aesthetic of deferral, endless or otherwise), confers on such labors a time-sense only recognizable *in the future*, or at some other time after the time of conception. Most assuredly this accounts for aspects of literary production that are acknowledged retrospectively, an *as if* present in the work at the time of conception, yet an *as if* that may only become an *as is* through the passage of conventional time. Therefore, its intermediate state is the *as it might be*, arguably the time-sense of the universal.

Thus, theological texts (as well as some highly figurative metaphysical texts) display a complexity of verbal tenses that are difficult, if not impossible to parse via translation or the usual rules of Western epistemological or philological archaeology. Chronology is typically the first stumbling block for interpretation of works that carry the impress of multiple time-senses—the "chronogenic" senses conflicting with rote chronology, as iconology often conflicts with iconography. Furthermore, as in the case of authorized textual traditions (compilations that exhibit an orthodoxy attributable to their authors), exclusions and occlusions occur, which then set in motion the reductivism of scholarship in service to low-level formations of ideological usurpation.

The New Testament is one such example. But so are other attempts to hypostasize complex times (to historically ground periods where the "landscape hovering above the landscape" confers unease), such as the Renaissance or the Enlightenment or Modernism, whereas in the case of Modernism the instances of anti-modernism are of far greater interest than the orthodox or canonical works for reasons that the rational disposition of the corpus actually fails, revealing other moments and the proverbial lost causes or ghosts, just as the Gnostic gospels create enormous tension within New Testament scholarship, or just as when reading the surviving documents of the Franciscan order (including the Rule) one finds all manner of mischief in burying the originary vision (Francis' actual words) in scholastic verbiage. The strangest effects, however, within these documents considered *the* Franciscan canon is that passages that have been overwritten contain peculiar and electrifying phrases and/or whole sentences that register a time-sense that has *no* relation whatsoever to (no common valence with) the rationalist-doctrinal disposition or tenor of the overall document/screed.[2] This is the

---

[2] In purely secular terms, an excellent summary of a rigorously and scientifically policed but, arguably, *non-scientific* system of argumentation (a Rule) may be found in David Cronenberg's film, *A Dangerous Method* (2011), which concerns the differences between Sigmund Freud's and Carl Jung's attitudes toward the unconscious. The film is based on Christopher Hampton's play, *The Talking Cure* (2002), which in turn is based on the controversial book by John Kerr, *A Dangerous Method* (New York: Random House, 1993). The currents between the four protagonists—Carl Jung, Sigmund Freud, Otto Gross, and Sabina Spielrein—are reducible to a grand inquisition on rationality and its methods. For a review, see Philip French, "*A Dangerous Method* – Review," *The Guardian*, 2012, http://www.theguardian.com/film/2012/feb/12/dangerous-method-david-cronenberg-review. Notably, Kerr's treatment of this primal skirmish between Freud and Jung annoyed "Freudians" as much as the skirmish between Wolfgang Amadeus Mozart and Antonio Salieri in Peter

"secret concordance" that survives assimilation of avant-garde works (revolutionary, theological, pedagogical, etc.), commentaries either further burying the voice or freeing it

Shaffer's stage play *Amadeus* (1979), plus Miloš Forman's film version (*Amadeus*, 1984), thrilled and annoyed conventional neo-classicists or "Mozartians." Additionally, for the stalemate associated with the logical-positivist bias, see Ludwig Wittgenstein's exquisitely concise and elegant *Tractatus Logico-philosophicus*, trans. C.K. Ogden (London: Routledge and Kegan Paul, 1922), and its famous evocation of, and closure with "everything else" (about which we must remain silent, if we remain within the charmed circles of hyper-rationalist inquiry). "Wovon man nicht sprechen kann, darüber muss man schweigen" ["Whereof one cannot speak, thereof one must be silent"]: Wittgenstein, *Tractatus Logico-philosophicus*, 7.1. First published as "Logisch-Philosophische Abhandlung," *Annalen der Naturphilosophie* 14 (1921). Of course, Wittgenstein soon afterward turned to this self-same "everything else," much to the chagrin of his own father figure, Bertrand Russell. One day, perhaps, a film or novelistic treatment will be made of Russell and the stories circulating in Northwest Wales as of 2013 regarding his setting a place at his table for an invisible interlocutor; that is, an imaginative treatment regarding his own relationship to "everything else," including the radical pacifist politics at which he excelled. Such might free Russell from the historically imposed straightjacket of quintessential arch-rationalist and arch-atheist. Russell was semi-retired when "taking tea" with this imaginary presence (living near Penrhyndeudraeth, Gwynedd). Regarding Russell's pragmatics, however, in a simultaneous compliment and criticism of the Soviet Union, Russell stated in 1961 (at the age of eighty-nine): "The Russians, with even more success, were able to do what the Japanese had done at the turn of the century; they were able to utilize the scientific method for great technological advance but were unable to grasp its spirit." See Dannel Angus McCollum, "Tea with Bertrand Russell in 1961," *Escarpment Press*, n.d., https://escarpmentpress.org/russelljournal/article/download/1476/1503. See also Derek Jarman's film-portrait of Ludwig Wittgenstein in *Wittgenstein* (1993). For a similar cinematic portrait detailing the existential aspects of this *concordia discors* between the arts as non-discursive radical praxis (an alternative Rule) and the annals of Western rationality, see Derek Jarman, *Caravaggio* (1986).

from the confines of elaborate and circular verbiage.[3]

In the arts the same occurs. It proceeds, however, through the art-historical apparatuses of assimilation and elaboration, rarely ever preserving the impress of the time signature of the work. The retrospective gaze of art-historical scholarship is a deathly gaze, and few instances of the preservation of the spirit of the work under assimilation, calibration, and valorization survive this process. The survival, instead, is to be found in works that recuperate and assimilate through dynamic, often-subversive praxis the time-senses of the works—not the scholarship. Yet certain forms of scholarship provide assistance—for example, literary assimilation. Russian Formalism is one example; and the fate of the earliest progenitors of a Western avant-garde has fallen into two primary paths—one, the assimilation to the Western canon of the "emergence" of Modernism; and two, the periodic return of the formalist moment in works that directly or indirectly access the secret concordance within the subsequent transmission of what has fallen into traditional art-historical scholarship as a type of "red scare" averted (or subverted and commodified).[4]

---

[3] Regarding the hidden or buried Franciscan voice, see Keeney, "Part II: What is Franciscan Ontology?" in *Not-I/Thou: The Other Subject of Art and Architecture* (Newcastle upon Tyne: Cambridge Scholars Publishing, 2014). Regarding Pico della Mirandola's statements regarding the Medieval voice haunting Renaissance arts and letters, see Gavin Keeney, "The Origin of the Arts," in Gavin Keeney, *"Elsewhere": Essays in Art, Architecture, and Cultural Production 2002-2011* (Newcastle upon Tyne: Cambridge Scholars Publishing, 2011), 227–248.

[4] See, for example, the work of the Yugoslav-Slovene collective IRWIN and the occasional presence of Russian Formalism. Note as well the presence of Orthodox icons....

II. PRE- AND POST-MARXISM

America, why are your libraries full of tears?[5]

Allen Ginsberg

Between pre- and post-Marxism is *and was* Marxism proper. How does Marxism, however, include pre-Marxism and post-Marxism other than through the retrospective gaze of historical consciousness? Furthermore, how does Marxism appear out of pre-Marxism and move toward post-Marxism? Does not post-Marxism already exist within pre-Marxism and Marxism? And is post-Marxism not waiting over the horizon for Marxism? Does it have a station toward which moves Marxism proper, or do they move toward one another and meet at X? A certain antinomialism might demolish such circular arguments, arguments that resemble sophistry and/or metaphysical poetry, yet the facts remain the same no matter how the discourse creates proportionality or distributes effects historically.

What might be said to actually move is historical consciousness, yet again via its discourses concerning Marxism. The movement resembles the disk of light moving across the interior surface of the Pantheon, the light of the Sun entering through the oculus and drifting with the day, and days, to illuminate different paths within the domed structure. Marxism as phenomenon thus might be de-classified as historical

---

[5] Allen Ginsberg, "America," in Allen Ginsberg, *Howl and Other Poems* (San Francisco: City Lights, 1956); punctuation added. The immediate context for this lament from January 1956, when the poet was ostensibly down to "two dollars and twenty-seven cents," is: "America when will you be angelic? / When will you take off your clothes? / When will you look at yourself through the grave? / When will you be worthy of your million Trotskyites? / America why are your libraries full of tears?" The Whitman-esque aspects of this poem are emblematic of the Beat sensibility, yet Whitman as enlightened tramp. In this poem, Ginsberg effectively assimilates the voice from Walt Whitman's *Leaves of Grass*, but turns the high-Romantic exhortation of Whitman toward a dark lamentation.

materialism and re-classified as the phenomenological and/or structuralist project par excellence.

It was perhaps Jacques Derrida's *Specters of Marx* that first unearthed what Marx had buried or tried to bury in his written works—namely, Max Stirner and all that he represented as reprehensible to Marx and Engels.[6] Derrida's cause, far from resurrecting Stirner, was to resurrect Marxism, following 1989, as phenomenologically inflected historical discourse and anti-capitalist project. That Derridean Deconstruction (as a variant of High Post-structuralism, and as hermeneutic) is clearly haunted by High Structuralism is instructive, just as Post-phenomenology (and its theological turn) concerns exiting the circular exegesis of Husserlian Phenomenology.

Varieties of post-Marxism existed from Marx forward, with a notable proliferation after the Soviet invasion of Hungary in 1956—inclusive of a curious variant known as "Creative Marxism."[7] Indeed, Cold War rhetoric only instilled forms of post-Marxism that sought not so much a middle ground, as a ground that in many respects reconstituted aspects of pre-Marxism. If Marxist insurgencies around the planet failed in the 1970s, leading directly to the triumphalism of neo-liberal capitalism in the 1980s and beyond, various other disciplines and discourses took up the cause, and the schematic of the continuum, as above, the problems associated with "before,

---

[6] Jacques Derrida, *Specters of Marx: The State of the Debt, the Work of Mourning, and the New International*, trans. Peggy Kamuf (London: Routledge, 1994).

[7] See Gavin Keeney, "Anamnesis," in Gavin Keeney, *Dossier Chris Marker: The Suffering Image* (Newcastle upon Tyne: Cambridge Scholars Publishing, 2012), for a discussion of varieties of post-Marxism: "Creative Marxism was distinguished by the late-1950s' and early-1960s' turn toward 'theoretical and conceptual issues,' and was a distinct event in the West, versus the East, insofar as it was further distinguished by its 'openness' to reflection 'without being foreclosed by party-line polemics or divisive political loyalties'" (45); with reference to Göran Therborn, "Critical Theory and the October Revolution," in Göran Therborn, *From Marxism to Post-Marxism?* (London: Verso, 2008), 90–91 [90–92].

during, and after X," moved into discursive and artistic milieux, more definitively perhaps, given that such disciplines and discourses were always present in the multiple arts throughout the Marxist insurgencies noted. Indeed, there might even be an ur-Marxist literature hidden in avant-garde practices from the 1950s forward, but hidden because such works invoke pre-, X, and post-X—or, such works irreducibly engender a meditation on time and time-senses that are spectrally Marxist works versus overtly Marxist works.

The time-sense of Alain Robbe-Grillet's screenplay for *Last Year at Marienbad*[8] is but one example, as Chris Marker's *La jetée*[9] is another, both films situated astride the year 1962. The implosion of narrative conventions in the former is matched by the wholly and holy liquidation and redemption of the world in *La jetée*—a liquidation and redemption through memory and its multiple "stations" (Stations of the Cross in an irreligious manner, but Stations of the Cross nonetheless). That Marker's protagonist in *La jetée* returns to the past before venturing into the future is not coincidental to the sci-fi scenario involving time travel. That the beginning of this tale conjoins to its closure, with one major difference (the conscious age of the protagonist in otherwise identical scenes), invokes consciousness within consciousness, or, hyper-consciousness. Revelation, then, returns to Marxism through the aegis of multiple time frames or the evocation in works of art and literature of time-senses that make no real sense to the rationalist bias of historical materialism or conventional dialectics as such. Synthesis or Utopia is no longer the issue. The strange virtues of Hegel's *Phenomenology of Spirit*, as they migrated to the left *and* to the right, might be seen as evidence of the pre-Marxist aspects of Marxism as such, insofar as the judgment that Marx turned Hegel upside-down is true.

---

[8] Alain Resnais, *L'année dernière à Marienbad* (1961).

[9] Chris Marker, *La jetée* (1962). For the commonality of *La jetée* and *L'année dernière à Marienbad*, see Gavin Keeney, "Séance 'C.M.'," in Keeney, *Dossier Chris Marker*, 223–232.

If the purpose of Marxism or Marxian praxis is sociocultural autonomy (above and beyond everyday socio-economic justice), and over and against capitalist determinism, the great modernist project of Structural Linguistics and its focus on word and mnemonic image would seem to be the foremost address for the insurgency, inclusive of the failed quest for deep grammars.[10] The psycho-mnemonic resources of language prefigure autonomy or enslavement, and the circularity of developed discourse is quite often the primary objection posed by avant-garde artistic and scholarly projects. Structural Linguistics crosses the entire "continent" of the twentieth century. As meta-discipline, it also crosses other disciplines. From Dadaism to Minimalism, from Modernism to Post-modernism, with all manner of anti-modernisms thrown in for good measure, the multiple arts generally, and when practiced under self-imposed duress, serve the singular cause of focusing a light on the shadowy origins of language—the

---

[10] It is autonomy for nominally closely argued disciplines and systems, with their attendant repressions or sublimations, that represents the greatest stumbling block in arguing for or against systems. The utility of the system often substitutes for its possible sublimity. In the same manner, formalism is an elective means for developing the inherent resources of a system or discipline (its internalizing time-senses), or for erasing the self-same; yet formalism is as often utilized as a convenience or an excuse for closing off the outside from the inside, precipitating further repressions. Thus, forms of high and low formalism may be found strewn across the history of scholarship and the arts—with the higher forms marked by dialectical sublimation and the lower forms marked by continuous repression. See Gaston Bachelard on Novalis in Gaston Bachelard, *The Psychoanalysis of Fire*, trans. Alan C.M. Ross, preface by Northrop Frye (Boston: Beacon Press, 1964). First published as *La psychanalyse du feu* (Paris: Éditions Gallimard, 1938). "One can study only what one has first dreamed about": Bachelard, *The Psychoanalysis of Fire*, 22. See also Cristina Chimisso, *Gaston Bachelard: Critic of Science and the Imagination* (London: Routledge, 2001). This statement by Bachelard was used by Hayden White as the epigraph for his *Metahistory: The Historical Imagination in Nineteenth-century Europe* (Baltimore: Johns Hopkins University Press, 1973), v.

moods, the premonitions, the specters, and the absences that generate language. The finger pointing at the moon and the moon entangled in the trees are images of an order of such premonitions for the arts—strictly apolitical premonitions that migrate through linguistic forms to socio-cultural formations that then instill further delimitations (productive orders, agendas, factions, genres, and such). The perennial quest for an ur-language in philology is not dissimilar. In the arts this quest takes the form of renegotiating a relationship with the idealist gambit of pure subjectivist inquiry—speaking to oneself in the abstruse pre-linguistic register of premonition, admonition, and exaltation.[11] Reverie and Revelation. This level or semi-privileged, apparently hyper-logical position within thought is precisely the functional equivalent of pointing to the moon entangled *in* the treetops, as it combines two gestures at once (the subjective condition or origin of the act and the non-subjective condition or phenomenal address of the act, the latter being its ideo-grammatical form, while the former is formless).[12]

---

[11] For the phantasmagorical implications of the idealist gambit, see Stefan Andriopoulos, *Ghostly Apparitions: German Idealism, the Gothic Novel, and Optical Media* (New York: Zone Books, 2013).

[12] See the various works assembled around this theme of "formless." For example, Yve-Alain Bois and Rosalind E. Krauss' exhibition and book based on themes to be found in the work of Georges Bataille but extrapolated to address modern and contemporary art works by "Jackson Pollock, Andy Warhol, Cy Twombly, Lucio Fontana, Cindy Sherman, Claes Oldenburg, Jean Dubuffet, Robert Smithson, and Gordon Matta-Clark, among others": "Formless: A User's Guide," *Zone Books*, 2014, http://www.zonebooks.org/titles/BOIS_FOR.html. See also Yve-Alain Bois and Rosalind E. Krauss, *Formless: A User's Guide* (New York: Zone, 1997). "In a work that will become indispensable to anyone seriously interested in modern art, Yve-Alain Bois and Rosalind Krauss convincingly introduce a new constellation of concepts to our understanding of avant-garde and modernist art practices. *Formless: A User's Guide* constitutes a decisive and dramatic transformation of the study of twentieth-century culture. Although it has been over sixty years since Georges Bataille undertook

III. JUDGMENT AND JUSTIFICATION

The finger pointing to the moon, the moon entangled in the treetops, and the finger pointing to the moon entangled in the treetops are three versions of an ideo-grammatical hypostasization of conscious and pre-conscious discourse (thought as word-image). The finger pointing to the moon is the instantiation of the gesture of speech, whereas the moon entangled in the treetops is a consciously observed phenomenon suffused with subjective agency, conjoining two spatial realities. The finger pointing to the moon entangled in the treetops is the convergence of the pre-conscious mood or state preceding language and the will to language—its creative force. Not vitalism in its classic sense, this conflation produces nonetheless the specter of vitalism through the subversion of the Real. The ideo-grammatical construction of the image includes time-senses that elude rational disposition or conveyance via rational discourse. The moon remains an orb circling the Earth, but it comes inexplicably closer by virtue of being hung up in the treetops. The gesture toward this phenomenal object (a montaged object, after all) is conditional—the observation is infused with intention. The intentionality is purely verbal, the will to language a combination of mood and observation.[13]

---

his philosophical development of the term *informe*, only in recent years has the idea of the 'formless' been deployed in theorizing and reconfiguring the very field of twentieth-century art. This is partly because that field has most often been crudely set up as a battle between form and content, whereas 'formless' constitutes a third term that stands outside the opposition of form and content, outside the binary thinking that is itself formal": "Formless: A User's Guide."

[13] See "2. The Paradox of the Intentional Object," in Vincent Descombes, *The Institutions of Meaning: A Defense of Anthropological Holism*, trans. Stephen Adam Schwartz (Cambridge: Harvard University Press, 2015). "2.1. What Husserl calls 'the paradox of the intentional object' is the fact that the perceived tree, taken as such, unlike the tree itself, does not have the natural powers of a physical thing (it can be seen to be burning up, but it cannot burn up). How is

Thus, the times that are present in the ideo-grammatical formation are multiple, and the figure of the moon in the treetops becomes preternatural. The image returns to its origins with multiple times fused through the movement of gesture, gaze, and return gaze—a Levinasian economy of transpersonal import. This elemental, almost gothic presentiment is somewhere at the foundation of all mimetic exercises; whether addressed to empirical antecedents or projected into a futural system under construction via the mimetic exercise. Subjective agency conditions the subsequent report: the scientist determining the proper location of moon and tree; the artist or poet determining the absolute and contingent markers for the supposition that the moon is caught in the treetops. These markers are strangely absolute and contingent, at once, due to their compromise with space-time. The transpersonal imprint that sustains the image is what permits the image to return the gaze. This economy is the foundation for ethics. When transferred to the socio-cultural it is the beginning of every revolt against hegemony and its variants—the locus for the skirmish always a socio-economic terrain, whereas the finger that points to the moon entangled in the treetops is the dynamic and hyper-conscious address for artistic and scholarly praxis as revolutionary praxis.

Underwriting a metaphysics of perception (or a phenomenology of metaphysics), the word-image is an expression of atonement. This is also why it is possible to say that the eagle and the sky are one thing. Revolutionary praxis that is also enlightened or ethical and moral praxis substitutes one form of consilience for another. Entanglement becomes liberty. The hypostasizations of the former call to the latter across

---

this doubling of the tree—into both an object of physical actions and an object of mental operations—to be avoided?" "2.2. According to Husserl, the only tree that can be seen in the garden is the intentional object." "2.3. Intentional objects are not entities endowed with a specific mode of existence. It is meaningful to ask 'Where is the tree perceived?' but meaningless to ask 'Where is the perceived tree?'"

multiple times but through the ideo-grammatical time-sense of the singular image.

Consider for a moment the possibility of "The Moment," or every historical moment past, present, and future combined; and add to this world-historical continuum every subjective moment lived by every subject past, present, and future. Is this not the very image of the All-Knowing, of the Absolute, of both pantheism and monotheism (and, by negation, elevated forms of nihilism and atheism)? Is such the measure of finitude or infinity? To answer, time would have to have either an End and a Beginning, or no End and no Beginning, *for subjects*. Is this simultaneity of historical and subjective times consistent with Hegelian Pleroma? Does it only exist in literary ventures? Thus the (im)possibility of all times in one time—the very definition of Revelation—and the relative poverty of materialist and reductivist systems that do not contain the imprint of this considered, all-knowing moment that re-subjectivizes collective experience. Such is a judgment and justification for scholarship in service to no singular this-worldly master. Such also makes the production of knowledge under the spell of such auspices utterly transpersonal and de-singular (Tristan Tzara's gift). Paradoxes ensue, and tautologies multiply. Similarly, the sense of normative subjectivity constituted as "Being, stranded between two infinities" (from Pascal to Nabokov) collapses.[14]

---

[14] "The cradle rocks above an abyss, and common sense tells us that our existence is but a brief crack of light between two eternities of darkness": Vladimir Nabokov, *Speak, Memory: An Autobiography Revisited* (New York: Vintage, 1967), 19 (first published in 1951 and "assiduously revised" in 1966). For nuanced semi-Proustian readings of Nabokov's literary exploration of themes related to such a moment, see, for example, Sigi Jöttkandt, "Topographies of a Cinematic City: Vladimir Nabokov's 'A Guide to Berlin'," *Symplokē* 22.1-2 (2014): 181–199, and David Shields, "Autobiographic Rapture and Fictive Irony in *Speak, Memory* and 'The Real Life of Sebastian Knight'," *Iowa Review* 17.1 (Winter 1987): 44–54. See also Cronenberg's *A Dangerous Method*, which deconstructs the Jungian version of this spectral-noetic complex formalized by Carl Jung as the Collec-

That distinguished scholars of the caliber of Wilhelm Dilthey and Pierre Bourdieu could confer such a moment on both historical and cultural exegesis preempts any objections or accusations of bathos for considering speculations regarding an ur-time of this order inherent to speculative thought itself. That film noir specializes in the same, and that David Lynch has made a career out of mining this presentiment of infinitude in finitude (and finitude in infinitude), only confirms the frightful or psychotic prospects for singular and notional forms of Cartesian consciousness, always haunted anyway by its Double. Furthermore, the instantiation of the Multiple, by austere and abstract means in Alain Badiou and others, confers an aspect of Revelation upon logic and its analogues further delimiting the mark of such a moment. Indeed, without the moral and ethical precepts invoked long ago by Pascal, to counter Descartes, Hegel's Night of the World is full of bloody heads, and all cows returning "home" (or chickens returning "to roost") are black.

"Render unto Caesar what is Caesar's...."

tive Unconscious. In this regard, it would be interesting to bang *The Red Book* of Jung up against the Black Books of Martin Heidegger to see what might "fall out."

IV. "THE KINGDOM, THE POWER, AND THE GLORY"

> Memory has the capacity to recognize intuitively and directly the images we keep of the impression the past makes on us, with all the uncertainties stemming from its questionable reliability. This problem concerns all stages of the historiographic process: testimony and archives—explanation/comprehension—, narrative and rhetorical representation during the writing of the historian's final text. But one thing remains certain, it is impossible to give priority to either memory or history.[15]
>
> Paul Ricoeur

If Giorgio Agamben's neo-Foucauldian project of dynamiting discourses to extract the *dynamis* or operative power embedded within them is a philosophical-archaeological project starting roughly with the opening of the *Homo Sacer* project in 1995 (with *Homo Sacer: Sovereign Power and Bare Life*), it reaches (for or against Power and Law) an uneasy and retrospective apotheosis in *The Signature of All Things* (2009). Indeed, to convert the concept of *dynamis* (derived from Old and New Testament patristics) to time-sense, or time-senses, is wholly consistent with his extraordinarily complex "intercessionary" work, outside of, but coincidental to *Homo Sacer*, *The Time that Remains* (2000).[16] Over the course of *Homo*

---

[15] Paul Ricoeur, "L'écriture de l'histoire et la réprésentation du passé," *L'École des Hautes Études en Sciences Sociales*, n.d., http://cmb.ehess.fr/95; abstract for a paper of the same title presented by Ricoeur at the XXIIᵉ Conférence Marc-Bloch, June 13, 2000. See also Paul Ricoeur, "L'écriture de l'histoire et la réprésentation du passé," *Annales: Histoire, Sciences Sociales* 55.4 (July-August 2000): 731–747. The abstract, as cited, begins: "The problem of the representation of the past does not begin with history, but with memory."

[16] Giorgio Agamben, *The Signature of All Things: On Method*, trans. Luca D'Isanto, with Kevin Attell (New York: Zone Books, 2009). See also Giorgio Agamben, *Il tempo che resta* (Turin: Bollati Boringhieri, 2000). For a review of *The Signature of All Things*, see John V. Garner, "Giorgio Agamben: *The Signature of All Things*," *Continental Philosophy Review* 43.4 (November 2010): 579–588. "Agamben initi-

Sacer, 1995-2013, Agamben has effectively moved from the elevated nihilist postures of High Post-structuralism toward a seemingly unavoidable confrontation with the conferral of sentience to discourses via theological precepts buried within secular practices—political, economical, and cultural. One almost sees history and its commentaries coming to life and defending themselves through such work—but defending principles of historicity, not episodes. The implied dereliction of duty for historians is profound. As a result, the extolling of the virtues of divine madness in artists and poets (their conversion to holy fools) by post-structuralist critics begins to make sense, on the one hand, while, on another level, it begins to instill pathos and a lachrymose sensibility that all attempts to reach the Absolute (Truth) through creative praxis are doomed to failure—a failure that may or may not have anything to do with socio-economic conventions and their

ates *The Signature of All Things* by defining the philosophically genuine as 'its capacity for elaboration' and by reproposing, in terms that again challenge the generic foundations of contemporary academic discourse, the onto-epistemic relation between thought and interpretation": Nicola Masciandaro, "Conjuring the Phantasm," *Theory and Event* 13.3 (2010), http://muse.jhu.edu/journals/theory_and_event/v013/13.3.masciandaro.html. See also the discussion regarding the magico-religious vis-à-vis Aby Warburg's Mnemosyne Atlas in Gavin Keeney, "The Semi-divine Economy of Art," in Keeney, *Not-I/Thou*, 75–92. Agamben's time at the Warburg Institute, c. 1974-1975, or during the years Frances A. Yates was also in residence, has as much significance to his overall project as the usual recourse of commentators to citing his spiritual heirs as Michel Foucault and/or Walter Benjamin, as does whatever Agamben felt or saw as an extra on the set of Pier Paolo Pasolini's *Il Vangelo Secondo Matteo* (1964). Notably, Yates wrote and published, between the late 1950s and the early 1970s (and while associated with the Warburg Institute), *Giordano Bruno and the Hermetic Tradition* (1964), *The Art of Memory* (1966), *Theatre of the World* (1969), and *The Rosicrucian Enlightenment* (1972). Yates and Agamben act as "mediums" for their respective disciplines, reading the invisible concordances that inhabit texts and intellectual traditions. Their works are marked by fearlessness (but with respect) before (and for) tradition.

reduction of all things to rote instrumentality (plus the conversion of imagination to sentimentality). Agamben's project, therefore, appears to bring us to the brink of madness, where we are staring into an abyss.

Mediation or "mediumship" in the Arts and Humanities progresses by way of the analogical and the anagogical, a position that is roughly equivalent in present-day terms to the ravages or skirmishes associated with iconography and iconology in art-historical discourses—the former being referential and the latter utterly dynamic and topological. It is for this reason that Chris Marker divides *Le tombeau d'Alexandre* (1993) into "The Kingdom of Shadows" and "The Shadows of the Kingdom."[17] The division invokes, with artistic license and temporal slippage, the Spinozian conceit, *sub specie aeternitatis*, plus its corollary, *sui generis*—yet in reverse, and "The Kingdom" (or, Truth) denoted by its representations (the shadowy realm of cinema), connoting, in turn, the responsibility of representational orders to speak of Truth ("The Kingdom"). The film concerns Marker interrogating Alexandre Medvedkine, a friend, yet several years after his death in 1989. The Russian filmmaker's legacy, as avant-garde filmmaker (at first renowned and then forgotten for his *ciné-train* experiments in the Soviet Union in the 1920s), is what concerns Marker on one level, while the truth-telling apparatus of cinema is the primary concern. Marker's film is a *détourned* séance, as he is conjuring up Medvedkine's ghost to answer questions that could not be posed while he was alive.[18] Or, at

---

[17] *Le tombeau d'Alexandre* (1993). Written, directed, and edited by Chris Marker (with Andrei Pachkevitch). See Barthélémy Amengual, "*Le tombeau d'Alexandre*: Une tragédie optimiste," *Positif* 391 (September 1993): 56–59; François Lecointe, *"Le tombeau d'Alexandre": Cinéma, mémoire, histoire* (Saint-Martin-d'Hères: Institut d'Études Politiques, 2000); and Chris Marker, "Six lettres à Alexandre Medvedkine (*Le tombeau d'Alexandre*)," *Positif* 391 (September 1993): 49–54.

[18] Regarding Medvedkine, the Russians, and Marker, see Gavin Keeney, "Something about Nothing," in Keeney, *Dossier Chris Mark-*

least that is the premise of the six letters that comprise the overall structure of the film. More importantly, *tombeau* is an elegiac musical form, and Marker is using it for its obvious semantic indeterminancy. The English title is even more surreptitious in this regard; for, to "translate" or transform the title to *The Last Bolshevik* alters the linguistic and mnemonic terrain significantly, while also offering red bait to its Western (English-speaking) audience.[19] Why *last* Bolshevik? Notably, the film works its way all the way through to 1989 and the collapse of the Soviet Union shortly afterward, when the questions Marker poses no longer concern Medvedkine and they become doubly troubling because they approach the spectacle of post-Soviet duplicity in declaring the past dead. Medvedkine escapes witnessing this debacle by dying. ("Die at the right time: so teaches Zarathustra.") Marker then visits his grave and time implodes, via the screen, in an exquisite evocation of 1920s-style, Soviet-era montage—Medvedkine's cavalry past generating war horses superimposed and gallop-

er, 151–213.

[19] In Markerian terms, the "linguistic" content (or, voice-over) is the primary discursive terrain of the work, while the rhetorical "ray" (André Bazin's term) wavers and often turns lyrical or ironical. See André Bazin, "Chris Marker, *Lettre de Sibérie*," in André Bazin, *Le cinéma français de la libération à la Nouvelle Vague* (Paris: Cahiers du Cinéma, 1983), 179–181. Bazin's much-problematized "three rays" of cinema, as utilized to extraordinary effect in Marker's first solo film, *Lettre de Sibérie* (1958), are the visual, the verbal, and the aural. As semi-independent forms of knowledge, they converge in *Lettre de Sibérie*. To expand upon Bazin's schematic, the "mnemonic" content, while not solely confined to the visual spectrum, is either discursive or non-discursive. In the former, discursive instance the mnemonic image is, nominally, referential; while in the latter, non-discursive case it is mesmeric and, decidedly, non-referential. The so-called irrationality of the mesmeric image opens, in turn, onto multiple readings. Here, Badiou's concept of the Multiple coincides with cinema's relationship to narrativity and its Other—not-knowledge (that is, cinema's inherent revelatory aspects, which are effectively literary, arrayed against any singular reading).

ing across the face of his tomb and the Russian steppe. Marker's revenge is to forgive Medvedkine his crimes (primarily related to the Stalinist years of repression) and to proclaim the last Bolshevik immortal (though interred in the very history of agit-prop cinema).

The analogical *circles*, while the anagogical *rises*.[20] The anagogical belongs, or is inherent to theological exegesis, while the analogical is often applied to scholastics (including theological disputation). It is the apophatic path in theological and socio-cultural critique that is, perhaps, most interesting in this respect, for the elective and elevated nihilism of its model is anti-system, or proto-anarchistic in both the development of anti-systems and the sounding of an existential-metaphysical *rapport* (report) on the state of things and possible measures toward other states.[21]

Thus, Glory appears in the form of valorizing (glorifying) other states; or, it appears as spectral operational power in formalizing a reading of another, primordial state buried with-

---

[20] *Anagoge*, from the Greek ἀναγωγή—"to climb." Regarding anagogical exegesis, see Bonaventure (who derived the method from the works of Dionysius the Areopagite). Regarding Bonaventure's reading of Francis of Assisi's stepping outside the law (his first moves in Assisi to disassociate himself from his own times), see Hester Goodenough Gelber, "A Theater of Virtue: The Exemplary World of St. Francis of Assisi," in John Stratton Hawley, ed., *Saints and Virtues* (Berkeley: University of California Press, 1987), 31 [15–35].

[21] Such is the origin of Guy Debord's *Rapport* (1957) on behalf of the Situationist International: Guy Debord, *Report on the Construction of Situations and on the Terms of Organization and Action of the International Situationist Tendency* (1957). The English title varies slightly depending upon the source. Published in Tom McDonough, ed., *Guy Debord and the Situationist International: Texts and Documents* (Cambridge: MIT Press, 2002). This book includes an essay by Giorgio Agamben on Debord's films: Giorgio Agamben, "Difference and Repetition: On Guy Debord's Films." See also Guy Debord, *Correspondence: The Foundation of the Situationist International (June 1957-August 1960)*, trans. Stuart Kendall and John McHale (Los Angeles: Semiotext(e), 2009). First published as *Correspondance, Volume 1 (Juin 1957-Août 1960)* (Paris: Librairie Arthème Fayard, 1999).

in current states, broken or otherwise. In Gnosticism it is productive of angels and archons....The political emerges as this possible state within states (*terroir* or cultivated ground being its base, or its socio-economic expression, while the "void" of contemporary re-visitations of Lucretius et al. is an evocation of the potential *for* other states within an ultra-primordial state provisionally configured as becoming or "to come"). *Thus* angels and archons.

For this reason, Agamben has excavated Glory as the hidden spring in secular practices that are actually deformed theological practices.[22] The winged white horse of Greek mythology (Pegasus) striking its hoof atop the mountains to produce the Muses seems to claim the same origin for the arts. The same dynamic principle, therefore, underwrites any and all written exegesis of/for other worlds—yet virtuous worlds that serve as judgment and justification for moral and ethical insurrection (that is, stepping outside of the law to point to a "higher" law).[23]

---

[22] Giorgio Agamben, *The Kingdom and the Glory: For a Theological Genealogy of Economy and Government*, trans. Lorenzo Chiesa, with Matteo Mandarini (Stanford: Stanford University Press, 2011). First published as *Il Regno e la Gloria*, Homo Sacer II, 2 (Turin: Bollati Boringhieri, 2009).

[23] Jean-Luc Godard's *L'origine du XXIème Siècle (pour moi)* (2000) speaks to this complex, as does Patti Smith's 2012 appropriation of this short, mesmerizing film/video. *L'origine du XXIème Siècle (pour moi)* is a 15-minute, 44-second film (versions vary in length) commissioned for the 2000 Cannes Film Festival. See http://vimeo.com/19332340. Smith appropriated the film, trimmed it to four minutes and six seconds, both reversing and speeding it up, and set it to her rendering of Neil Young's "After the Gold Rush," leaving out the verse about "lying in a burned-out basement" and shifting the vision forward to the twenty-first century. See Patti Smith, *After the Gold Rush*, https://www.youtube.com/watch?v=wLqcClh3qKQ. The altered refrain, "Look at Mother Nature on the run in the twenty-first century," repeats six times, with children joining as chorus, to close Smith's assimilation and appropriation—her otherworldly crosspollination of Godard and Young. Godard's film moves forward, toward its polemical conclusion, by moving backward in time—the carnage of war

As Friedrich Nietzsche, arguably the father or fountainhead of modernist and post-modernist nihilism and/or *fin-de-siècle* egoism, stated, "Even the hollowest nut wants to be cracked."[24] While this was addressed to the Last Men, it also, perhaps, implies that "all broken promises wish to be fulfilled."[25] Some things are, *pace* Nietzsche, more important than others. The anagogical might be seen, then, as the secret path within the analogical. Metaphors, when re-conjoined to their missing referents, vanish—the metaphors of analogical thought being, thus, productive mirages. So too circular discourses and petty squabbles, plus all non-productive nagging rejoinders and obsessive emendations (or, qualifications). Eventually endless commentaries must end....

Eventually, and/or in a certain light, the invisible concordance in all things (Agamben's "signature of all things") crosses and marks all representational systems (all discourses and all creative practices given to the Arts and Humanities). Thus, from Tertullian's remarks on the radiance of the visible to Dante's oppressive dark wood, from the high poetics of Shakespeare's *Cymbeline* to Tennyson's faux-medieval "Lady of Shallot," from Rimbaud's "Drunken Boat" to Godard's *L'origine du XXIème Siècle (pour moi)*, what Susan Sontag saw in a reverence or fascination for images *of the truth* ver-

---

interlaced with moments of sublimity. Smith's music video moves forward, toward its own polemical conclusion, by erasing things (by racing *backward* through Godard's film and forward toward the end of the twentieth century).

[24] Friedrich Nietzsche, *Thus Spoke Zarathustra: A Book for All and None* (1883-1891).

[25] "The messiah comes for our desires. He separates them from images in order to fulfill them. Or rather, in order to show they have already been fulfilled. Whatever we have imagined, we already had. There remain the (unfulfillable) images of what is already fulfilled. With fulfilled desires, he constructs hell; with unfulfillable images, limbo. And with imagined desire, with the pure word, the beatitude of paradise": Giorgio Agamben, "Desiring," in Giorgio Agamben, *Profanations*, trans. Jeff Fort (New York: Zone Books, 2007), 54 [53–54].

sus the *truth itself* (Tertullian's point) registers both a restlessness and a liminal discontent with verisimilitude and similitude versus its referent.[26]

What is the referent, when all of the above share a register in thought that creates holes in knowledge that seem permanent? Are these holes not doubly negative forms of not-knowledge (the generative Other to rational thought per se, or that which sustains/underwrites rational thought)? Is this skepticism regarding the image or its corollary in scholarship, near-endless circular discourses, warranted? Yes and no. For, the image circulates in the shadow of the Kingdom (Truth). The tragic fate of the Lady of Shallot may be "Tennyson's" fate, a projection, insofar as Tennyson saw poetry as a reflective immersion in images, as opposed to the heroic pursuits of "knights errant" (whatever the equivalent was in his own day). And Godard may try to reverse time and throw the twentieth century on the scrap heap, but his works belong to the twentieth century, as do Marker's. Due to the very fact that Godard and Marker traffic in images is proof enough that there is still something to say with images, even if it often requires a barrage of words to say it, and even if that barrage of words comes in the form of primitively animated intertitles (the words or letters rearranged and shuffled like acrostics) that bark orders at the viewer/audience or confound them with gnomic, brilliant, and annoying utterances. Doubly so if those words attached to images speak against the images they comment on.

One last way to see the invisible concordance, as above, is to *look past it*—not to ignore it, but to *not look* directly at it. Oblique vision is one of the keys to such vision (to Revela-

---

[26] "Either you are merely the visible, in which case I will abhor you as an idol, or you open onto the radiance of the visual, in which case I will acknowledge in you the power to have touched me deeply, to have made a moment of divine truth surge forth, like a miracle": Tertullian, in Georges Didi-Huberman, *Confronting Images: Questioning the Ends of a Certain History of Art* (University Park: Pennsylvania State University Press, 2004), 28.

tion). In fact, it is axiomatic that one can never take the measure of the immeasurable. Even Plato admitted such in admitting that most people will return to the cave anyway upon seeing the origin of the kingdom of shadows.[27] The image in its "hollow" utilitarian character has a peculiar relationship to the phantasmatic side of History (and historicity). This does not excuse images of truth versus Truth itself. Yet it begins to show how scholarship and the arts may approach the truth through moral and ethical praxis. Scholarship in the Arts and Humanities has a strange relationship to the secret concordance in all things—by denying or defying it, scholarship reinforces its own limited resources and/or its spectral indexicality (through deconstruction and negation). By defiling it, scholarship only creates the maximum distance from which to look back and gain perspective, or (but not and/or) to circle forever in the dark wood. Via the oblique approach, however, scholarship engages in that mesmerizing game of cat and

---

[27] This nominal "return to the cave" is played out in a dialectical fashion in Hegel's deconstruction of the Master/Slave relationship, with the liberated Slave becoming a Master but then returning to self-directed activity (a *commercium* of interests)—that is, a voluntary return to subjection via ethical works toward/on behalf of Spirit. "Spirit" in Hegel's *Phenomenology of Spirit* is collective speculative praxis, plus its everyday analogues. See Fredric Jameson, "The Ethics of Activity," in Fredric Jameson, *The Hegel Variations: On the Phenomenology of Spirit* (London: Verso, 2010), 61–68 [51–68]. Once establishing the universal nature of speculative thought, the liberated subject returns to processes of subjectivization (contextualized praxis) associated with immanence and the Real. The short circuit in German Idealism nonetheless leaves traces of the transcendental in the immanent—neutralizing, as it were, high-subjective idealism proper, which often (yet not always) veers close to the Saturnine pull of rote solipsism and/or abject egoism. "I externalize myself, to the attention and interest of other people: 'actualization is...a display of what is one's own in the element of universality, whereby it becomes, and should become, the affair of everyone'" (Jameson, "The Ethics of Activity," 66); with reference to G.W.F. Hegel, *Phenomenology of Spirit*, trans. A.V. Miller (Oxford: Oxford University Press, 1977), 251. This justifies the Hegelian tautology, "The Ideal is the Real."

mouse that Marker played so well, and which Godard was less gifted (or slightly ham-fisted) at.

The animosity of iconoclasm makes sense and no sense. Thus Mallarmé's great dictum (and bold-paradoxical assertion): "Deny the unsayable, it lies...."[28]

The possibility of radical scholarship rises or falls on the availability of "access to" the invisible concordance. It requires, therefore, that the scholar-artist or artist-scholar look away from the world, at least on occasion, and disappear into

---

[28] "Là-bas, où que ce soit, nier l'indicible, qui ment": Stéphane Mallarmé, "Music and Letters (La musique et les lettres)" in Stéphane Mallarmé, *Mallarmé in Prose*, ed. Mary Ann Caws, trans. Jill Anderson et al. (New York: New Directions, 2001), 44. Anderson translation modified in Alain Badiou, "Language, Thought, Poetry," in Alain Badiou, *Theoretical Writings*, trans. Ray Brassier and Alberto Toscano (London: Continuum, 2014), 241 [233–241]. Badiou closes his essay, with a lightning bolt, by way of this statement by Mallarmé. The awe-inspiring torsion within this declaration, appropriated by Badiou to great effect, is based on its unequivocal relation to belief and utterance—the poet's purview. Yet that unequivocal relation is doubled, if not tripled or quadrupled. If one believes what the unsayable says, the implication is that one will remain silent because it is unsayable (one cannot speak for it), and/or out of respect for the inexpressible. If the unsayable lies, however, it is actually not unsayable. If it lies in speaking such (claiming unsayability) why does it lie? Is the lie, then, not its truth? If it lies, then it is sayable. Furthermore, the unsayable connotes silence or what is beyond verbal representation. For it to lie means it speaks (through its silence or otherwise). For it to speak means its lies, etc. Mallarmé's speaking for it places him in direct relation to its unsayability. The koan-like crystalline structure of the statement is pure poetic utterance. From the great Symbolist poet, it makes sense. Thus also Nietzsche's "Truth and Lies in the Non-moral Sense" (1873), wherein the lie is often true and the true is often a lie; or, when a higher morality is to be found in so-called amorality or immorality. The misreading of Nietzsche as arch-enemy of morality is, nonetheless, absurd. Early Nietzscheans were extraordinarily moral— for example, Vladimir Solovyov, William Butler Yeats, and George Bernard Shaw. Nietzsche's "Truth and Lies in the Non-moral Sense" is coterminous with his *Untimely Meditations* (written between 1873 and 1876).

the vault or archive of past practices—the so-called old ways. This means whatever it means, for it means different things under different times. What it always means, however, is that the invisible concordance runs through visible and invisible libraries (the real and irreal libraries of "Aguascalientes").

We do not go back the way we came....*We die into the future.*[29] The secret concord in experience that underwrites all discourse is experience (the existential-metaphysical chord); it animates artistic and humanistic discourses (which also die through assimilation or abandonment) by its variable, creative time-senses, modalities that nonetheless speak of all times in one time, *and* vice versa. Hence the various versions and valences of/for "those who cannot learn from history are doomed to repeat it."[30] Substitute the word *experience* for the word *history* and the weak justifications for endless and circular commentaries collapse. What moves into view is the mystery of historicity as collective experience, Schopenhauer's darkening world of will and representation its mere shadow.

March 1, 2015

---

[29] "And yet the world is nothing but a tempestuous sea; time is naught but a bridge thrown over the abyss connecting the negation that preceded existence with the eternity that is to follow it. The slightest inadvertence can precipitate him who crosses this bridge into the abyss": Jedaiah ben Abraham Bedersi, "Sefer Beḥinat Olam" ("The Book of the Examination of the World") (1306), trans. Tobias Goodman (London, 1806), in Richard Gottheil, Isaac Broydé, "Bedersi, Jedaiah ben Abraham," *Jewish Encyclopedia*, n.d., http://www.jewishencyclopedia.com/articles/2726-bedersi-jedaiah-ben-abraham.
[30] G.W.F. Hegel, George Santayana et al.

Appendix A

Agence 'X' Publishing Advisory

I. Précis—*In Media Res* ...

II. Academic Publishing & E-books

III. Academic Peer Review & Research Standings

IV. Intellectual Property

V. Publishing Law

VI. Digital Archives & Databases

VII. Edufactory—Passim

VIII. Summary

IX. A Curious Scenario

X. Addenda

Appendix A

Agence 'X' Publishing Advisory[1]

I. PRÉCIS—*IN MEDIA RES* ...

Agence 'X' provides not-for-profit, experimental consulting services for artists, architects, and scholars toward publication across multiple platforms, inclusive of both print and digital media. The primary focus of the advisory is to tailor the production of written and visual media for non-commercial (not-for-profit), peer-to-peer distribution, avoiding the present-day predatory practices of commercial and academic publishing. Intentionally oriented toward emergent alt-academic and alt-art practices, the advisory invites strategic alliances with institutions and individuals engaged in the preservation and privileging of the Seven Liberal Arts via high scholarship (the so-called old ways).

Shifts in both academic and commercial (trade) publishing today privilege conventional and unconventional texts and visual media as part of overall cultural production, a broad *field* of activity that eludes traditional categories and places the author or artist in the position of selecting the most appropriate means for disseminating research and art works.

---

[1] All URLs in this document were operable as of late 2014.

Agence 'X' proposes a multi-platform model for works of scholarship as work of art and art work as form of scholarship. The principal focus of the former is the high-Romantic "literary work of art," while the principal focus of the latter is the pre-modernist and early modernist folio, edition, and/or experimental exhibition.

Combining literary values with critical exegesis, the Publishing Advisory is aimed at meeting and exceeding existing standards for academic publishing and art and architecture monographs. Working with the author or artist, and liaising with not-for-profit or alternative for-profit presses, the Advisory emphatically and radically undermines and subverts the prevailing models for author-pay or artist-pay publishing (journals, books, exhibitions), e-aggregation (EBSCO et al.), and e-books (at the expense of print editions). As such, the primary focus is the protection of Intellectual Property Rights from Big Capital and Big Data. In terms of discursive forms of academic scholarship, and primarily tailored for alternative forms of critical research, the Advisory offers structural editorial services and advice toward digital and print publication. In the case of the production of unique or editioned publications (artist book, folio, etc.), the Advisory's goal is to combine discursive and non-discursive (textual and visual) models. Additionally, services are offered for converting novel and classical forms of written and visual research to physical and archival artifacts (editioned books, folios, and dossiers). The Advisory also includes the development of peer-to-peer platforms (digital and otherwise) for artists, architects, and scholars concerned with circumventing and/or evading the assimilation of their works to commercial and/or open-source publishing.

November 1, 2014

II. ACADEMIC PUBLISHING & E-BOOKS

With the shift underway in academic publishing toward "author-pay" models (for both journals and books) it is imperative that authors develop multiple strategies for circulating their works, bypassing or subverting predatory publishers. Stand-alone print publications (traditional monographs) are fast becoming a thing of the past. Additionally, traditional print platforms (including journals) are increasingly being undermined by digital publication models, often in concert with print models. While scholarship itself has not changed, author rights are slowly being eroded and all profits from such publications today generally go to the publisher and the distributor. Academics are expected to publish for free to burnish resumes and chase tenure, while tenured positions are vanishing worldwide and resumes are relative to what one wishes to achieve.

Scholarly publication is, in many respects, undergoing the same stresses as mass-market or trade publishing, but with the additional problem that academics are expected to donate content (plus peer review and editorial services) to for-profit publishers. The consolidation of academic presses through acquisition has also led to the problem of intellectual property being owned and managed by fewer and fewer global corporations, who then market it to the very institutions and individuals that produced it. Combined with these problems are the emergent pre-print, not-for-profit platforms and databases which generally are file-sharing operations with a not-so-secret private and proprietary agenda of text- and data-mining.

In terms of digital or electronic publications, and with utter disregard for traditional author rights, these same global publishing empires are in the process of licensing works (short and long term), a practice that undermines the sales of print and digital books. An academic author who signs a contract with a publisher for a print and digital (e-book) edition stands the chance of never reaching the threshold for royalties (typically 500 copies for a print edition and 500 copies for an e-book) due to the fact that libraries can now license ("rent") an e-book from companies such as EBSCO, who "buy" one copy of the e-book and then lease it to hundreds of libraries. Additionally, college and university libraries are increasingly creating regional consortiums that then share a single license to the e-book among members. While this may be, arguably, "good" for disseminating scholarly work widely, the erosion of conventional copyright, plus the author's moral rights (regarding derivative works), is self-evident. These e-licensing practices are generally permitted through arrangements with publishers, who technically own the intellectual rights to the published version of the work (via copyright transfer), but who also license e-books for an undisclosed percentage of the fees paid by libraries. Most contracts stipulate that the author will receive royalties on sales (as above) but not on licensing through such practices as those developed by, for example, EBSCO, primarily through their so-called Academic E-book Collection.

The answer to this problem for authors wishing to prevent e-aggregators from diluting sales and profiting from their work is to sign contracts that prohibit e-books outright or prohibit e-licensing.

TANGENTS / LINKS

For the market details of the e-book model, see:

> http://cyber.law.harvard.edu/sites/cyber.law.harvard.edu/files/E-Books%20in%20Libraries%20(O'Brien,%20Gasser,%20Palfrey)-1.pdf

Regarding EBSCO's early dance with copyright violation, as part owner of the short-lived Contentville, see:

> http://www.villagevoice.com/2000-07-25/news/partners-in-copyright-scam/

http://online.wsj.com/article/SB965263477520525910.html

ebrary's Academic Complete[2]:

http://www.ebrary.com/corp/models.jsp

ebrary's policies are transparent (open to public scrutiny), and include numerous provisions regarding copyright and fair use, whereas EBSCO's are not:

> If you believe that a work has been copied and is accessible on this site in a way that constitutes copyright infringement, you may notify ebrary's designated agent, Juliette Hirt, Esq., at the address below or by phone: 650-475-8700, fax: 650-475-8881, or e-mail (with confirmation of receipt requested) to CopyrightClaim@ebrary.com. This site is operated by ebrary, 318 Cambridge Avenue, Palo Alto, California 94306-1505.
>
> Materials available on this Web site are the property of their respective copyright holders. Please see the individualized copyright notice that is printed within or appears with each document, and read the 'EBRARY TERMS OF SERVICE' for information about what you may and may not do with the Materials available on this site. All rights not expressly granted herein are reserved to the copyright holders.
>
> ebrary titles are protected by copyright laws, and your access is allowed under 'Fair Use' limitations.
>
> The ebrary service is designed for end-users conducting research, and it is not intended as a substitute for purchasing your own copy of a printed or digital book. While you may

---

[2] All ebrary citations refer to the company website as of late 2014. Although ProQuest purchased ebrary in 2011 for an "undisclosed sum," the ebrary website was not immediately phased out.

read an entire ebrary title online with the ebrary Reader™, ebrary places these restrictions on content usage to prevent misuse and protect our publishing partner's copyrights:

- You are not allowed to print out or copy the entire book.
- There are limitations on the number of pages you may print and copy.

Any attempts to circumvent ebrary's print or copy restrictions may subject you and/or your institution to legal action including civil or criminal penalties. Additionally, it may result in suspension of the ebrary service.

http://www.ebrary.com/corp/legal.jsp

The European Commission, "Copyright: Commission Urges Industry to Deliver Innovative Solutions for Greater Access to Online Content" (December 18, 2012):

The digital economy has been a major driver of growth in the past two decades, and is expected to grow seven times faster than overall EU GDP in coming years. Online there are new ways of providing, creating and distributing content, and new ways to generate value. The emergence of new business models that use the internet to deliver content represents both a challenge and an opportunity for the creative industries, authors and artists. This is why the European Commission is acting today to ensure that copyright and licensing stay fit for purpose in this new digital context.

http://europa.eu/rapid/press-release_IP-12-1394_en.htm?locale=en

http://ec.europa.eu/digital-agenda/

The European Commission, "Copyright and Neighbouring Rights" (January 30, 2014):

> The European Commission is also responsible for conducting negotiations on industrial and intellectual property within World Intellectual Property Organisation (WIPO) (e.g. audiovisual, broadcasting, resale right, databases, etc.), for participating in the relevant WIPO General Assemblies, and for contributing to the work of other international fora on IPR related matters with a view to ensuring adequate protection of intellectual property rights (IPR) internationally.

> http://ec.europa.eu/internal_market/copyright/index_en.htm

Peter Brantley, "Academic E-books: Innovation and Transition," *Publishers Weekly* (February 3, 2012):

> http://www.publishersweekly.com/pw/by-topic/digital/content-and-e-books/article/50486-academic-e-books-innovation-and-transition.html

Clifford A. Lynch, "Imagining a University Press System to Support Scholarship in the Digital Age," *Reimagining the University Press* 13.2 (Fall 2010):

> http://quod.lib.umich.edu/j/jep/3336451.0013.207?rgn=main;view=fulltext

For an out-of-date synopsis of what c. 2008 seemed promising but has since become a plague, see Richard N. Katz, ed., *The Tower and The Cloud* (Educause, 2008):

> http://www.educause.edu/research-and-publications/books/tower-and-cloud

Jennifer Howard, "Who Gets to See Published Research?" *Chronicle of Higher Education* (January 22, 2012):

http://chronicle.com/article/Hot-Type-Who-Gets-to-See/130403/

For authors' rights in terms of e-books, see:

http://www.authorsguild.org/services/legal-services/electronic-rights/

Concerning the Bodleian Libraries' e-book trials in 2013, see:

http://www.bodleian.ox.ac.uk/notices/2013-mar-22

For a list of "potential, possible, or probable predatory publishers," see:

http://scholarlyoa.com/publishers/

Concerning the status of the reader, plus a swipe at academic authors, see:

http://www.nytimes.com/2014/01/05/opinion/sunday/the-loneliness-of-the-long-distance-reader.html?hp&rref=opinion&_r=0

Concerning the University of California's Open Access Policy of July 2013, see:

http://osc.universityofcalifornia.edu/open-access-policy/

Text-mining and data-mining comes to academic publishing (care of Elsevier):

http://www.elsevier.com/connect/elsevier-updates-text-mining-policy-to-improve-access-for-researchers

Elsevier buys Mendeley and threatens Academia.edu (2013):

http://chronicle.com/blogs/wiredcampus/posting-your-latest-article-you-might-have-to-take-it-down/48865

http://scholarlykitchen.sspnet.org/2013/12/11/has-elsevier-signaled-a-new-era-for-academia-edu-and-other-professional-networks/

III. ACADEMIC PEER REVIEW & RESEARCH STANDINGS

Academics are generally expected to indulge in so-called peer review while the entire apparatus of peer review involves blind submissions to journals and publishers that enlist the assistance of a narrow swathe of scholars with established and/or intractable biases. The alternative is to network works while in production, versus submit works for peer review after they are more or less complete. Typically peer review means a few shallow remarks regarding the structure or integrity of the submitted work and not all recommendations for changes are valid. It is also not necessary to change everything to meet peer-review standards and authors have the right to refuse to make changes that will alter the tenor or intention of the work reviewed. The outcome, while often a tussle between author and peer, may vary, with the author risking the refusal of publication upon revision. Additionally, normal peer-review practices are almost irrelevant in the case of experimental works.

The better, emerging standard for scholars not concerned with seeking tenure and/or impressing peers is to avoid journals altogether that have a stable of biased peers and seek out alternative platforms for publication. The problem that arises in such cases is that universities are increasingly using an authorized list of journals and publishers that confer respectability to a handful of journals, more or less marginalizing or ignoring all others. In some cases this practice forces lesser-known journals out of business, cutting off access to scholars who will only submit their work to the university-authorized publications. While the lists can be extensive, the rankings are effectively incapable of acknowledging experimental or avant-garde publications.

Research standards in universities, used to rank departments and faculties (and used to weigh PhD production), have recently become the target of severe criticism for favoring established journals and publishers at the expense of new or less-prestigious outlets for research.

In the case of scholarly monographs the situation is similar, with university-generated lists favoring publishers that utilize peer review and provide hands-on, substantive editorial oversight. Smaller presses that accept work based on an abstract and review by an editorial board are notably placed low on the lists or are missing altogether. Most publishing houses (academic and trade) have cut editorial services and authors are expected to edit their own works or hire a professional editor. While the issue of serious or laissez-faire editorial policy for academic presses, and the presence or absence of text editors for authors of scholarly monographs, leads to implicit and explicit judgment visited upon publishers by scholars and by universities, the trend is nonetheless toward "no editorial assistance whatsoever," with the high-end presses garnering the majority of established authors who can write or who can afford to hire or otherwise engage assistants for the technical production of the text. The presence of thematic series within academic presses, produced with a credible series editor and a credible editorial board (independent of the publisher), is an established practice that continues to provide an additional layer of credibility for both author and press, while it does not necessarily guarantee nor suggest that the work will receive substantive editorial assistance. While the work will be measured by the standards of the series and the editorial board, the implication for the model is that it constitutes de facto peer review.

It is, therefore, the author/scholar's prerogative to choose to move "down market to go upstream." Such a strategy involves working with publishers that may or may not show up on the authorized lists issues by universities but which do not engage in predatory practices (such as the "author-pay" model noted above). A possible outcome for such a strategy might be that works that would normally be altered beyond repair by peer review and/or refused by mainstream publishers will find a niche that permits their modest circulation in libraries by print or electronic edition. The downside of this stratagem is that the down-market presses one might choose will invariably offer no royalties or royalties based on sales numbers that will never be and never can be achieved in the academic market.

The agenda noted above suggests a more subtle approach for authors who are not in pursuit of tenure and who do not write for money. It also suggests the perhaps utterly radical gesture of the author who writes to be read, and the author who (in the Franciscan tradition) presumes the right to have no rights (but also does not cede his/her rights to Capital).

TANGENTS / LINKS

For generally nuanced remarks on so-called Open Peer Review, see Peter Brantley, "Back Doors to Transformation," *Publishers Weekly* (January 30, 2012):

> Fundamental aspects of the publishing process could change. In an open peer review system, the status of reviewers could be far greater than it is today. Ultimately curation is the most highly valued product of publishing, and thoughtful reviewers might well become the most essential arbiters of quality. Publishing concerns would seek to form alliances with specific individual reviewers or reviewer collectives, even above association with specific authors, as authorship shifts into web-based practice.

> http://blogs.publishersweekly.com/blogs/PWxyz/2012/01/30/back-doors-to-transformation/

For a generally commendable analysis of the corruption of academia by neo-liberal capitalism, see Max Haiven, "The Ivory Cage and the Ghosts of Academe," *Truthout* (April 30, 2014):

http://www.truth-out.org/news/item/23391-the-ivory-cage-and-the-ghosts-of-academe-labor-and-struggle-in-the-edu-factory

For possible alternative models of research, see Max Haiven, Alex Khasnabish, "Fomenting the Radical Imagination with Movements," *Roar Magazine* (July 31, 2014):

http://roarmag.org/2014/07/fomenting-the-radical-imagination-with-social-movements/

IV. INTELLECTUAL PROPERTY

Intellectual property is cultural capital. In the present climate of "rent-seeking" neo-liberal capitalist practices, and given the emergence of global e-aggregation of intellectual property, it is the author's prerogative to opt-out of predatory practices that are built atop the outdated justifications for intellectual copyright.

With the emergence of open-source publishing, and the attendant justifications for the same (by alternative presses and by universities), plus the arguments for and against academic scholarship being freely available in the public domain (because it was "funded" by universities), the situation for the solitary author becomes increasingly slippery. There is little question that e-aggregation and academia are on a collision course, foremost in terms of the production of knowledge and its distribution. For corporatized universities to question the practices of corporatized publishing is, in fact, a paradox. For the author, the solution is to step aside and protect one's so-called moral rights. Moral rights are not transferrable, and if copyright is increasingly undermined through e-aggregation and fair-use practices, moral rights for authors represent the last frontier.

The present model for publishers engaging in "licensed sales" will without doubt change, and contracts with authors may or may not be supplemented to account for e-licensing. Whether minor and/or emerging authors/scholars will ever see any of the proceeds from e-licensing and e-books is in question. Digital Rights Management for publishers includes the unwritten right to "market" their product by way of multiple platforms. The "long-tail" marketing model suggests that all minor authors/scholars will see their works given away. Whereas licensing previously meant secondary (non-literary) usages for written works, and profits were shared accordingly (usually 50-50), the current marketing strategies of publishers have not caught up with multi-platform publishing and distribution.

The author's moral rights are immemorial. They transcend copyright and they will remain inviolable insofar as Capital is incapable of finding a purchase in the actual production of knowledge versus its management and distribution.

The parallel here is the art world and what is occurring in the secondary market (the auction houses). Art works bought by collectors as investment vehicles are resold in the secondary market after a period of time typically dictated by the inflation of the artist's reputation (often an outcome of collusion between the galleries and the auction houses). The artist (the author) enjoys none of the benefits of sales on the secondary market (other than the perverse satisfaction of seeing his/her works sold for a premium, plus any knock-on effects such as higher sale prices in the primary market).

The right to have no rights, then, is the most radical gesture available to the author (and the artist). Copyright and moral rights must be separated. Copyright must be protected from Capital and moral rights must be safeguarded through resistance to the recursive practices to come that will no doubt involve "employers" (corporatized universities, publishers, agents, e-marketeers) commanding ownership of creative works due to the mere fact that they control the mechanisms of branding, marketing, and distribution.

Centre for Media Pluralism and Media Freedom (CMPF)—European University Institute (EUI):

> The aim of the EUI Centre for Media Pluralism and Media Freedom is to enhance the awareness of the importance of freedom and pluralism of the media, to contribute to its protection and promotion and to develop new ideas among academics, policy makers, regulators, market stakeholders, journalists, and all other directly involved professionals who take part in the public debate.
>
> http://cmpf.eui.eu/Home.aspx

Policy Report: European Union Competencies in Respect of Media Pluralism and Media Freedom (CMPF):

> This independent policy report, written at the request of the European Commission, presents the phenomena of media freedom and pluralism, and the major academic and policy debates surrounding their social, political, economic role and implications. It highlights the importance of media freedom and pluralism for the functioning, sustainability and legitimacy of a democratic government, and therefore the necessity for relevant policy actions.

> http://cmpf.eui.eu/publications/policyreport.aspx

World Intellectual Property Organization (WIPO)—Berne Convention for the Protection of Literary and Artistic Works (Paris Act 1971, Amended 1979):

> http://www.wipo.int/treaties/en/ip/berne/trtdocs_wo001.html

Signatories to the Berne Convention, World Intellectual Property Organization (WIPO):

> http://www.wipo.int/treaties/en/ShowResults.jsp?treaty_id=15

Internet Intermediaries and Creative Content, World Intellectual Property Organization (WIPO):

> http://www.wipo.int/copyright/en/internet_intermediaries/

Copyright Licensing in the Digital Environment, World Intellectual Property Organization (WIPO):

http://www.wipo.int/copyright/en/activities/copyright_licensing.html

Eileen A. Joy, "Let Us Now Stand Up for Bastards: The Importance of Illegitimate Publics," *Chiasma: A Site for Thought* 2 (2015):

https://westernchiasma.files.wordpress.com/2015/05/2.pdf

V. PUBLISHING LAW

Regarding "contract updates for the e-book era", see the following article by Steve Gillen (Independent Book Publishers Association):

http://www.ibpa-online.org/article/contract-updates-for-the-e-book-era/

Regarding copyright of academic works, see the following article by Steven Shavell (Samuel R. Rosenthal Professor of Law and Economics, Harvard Law School):

http://cyber.law.harvard.edu/sites/cyber.law.harvard.edu/files/Copyright%207-17HLS-2009.pdf

World Intellectual Property Organization (WIPO)—Guide on the Licensing of Copyright and Related Rights:

http://www.wipo.int/export/sites/www/freepublications/en/copyright/897/wipo_pub_897.pdf

World Intellectual Property Organization (WIPO)—Intellectual Property Issues Related to Electronic Commerce:

http://www.wipo.int/export/sites/www/sme/en/e_commerce/pdf/ip_ecommerce.pdf

World Intellectual Property Organization (WIPO)—Understanding How Intellectual Property (IP) Relates to E-Commerce:

http://www.wipo.int/sme/en/e_commerce/ip_ecommerce.htm

Mathias Döpfner (Axel Springer)/Shoshanna Zuboff (Harvard Law School)—Regarding Google and the EU:

Mathias Döpfner, "An Open Letter to Eric Schmidt: Why We Fear Google," http://www.faz.net/aktuell/feuilleton/debatten/mathias-doepfner-s-open-letter-to-eric-schmidt-12900860.html

Shoshanna Zuboff, "Response to Mathias Döpfner: Dark Google," http://www.faz.net/aktuell/feuilleton/debatten/the-digital-debate/shoshanna-zuboff-dark-google-12916679.html

VI. DIGTAL ARCHIVES & DATABASES

HathiTrust—Academic repository for electronic books and other digital content (based at the University of Michigan), many scanned by Google Books Library Project:

http://www.hathitrust.org/

"Authors Groups From U.K., Canada, Norway and Sweden Join Authors Guild, Australian Society of Authors, and Quebec Writers Union in Suit Against HathiTrust," Authors Guild (2011):

http://www.authorsguild.org/advocacy/authors-groups-from-u-k-canada-norway-and-sweden-join-authors-guild-australian-society-of-authors-and-quebec-writers-union-in-suit-against-hathitrust/

WorldCat—For tracking books in academic libraries worldwide, including e-books:

Can I get into electronic databases?—Some WorldCat libraries make their specialized reference databases available on their Web sites, but only to library members. Your search on WorldCat.org may produce direct links to articles and other resources in these databases. To access these resources, though, you may first be required to log in with a valid library membership.

http://www.worldcat.org/

Thomson Reuters—Proprietary databases for citations in the Social Sciences and Science; 53% owned by The Woodbridge Company (Thomson Reuters, US$ 13.27 billion gross income in 2012):

http://thomsonreuters.com/social-sciences-citation-index/
http://science.thomsonreuters.com/cgi-bin/jrnlst/jloptions.cgi?PC=K

Taylor & Francis—Proprietary databases for online (toll-access) journals; owned by Informa (Informa, £1,232.5 million gross revenue in 2012):

http://www.tandfonline.com/

Elsevier—Proprietary databases for online (toll-access) journals plus text- and data-mining platforms; parent company, Reed Elsevier (Reed Elsevier, £2,063 million gross income in 2012):

http://www.elsevier.com/

JSTOR—As of early 2014, JSTOR, a not-for-profit e-aggregator, announced they would begin offering e-books. The likely outcome is that JSTOR will become the antidote to EBSCO et al. As a not-for-profit enterprise, and given that they offer free access to their databases for Third World universities, JSTOR is positioned to lower the profile of the predatory giants. In some respects, JSTOR is the compromise position between the earlier attempts by universities to privilege Open Access and the subsequent corporate takeover of academic research.

> JSTOR is a shared digital library created in 1995 to help university and college libraries free up space on their shelves, save costs, and provide greater levels of access to more content than ever before. More generally, by digitizing content to high standards and supporting its long-term preservation, we also aim to help libraries and academic publishers transition their activities from print to digital operations. Our aim is to expand access to scholarly content around the world and to preserve it for future

generations. We provide access to some or all of the content free of charge when we believe we can do so while still meeting our long-term obligations.

http://www.jstor.org/

VII. EDUFACTORY—PASSIM

Keith Thomas, "Universities under Attack," *London Review of Books* (November 28, 2011):

http://www.lrb.co.uk/2011/11/28/keith-thomas/universities-under-attack

Peter Conrad, "*What are Universities For?* by Stefan Collini—Review," *The Guardian* (February 18, 2012):

http://www.theguardian.com/books/2012/feb/19/what-universities-for-collini-review

Alan Ryan, "*What are Universities For?*—Review," *The New Statesman* (February 27, 2012):

http://www.newstatesman.com/books/2012/02/universities-university

Ben Etherington, "Universities on the Block," *Sydney Review of Books* (May 23, 2014):

http://www.sydneyreviewofbooks.com/universities-and-the-block/

Kylar Loussikian, "ACU Research Row Boils Over," *The Australian* (November 26, 2014):

"ACU management have resorted to the dubious strategy of approaching a select group of world-renowned professors and offering them lucrative fractional appointment," the academic wrote.

"In exchange for their lengthy CVs, these academic 'stars' are required to do very little and spend even less time on the ground with staff and students. Management, in an effort to outdo the (Australian Research Council), refused any process of independent peer review of staff publications and paid no attention to the content of the research," the academic wrote.

"Instead, a staff member's research was measured purely on the basis of the outlet of the publication—that is, where it was published, with which journal or with what publishing house."

Dr Buckle said the "punitive nature" of the new provisions made it obvious management regarded academics "with contempt."

http://www.theaustralian.com.au/higher-education/acu-re search-row-boils-over/story-e6frgcjx-1227134767476

Julie Hare, "Visa Rort Alert as Foreign Students bring in $16bn," *The Australian* (November 26, 2014):

http://www.theaustralian.com.au/higher-education/visa-rort-alert-as-foreign-students-bring-in-16bn/story-e6frgcj x-1227134730910

"Publish and Perish at Imperial College London: The Death of Stefan Grimm," *DC's Improbable Science* (December 1, 2014):

http://www.dcscience.net/2014/12/01/publish-and-perish-at-imperial-college-london-the-death-of-stefan-grimm/

"Grimm's Tale," *Plashing Vole* (December 2, 2014):

http://plashingvole.blogspot.co.uk/2014/12/grimms-tale. html

Lawrence Wittner, "The $7 Million University President," *CounterPunch* (December 15, 2014):

http://www.counterpunch.org/2014/12/15/the-7-million-university-president/

VIII. SUMMARY

Refuse to participate in digital publishing and ignore the Digital Humanities. Publish actually existing books that are accessioned to actually existing libraries....

IX. A CURIOUS SCENARIO

The Berne Convention for the Protection of Literary and Artistic Works (Paris Act 1971, Amended 1979)[3] states that the production of "derivative works" of primary written, musical, and other literary and artistic works[4] requires the explicit permission of the author/creator (Article 14). With trade conventions typically conferring additional compensation (via contractual stipulations) up to 50% of proceeds (shared by publisher and author/creator), the definition of derivative works has not been sufficiently updated to reflect practices in digital publishing. If digital licensing of books and texts was to be characterized as "derivative works" (which it clearly is in almost all cases), all publishers and/or all owners of proprietary, for-profit digital platforms for the dissemination, exploitation, and/or text- and data-mining of copyrighted works would be required to pay copyright holders a substantial share of the fees levied for access by subscribers. If many of the current databases and online exchanges for digital versions of copyrighted works were to be included in a redefinition of "derivative works" (secondary marketing of pri-

---

[3] "Berne Convention for the Protection of Literary and Artistic Works," World Intellectual Property Organization (WIPO), http://www.wipo.int/treaties/en/ip/berne/trtdocs_wo001.html.

[4] Article 2: "(1) The expression 'literary and artistic works' shall include every production in the literary, scientific and artistic domain, whatever may be the mode or form of its expression, such as books, pamphlets and other writings; lectures, addresses, sermons and other works of the same nature; dramatic or dramatico-musical works; choreographic works and entertainments in dumb show; musical compositions with or without words; cinematographic works to which are assimilated works expressed by a process analogous to cinematography; works of drawing, painting, architecture, sculpture, engraving and lithography; photographic works to which are assimilated works expressed by a process analogous to photography; works of applied art; illustrations, maps, plans, sketches and three-dimensional works relative to geography, topography, architecture or science" ("Berne Convention").

mary works), Elsevier, Taylor & Francis, Thomson Reuters et al. would be required to distribute a share of their earnings for the dissemination and licensing of digital works and subsequent products to the copyright holders of such works.

Notably, Article 6[bis] of the Berne Convention for the Protection of Literary and Artistic Works concerns "moral rights", which include: "1. To claim authorship; to object to certain modifications and other derogatory actions; 2. After the author's death; 3. Means of redress". "Certain modifications and other derogatory actions" certainly describes the digitization and exploitation of primary works by e-aggregation and licensing.[5]

Given that many publishers require that authors sign over copyright for their works or pay a substantial fee to retain the same, the Berne Convention is of particular interest in that it states that moral rights are nontransferable. All authors pressed by circumstances or established practices to relinquish their moral rights are, therefore, in breach of the Berne Convention. Additionally, all publishers who demand ownership of copyright (for all of the reasons noted above regarding "derivative works") are in violation of the author's moral rights insofar as they market the primary work through derivative means.[6]

It is likely, then, that a re-definition of "derivative rights" would clarify once and for all the legal status of interrelated predatory practices in contemporary publishing and related industries.

---

[5] Article 3: "The performance of a dramatic, dramatico-musical, cinematographic or musical work, the public recitation of a literary work, the communication by wire or the broadcasting of literary or artistic works, the exhibition of a work of art and the construction of a work of architecture shall not constitute publication" ("Berne Convention").

[6] Article 6[bis]: "(1) Independently of the author's economic rights, and even after the transfer of the said rights, the author shall have the right to claim authorship of the work and to object to any distortion, mutilation or other modification of, or other derogatory action in relation to, the said work, which would be prejudicial to his honor or reputation" ("Berne Convention").

X. ADDENDA

EC Copyright Modernization:

> As of December 2013 the European Commission began "a public consultation on the modernisation of copyright (deadline: 5 March 2014)." Additionally, the remuneration of authors was "one important topic included in the consultation." "In particular, the consultation document recognises that concerns continue to be raised that authors and performers are not adequately remunerated, in particular but not solely, as regards online exploitation. Many consider that the economic benefit of new forms of exploitation is not being fairly shared along the whole value chain. Another commonly raised issue concerns contractual practices, negotiation mechanisms, presumptions of transfer of rights, buy-out clauses and the lack of possibility to terminate contracts."[7]
>
> http://ec.europa.eu/internal_market/consultations/2013/copyright-rules/index_en.htm

Jerome McGann, *A New Republic of Letters: Memory and Scholarship in the Age of Digital Reproduction* (Cambridge, MA: Harvard University Press, 2014):

> From Harvard University Press' description of the book:
>
> A manifesto for the humanities in the digital age, *A New Republic of Letters* argues that the history of texts, together with the methods by which they are preserved and made available for interpretation, are the overriding subjects of humanist study in the twenty-first century. Theory and philosophy, which have grounded the humanities for

---

[7] E-mail from Philipp Runge, Policy Officer, European Commission, DG CONNECT, Converging Media and Content, Brussels, Belgium, March 4, 2014.

decades, no longer suffice as an intellectual framework. Jerome McGann proposes we look instead to philology—a discipline which has been out of fashion for many decades but which models the concerns of digital humanities with surprising fidelity.

For centuries, books have been the best way to preserve and transmit knowledge. But as libraries and museums digitize their archives and readers abandon paperbacks for tablet computers, digital media are replacing books as the repository of cultural memory. While both the mission of the humanities and its traditional modes of scholarship and critical study are the same, the digital environment is driving disciplines to work with new tools that require major, and often very difficult, institutional changes. Now more than ever, scholars need to recover the theory and method of philological investigation if the humanities are to meet their perennial commitments. Textual and editorial scholarship, often marginalized as a narrowly technical domain, should be made a priority of humanists' attention.

About the Author:

Jerome McGann is University Professor and John Stewart Bryan Professor of English at the University of Virginia.

Reviews:

"McGann critiques encoded writing and digital humanities and asks how electronic formats can handle diverse literature from a scholarly point of view. His style reveals a well-read thinker who examines the act of the reader on the page with asides and constant allusions to other writers such as Dante Gabriel Rossetti, Marianne Moore, and Friedrich Nietzsche. He approaches his thesis from the angle of philology, which he asserts remains the best position because it offers perspectives on human production and socially constructed artifacts of all types and allows for a culturally relativistic attitude of those objects. He fully acknowledges that research libraries and archives, globally, are reformatting their collections into digital and suggests that our limited electronic tools open new doors for the humanities because there are no coded structures that represent a work's historical 'facticities.'...This book is for readers specifically attuned to the digital 'crisis' affecting humanities departments and related theoretical debates." (Jesse A. Lambertson, *Library Journal*, starred review)

"This is an awe-inspiring work, courageous, ambitious, startling, and full of learning, wit, and even fun. It will surely be regarded as the major realization of the several strands of McGann's distinguished career, and will be the single most significant contribution to the literature of memory and the archive in the early twenty-first century." (David Greetham, author of *The Pleasures of Contamination: Evidence, Text, and Voice in Textual Studies*)

"In a very plain sense, this is the book McGann has been writing his entire career; a book whose force of vision and depth of learned commitment make many so-called debates in digital humanities seem small by reconnecting both our momentary enthusiasms and our presentist anxieties with at least two centuries of programmatic continuity—philology, yes, but also poetry." (Matthew G. Kirschenbaum, University of Maryland)

Table of Contents:

Preface

Abbreviations

Introduction

I. From History to Method

1. Why Textual Scholarship Matters
2. "The Inorganic Organization of Memory"
3. Memory: History, Philosophy, Philology

II. From Theory to Method

4. The Documented World
5. Marking Texts in Many Dimensions
6. Digital Tools and the Emergence of the Social Text

III. From Method to Practice

7. What Do Scholars Want?
8. Philological Investigations I: The Example of Poe
9. Philological Investigations II: A Page from Cooper

Conclusion: *Pseudodoxia Academica*; or, Literary Studies in a Global Age

Notes

Acknowledgments

Index

http://www.hup.harvard.edu/catalog.php?isbn=9780674728691

February 12, 2015

Appendix B

Perpetual Petition for the Right of the Author to Have *No* Digital Rights

Appendix B

Perpetual Petition for the Right of the Author to Have *No* Digital Rights

Given the predatory practices of profit-making distributors and aggregators of digital works (books, texts, etc.), and given that publishers have yet to find a way of compensating authors for the licensing of electronic versions of written works (a practice that undermines the sale of print editions), SCHOLARS MINOR proposes an elective ban on all such practices, for authors, through a legally recognized opt-out clause, to be inserted into all contracts with publishers and to be conferred, upon proper evaluation, as a right within the Berne Convention for the Protection of Literary and Artistic Works, last updated in 1979.

Once such an elective opt-out clause is in force, either as standard practice through inclusion in contracts with publishers or by international treaty, permission to include an author's work in for-profit databases will require a signed release from the copyright holder. In the case of copyright being owned by a publisher, it will be the responsibility of the publisher to acquire a release from the author detailing compensation, both if no prior agreement exists between author and publisher and if an author wishes to agree to singular instances of e-distribution.

This right to have no digital rights is to augment out-of-date copyright law, plus moral rights, established before the arrival of the digital age and before academia embraced Cloud strategies for instruction. As opt-out clause, this right is also intended to confer upon the author the right to refuse exploitation of written works and research by for-profit entities that have had no role in the production of the work and/or have through spurious claims of Fair Use usurped the rights of authors to determine how their works are utilized. For-profit entities, in the latter case, also include schools and universities exploiting Cloud-learning strategies at the expense of traditional classroom-based studies and at the expense of faculty through the enforcement of adjunct teaching contracts that provide little or no security for scholars.

It is the intention of this petition to place responsibility for electronic reproducibility of works on the author versus the publisher, but also to reinforce the relationship of the author and publisher and reduce the role of the owners of digital platforms, databases, and Cloud-based networks.

It is a secondary concern of this petition to support libraries and universities in their quest to rein in costs associated with the acquisition of scholarly publications. As such, it is advised within the PETITION FOR THE RIGHT OF THE AUTHOR TO HAVE NO DIGITAL RIGHTS that Open Source be revisited for academic research that might be otherwise locked away in pay-per-view models controlled by profit-making aggregators of electronic academic journals and publications. The opt-out clause may, then, also be supplemented by an opt-in clause for open-access publishing in non-commercial environments, by authors. This opt-in clause will permit authors to give their work away, versus see their work exploited by for-profit, non-academic and academic entities.

It is further advised that authors also opt-out of any proprietary, for-profit practices that piggyback on the above-mentioned academic practices, plus dubious research standards imposed by School or University, until an acceptable and recognized clause is in force within academic presses and schools and universities toward the protection of author rights. It is also advised that authors avoid publishers that command sole copyright for works and/or employ author-pay models, both practices that undermine author rights. Avoiding such practices will, in turn, encourage the emergence of and recognition for presses that favor the moral rights of the author versus the potential profitability of the work.

In this manner, the PETITION FOR THE RIGHT OF THE AUTHOR TO HAVE *NO* DIGITAL RIGHTS is the renunciation of digital rights as means to counter the exploitation of authors by for-profit entities with no interest in the intellectual and/or moral rights of authors.

SCHOLARS MINOR

February 3, 2014

Appendix C

Symptom "A": The End

Appendix C

Symptom "A": The End

As the author-pay model spreads across academic publishing, what are the possible consequences? Will the current rage for open-source scholarship actually accomplish anything other than shifting the furniture around on the Titanic? Will not Open Source in combination with Digital Humanities further destroy the very idea of "slow" and "thoughtful" work in humanistic studies?

Is this model spreading because there is, finally, a revolt by academics serving for free as content providers, editors, and ex-officio peer-review panels for for-profit publishers of books and journals? Or is it spreading because of the tightening grip of neo-liberal capitalist control, with text- and data-mining procedures enforced from on high both from within academia and from without? Perhaps it is caused by symptoms operating in-between exploitation and revolt, as the revolt is, at best, episodic at the moment. If it is scholarly journals that are first to be hit with this model, with books trailing behind, will the book not be a probable "place" to counter the virulent aspects of this emergent symptom?

More to the point, it would seem that the author-pay model (formerly attributed to predatory publishers) is just another way of extracting tribute for the "privilege" of being published—enforceable only because academia has ratcheted up the stakes by enforcing research metrics and citations, in the public universities a practice that is primarily enforced by external "industrial" connections. Almost all public and private universities are heading toward measuring output with metrics—many academics now tailoring their CVs to show why they are "important," mirroring the social-media campaigns of celebrities and politicians, and many universities now citing their own "corporate" rankings when promoting their product (the University, the Institute, the Department, the Professor).

Where this is all going is toward increased precarity for anyone who does not play the game. Individual, solitary scholars will have few options.

The options for alternative models (such as modified open-access and a block-chain inspired "walled garden" for works that resist assimilation) will have to be vigorously networked—another manifestation of the same processes of converting scholarship to media—foremost on the peer-to-peer (P2P) and public-relations (PR) side. In adopting the necessity of the digital network, the product (books, not journals) will have to be kept in sight. The physical book is the only product that might benefit both the author and the alternative model proposed—against neo-liberal capitalist exploitation. Modified open-access publishing might become, in this scenario, the last stand for the immaterial rights of authors.

The great conundrum here is that socially generated forms of cultural production (retrospectively denoted "cultural heritage" or "cultural patrimony") have been hijacked, with atomization of scholars the intention of the machinic model enforced by Capital. Non-democratic, neo-liberal capitalism wants it two ways at once. It says to scholars and universities: We take the profit, you socialize the labor and risk. This is the exact premise or formula for what brought on the 2008 global economic catastrophe through the massive securitization of everything tangible and intangible. Must we now endure a global intellectual catastrophe as well? All signs point to the fact that we are already halfway there.

December 9, 2015

References

Adorno, Theodor W. *Notes to Literature, Volume 1*, ed. Rolf Tiedemann, trans. Shierry Weber Nicholsen. New York: Columbia University Press, 1991.

—. *The Stars Down to Earth and Other Essays on the Irrational in Culture*, ed. Stephen Crook. London: Routledge, 1994.

Agamben, Giorgio. *The Highest Poverty: Monastic Rules and Form-of-Life*, trans. Adam Kotsko. Stanford: Stanford University Press, 2013.

—. *The Kingdom and the Glory: For a Theological Genealogy of Economy and Government*, trans. Lorenzo Chiesa, with Matteo Mandarini. Stanford: Stanford University Press, 2011.

—. *Profanations*, trans. Jeff Fort. New York: Zone Books, 2007.

—. *The Signature of All Things: On Method*, trans. Luca D'Isanto, with Kevin Attell. New York: Zone Books, 2009.

—. "The Time that is Left." *Epoché* 7.1 (Fall 2002): 1–14.

—. *The Time that Remains: A Commentary on the Letter to the Romans*, trans. Patricia Dailey. Stanford: Stanford University Press, 2005.

Alter, Nora M. *Chris Marker*. Urbana: University of Illinois Press, 2006.

Amengual, Barthélémy. "*Le tombeau d'Alexandre*: Une tragédie optimiste." *Positif* 391 (September 1993): 56–59.

Andriopoulos, Stefan. *Ghostly Apparitions: German Idealism, the Gothic Novel, and Optical Media*. New York: Zone Books, 2013.

Aoudjit, Abdelkader. "*After Theory* by Terry Eagleton." *Philosophy Now* 55 (May/June 2006), https://philosophynow.org/issues/55/After_Theory_by_Terry_Eagleton.

Apocryphon of John. Nag Hammadi Codex II, 1 & Nag Hammadi Codex IV, 1, ed. Lance Owens, trans. Michael Waldstein and Frederik Wisse. *Gnosis*, n.d., http://www.gnosis.org/naghamm/apocjn-long.html.

Aristotle. *Nicomachean Ethics*, trans. H. Rackham. Loeb Classical Library, No. 73. Cambridge: Harvard University Press, 1934.

Audé, Françoise. "*Level Five*: La migraine du temps." *Positif* 433 (March 1997): 76–78.

Bachelard, Gaston. *The Psychoanalysis of Fire*, trans. Alan C.M. Ross, preface by Northrop Frye. Boston: Beacon Press, 1964.

Badiou, Alain. *Being and Event*, trans. Oliver Feltham. London: Continuum, 2005.

—. *Theoretical Writings*, trans. Ray Brassier and Alberto Toscano. London: Continuum, 2014.

Bauman, Zygmunt. *Liquid Modernity*. Cambridge: Polity, 2000.

Bazin, André. *Le cinéma français de la libération à la Nouvelle Vague*. Paris: Cahiers du Cinéma, 1983.

Bellour, Raymond. "Chris Marker and *Level Five*," trans. Adrian Martin. *Screening the Past*, 2009, http://www.screeningthepast.com/2013/12/chris-marker-and-level-five/.

—. *L'entre-images 2: Mots, images*. Paris: P.O.L., 1999.

Berlin, Isaiah. *The Roots of Romanticism*. A.W. Mellon Lectures in the Fine Arts, National Gallery, Washington, DC, 1965. Princeton: Princeton University Press, 1999.

Besson, Luc. *Lucy* (2014). DVD. Dir. Luc Besson. Universal City: Universal Studios Home Entertainment, 2015.

Blake, William. *The Complete Writings of William Blake: With*

Variant Readings, ed. Geoffrey Keynes (Oxford: Oxford University Press, 1966).

Bloom, Harold. *Anxiety of Influence: A Theory of Poetry*. Oxford: Oxford University Press, 1973.

Blümlinger, Christa. "The Imaginary in the Documentary Image: Chris Marker's *Level Five*," *Image [&] Narrative* 11.1 (2010), http://www.imageandnarrative.be/index.php/imagenarrative/article/view/51/32.

Bois, Yve-Alain and Rosalind E. Krauss. *Formless: A User's Guide*. New York: Zone, 1997.

Booth, Michael. "Dark Lands: The Grim Truth behind the 'Scandinavian Miracle'." *The Guardian*, January 27, 2014, http://www.theguardian.com/world/2014/jan/27/scandinavian-miracle-brutal-truth-denmark-norway-sweden.

Borges, Jorge Luis. *The Library of Babel*, trans. Andrew Hurley, engravings by Erik Desmazières, introduction by Angela Giral. Boston: David R. Godine, 2000.

Bove, Arianna and Erik Empson. "The Dark Side of the Multitude." *Future Nonstop*, October 4, 2003, http://future-nonstop.org/c/2300c934c6aec6cbea36f0436b8e5fca.

Bragg, Billy, with Wilco, Natalie Merchant et al. *Mermaid Avenue*. Audio CD. New York: Elektra, 1998.

Braudel, Fernand. *La Méditerranée et le monde méditerranéen à l'époque de Philippe II*. Paris: Colin, 1949.

Brody, Richard. *Everything is Cinema: The Working Life of Jean-Luc Godard*. New York: Metropolitan Books/Henry Holt & Co., 2008.

Cendrars, Blaise. *La fin du monde, filmée par l'ange N-D*. Paris: Éditions de la Sirène, 1919.

Chimisso, Cristina. *Gaston Bachelard: Critic of Science and the Imagination*. London: Routledge, 2001.

Chris Marker: A Grin without a Cat, eds. Chris Darke, Magnus Af Petersens, and Habda Rashid. London: Whitechapel Gallery, 2014. Exhibition catalogue.

"Contrôle de l'univers." In *Histoire(s) du cinéma*, ed. Jean-Luc Lacuve. *Le Ciné-club de Caen*, 2005, http://www.cineclubdecaen.com/realisat/godard/histoiresducinema4a.htm.

Cooper, Sarah. *Chris Marker*. Manchester: Manchester University Press, 2008.

Cronenberg, David. *A Dangerous Method* (2011). DVD. Dir. David Cronenberg. Culver City: Sony Pictures Home Entertainment, 2012.

Dauman, Anatole. *Anatole Dauman: Pictures of a Producer*, ed. Jacques Gerber, trans. Paul Willemen. London: British Film Institute, 1992.

Dawkins, Richard. *The Selfish Gene*. 2nd edn. Oxford: Oxford University Press, 1989.

De Sela, Lhasa. *The Living Road*. Audio CD. Montreal: Audiogramme, 2003.

Dean, Tacita. *Michael Hamburger* (2007). 16mm, color anamorphic 28-minute film with optical sound. *Film and Video Umbrella*, n.d., http://www.fvu.co.uk/projects/detail/commissions/michael-hamburger.

Debord, Guy. *Correspondence: The Foundation of the Situationist International (June 1957-August 1960)*, trans. Stuart Kendall and John McHale. Los Angeles: Semiotext(e), 2009.

Delahaye, Michel. "La chasse à l'I." *Cahiers du cinéma* 146 (August 1963): 5–17.

Denk, Jeremy. "Immortal Beloved." *The New York Times*, July 31, 2014, http://www.nytimes.com/2014/08/03/books/review/beethoven-by-jan-swafford.html.

Derrida, Jacques. *Specters of Marx: The State of the Debt, the Work of Mourning, and the New International*, trans. Peggy Kamuf. London: Routledge, 1994.

Descombes, Vincent. *The Institutions of Meaning: A Defense of Anthropological Holism*, trans. Stephen Adam Schwartz. Cambridge: Harvard University Press, 2015.

Deyhim, Sussan. "The Spilled Cup." In Bill Laswell, *Hashisheen: The End of Law*. Audio CD. Brussels: Sub Rosa, 1999.

Didi-Huberman, Georges. *Confronting Images: Questioning the Ends of a Certain History of Art*, trans. John Goodman. University Park: Pennsylvania University Press, 2005.

Eagleton, Terry. *After Theory*. New York: Basic Books, 2003.

Fanen, Sophian and Gregory Schwartz. "Next musique: Dix

albums pour bien finir 2014," *Libération*, August 19, 2014, http://next.liberation.fr/musique/2014/08/19/dix-albums-pour-bien-finir-2014_1076522.

Faure, Élie. *Histoire de l'art: L'esprit des formes*. Paris: G. Cres, 1927.

Fellows, Jay. *Ruskin's Maze: Mastery and Madness in His Art*. Princeton: Princeton University Press, 1981.

Fish, Stanley. *Is There a Text in This Class? The Authority of Interpretive Communities*. Cambridge: Harvard University Press, 1980.

Forman, Miloš. *Amadeus* (1984). DVD. Dir. Miloš Forman. Burbank: Warner Home Video, 1997.

"Formless: A User's Guide." *Zone Books*, 2014, http://www.zonebooks.org/titles/BOIS_FOR.html.

Foster, David. "'Thought-Images' and Critical-Lyricisms: The *Denkbild* and Chris Marker's *Le tombeau d'Alexandre*." *Image [&] Narrative* 10.3 (2009), http://www.kravanja.eu/pdf_files/ChrisMarker1.pdf.

Foundas, Scott. "Wildlife: Isild Le Besco." *Film Comment*, January/February 2011, http://www.filmcomment.com/article/wildlife.

Francis of Assisi and Clare of Assisi. *Francis and Clare: The Complete Works*, trans. Regis J. Armstrong, OFM Cap, Ignatius C. Brady, OFM. New York: Paulist Press, 1982.

Francovich, Allan. "The Mind's Eye: Chris Marker's *Level Five*." *Vertigo* 1.7 (Autumn 1997): 35–37.

French, Philip. "A Dangerous Method – Review." *The Guardian*, February 12, 2012, http://www.theguardian.com/film/2012/feb/12/dangerous-method-david-cronenberg-review.

Fulgentius of Ruspa. *Sancti Fulgentii episcopi Ruspensis Opera*, ed. Johannes Fraipont. Corpus Christianorum, Series Latina, 91, 91A. Turnhout: Typographi Brepols Editores Pontificii, 1968.

García Márquez, Gabriel, Roberto Pombo, and Subcomandante Marcos. "The Punch Card and the Hourglass: Interview with Subcomandante Marcos." *New Left Review* 9 (May-June 2001): 77.

Garner, John V. "Giorgio Agamben: *The Signature of All Things.*" *Continental Philosophy Review* 43.4 (November 2010): 579–588.

Gausa, Manuel et al., eds. *Rebel Matters/Radical Patterns.* Genoa: University of Genoa, 2015.

Ginsberg, Allen. *Howl and Other Poems.* Pocket Poet Series, 4. San Francisco: City Lights, 1956.

Godard, Jean-Luc. *Adieu au langage* (2014). *Goodbye to Language.* 2-disc DVD. Dir. Jean-Luc Godard. New York: Kino Lorber, Inc., 2015. ["Press Kit" (English), *Festival de Cannes,* 2014, http://www.festival-cannes.com/assets/Image/Direct/3e8f695c27127d94bb131c8bc8d27283.pdf.]

—. *Éloge de l'amour* (2001). *In Praise of Love.* DVD. Dir. Jean-Luc Godard. New York: New Yorker Video, 2003.

—. *Film Socialisme* (2010). DVD. Dir. Jean-Luc Godard. New York: Kino Lorber, Inc., 2012.

—. *Godard on Godard: Critical Writings*, eds. Jean Narboni and Tom Milne. New York: Viking, 1972.

—. *Histoire(s) du cinéma* (1988). DVD. Created by Jean-Luc Godard. St. Charles, IL: Olive Films, 2011.

—. *Histoire(s) du cinéma.* 4 vols. Paris: Gallimard/Gaumont, 1998.

—. *Jean-Luc Godard par Jean-Luc Godard*, ed. Alain Bergala. Paris: Éditions des Cahiers du Cinéma, 1998.

—. *JLG/JLG: Auto-portrait de décembre* (1995). DVD. Dir. Jean-Luc Godard. Neuilly-sur-Seine: Gaumont Vidéo, 2010.

—. *Notre musique* (2004). DVD. Dir. Jean-Luc Godard. New York: Wellspring Media, 2005.

Godard, Jean-Luc and Anne-Marie Miéville. *Four Short Films: De l'origine du XXIe siècle* (2000); *The Old Place* (1999); *Liberté et patrie* (2002); and *Je vous salue, Sarajevo* (1993). DVD. Dirs. Jean-Luc Godard and Anne-Marie Miéville. Munich: ECM, 2006.

Godard, Jean-Luc and Sarah Salovaara. "Watch: 45 Minutes of Jean-Luc Godard on *Goodbye to Language.*" *Filmmaker Magazine*, June 13, 2014, http://filmmakermagazine.com/86351-watch-45-minutes-of-jean-luc-godard-on-goodbye-to-language/#.U-elmaPQqM0.

Goodman, Matthew Shen. "Protesting the Guggenheim in Abu Dhabi: An Interview with G.U.L.F." *Art in America*, February 26, 2014, http://www.artinamericamagazine.com/news-features/interviews/protesting-the-guggenheim-in-abu-dhabi-an-interview-with-gulf/.

Gornick, Vivian. "The Interpretation of Freud." *The New York Times*, August 8, 2014, http://www.nytimes.com/2014/08/10/books/review/becoming-freud-by-adam-phillips.html.

Gottheil, Richard and Isaac Broydé. "Bedersi, Jedaiah ben Abraham." In *Jewish Encyclopedia*, n.d., http://www.jewishencyclopedia.com/articles/2726-bedersi-jedaiah-ben-abraham.

Graham, Peter, ed. *The New Wave: Critical Landmarks*. Garden City: Doubleday, 1968.

Grundy, Milton. *Venice: The Anthology Guide*. 6th edn. London: Gilles de la Mare, 2007.

Guillaume, Gustave. *Temps et verbe: Théorie des aspects, des modes, et des temps*. Suivi de L'architectonique du temps dans les langues classiques. Paris: Champion, 1970.

Hampton, Christopher. *The Talking Cure*. London: Faber and Faber, 2002.

Harbord, Janet. *Chris Marker: La Jetée*. London: Afterall Books, 2009.

Hartley, Hal. *No Such Thing* (2001). DVD. Dir. Hal Hartley. Santa Monica: MGM Home Entertainment, 2002.

Hawley, John Stratton, ed. *Saints and Virtues*. Berkeley: University of California Press, 1987.

Hegel, G.W.F. *Phenomenology of Spirit*, trans. A.V. Miller. Oxford: Oxford University Press, 1977.

Henrich, Dieter. *Hegel Im Kontext*. Frankfurt am Main: Suhrkamp, 1971.

Henry, Michel. *I Am the Truth: Toward a Philosophy of Christianity*, trans. Susan Emanuel. Stanford: Stanford University Press, 2003.

Hesse, Hermann. *Siddhartha: An Indian Poem*, trans. Susan

Bernofsky. New York: Modern Library, 2006.

Hirtle, Walter. *Language in the Mind: An Introduction to Guillaume's Theory*. Montreal: McGill-Queen's University Press, 2007.

Hugh of Digne. "*De finibus paupertatis* auctore Hugone de Digna." *Archivium Franciscanum Historicum* 5 (1912): 277–290.

Huysmans, J.-K. *Against Nature*, trans. John Howard. Auckland: The Floating Press, 2009.

Israel, Jonathan I. *Democratic Enlightenment: Philosophy, Revolution, and Human Rights, 1750-1790*. Oxford: Oxford University Press, 2011.

—. *Enlightenment Contested: Philosophy, Modernity, and the Emancipation of Man, 1670-1752*. Oxford: Oxford University Press, 2006.

—. *Radical Enlightenment: Philosophy and the Making of Modernity, 1650-1750*. Oxford: Oxford University Press, 2001.

Jameson, Fredric. *The Hegel Variations: On the Phenomenology of Spirit*. London: Verso, 2010.

Jarman, Derek. *Caravaggio* (1986). DVD. Dir. Derek Jarman. New York: Zeitgeist Films, 2008.

—. *Wittgenstein* (1993). DVD. Dir. Derek Jarman. New York, NY: Zeitgeist Films, 2008.

Jöttkandt, Sigi. "Topographies of a Cinematic City: Vladimir Nabokov's 'A Guide to Berlin'." *Symplokē* 22.1-2 (2014): 181–199.

Jousse, Thierry. "*Level Five* de Chris Marker: Mr and Mrs Memory." *Cahiers du cinéma* 510 (February 1997): 60–62.

Kämper, Birgit and Thomas Tode, eds. *Chris Marker: Filmessayist*. CICIM: Revue pour le cinéma français 45-47. Centre d'Information Cinémathographique de l'Institut Français de Munich. Munich: CICIM, 1997.

Kazantzakis, Nikos. *God's Pauper: St. Francis of Assisi*, trans. P.A. Bien. London: Faber & Faber, 1975.

—. *Report to Greco*, trans. P.A. Bien. New York: Simon and Schuster, 1965.

Keeney, Gavin. *Art as "Night": An Art-theological Treatise.* Newcastle upon Tyne: Cambridge Scholars Publishing, 2010.
—. *Dossier Chris Marker: The Suffering Image.* Newcastle upon Tyne: Cambridge Scholars Publishing, 2012.
—. *"Else-where": Essays in Art, Architecture, and Cultural Production 2002-2011.* Newcastle upon Tyne: Cambridge Scholars Publishing, 2011.
—. *Not-I/Thou: The Other Subject of Art and Architecture.* Newcastle upon Tyne: Cambridge Scholars Publishing, 2014.
—. "Séance 'C.M'." *Senses of Cinema* 64, September 2012, http://sensesofcinema.com/2012/feature-articles/seance-c-m/.
Keeney, Gavin and Parsa Khalili. "'Upstream': What is 'in' Formal Agency?" Agence 'X', 2010. Unpublished, privately circulated manuscript.
Kerr, John. *A Dangerous Method.* New York: Random House, 1993.
King, Karen L. *The Secret Revelation of John.* Cambridge: Harvard University Press, 2006.
Kristeller, Paul Oskar. *Renaissance Thought II: Papers on Humanism and the Arts.* New York: Harper Torchbooks, 1965.
Lacoue-Labarthe, Philippe. *Typography: Mimesis, Philosophy, Politics*, ed. Christopher Fynsk, introduction by Jacques Derrida. Stanford: Stanford University Press, 1989.
Lang, David. *The Little Match Girl Passion (for Chorus).* New York: Red Poppy, 2007. Musical score.
Lecointe, François. *"Le tombeau d'Alexandre": Cinéma, mémoire, histoire.* Saint-Martin-d'Hères: Institut d'Études Politiques, 2000.
Lupton, Catherine. *Chris Marker: Memories of the Future.* London: Reaktion Books, 2005.
—. "Terminal Replay: Resnais Revisited in Chris Marker's *Level Five*." *Screen* 44.1 (Spring 2003): 58–70.
Lupton, Catherine et al., "Total Recall: Film, Video and Multimedia Works by Chris Marker." *Film Comment* 39.4 (Ju-

ly-August 2003): 41, 45, 47, 49–50.

Lyotard, Jean-François. *Lessons on the Analytic of the Sublime: Kant's Critique of Judgment, [Sections] 23-29*, trans. Elizabeth Rottenberg. Stanford: Stanford University Press, 1994.

Magnusen, Finn. "On the Ancient Scandinavians' Division of the Times of the Day," trans. John M'Caul. *Mémoires de la Société Royale des Antiquaires du Nord* 1 (1839), http://www.cantab.net/users/michael.behrend/repubs/magnusen_day/pages/main.html.

Malevich, Kasimir. *The World as Non-objectivity: Unpublished Writings 1922-25*, ed. Troels Andersen, trans. Xenia Glowacki-Prus and Edmund T. Little. Copenhagen: Borgen, 1976.

"Malevich: Revolutionary of Russian Art." *Tate Modern*, July 15, 2014, http://www.tate.org.uk/about/press-office/press-releases/malevich.

Mallarmé, Stéphane. *Mallarmé in Prose*, ed. Mary Ann Caws, trans. Jill Anderson et al. New York: New Directions, 2001.

Malraux, André. *Voices of Silence*, trans. Stuart Gilbert. Garden City: Doubleday, 1953.

Marcin, "Interview with Guðmundur Óli Pálmason." *Muzyka Islandzka*, September 9, 2014, http://www.muzykaislandzka.pl/web/2014/09/16/interview-with-gudmundur-oli-palmason-from-solstafir/.

Marker, Chris. "*Bestiare* (1985–90)." *Electronic Arts Intermix*, n.d., http://www.eai.org/title.htm?id=2373.

—. *Chats perchés* (2004). *The Case of the Grinning Cat*. DVD. Dir. Chris Marker. New York: Icarus Films, 2006.

—. *iDead* (2011). Video (2 minutes 27 seconds). Created by Chris Marker. Music: "Hail! bright Cecilia!: 8. 'Wondrous Machine!'" by Philippe Herreweghe. Posted to YouTube under the pseudonym "Kosinki." *YouTube*, October 7, 2011, https://www.youtube.com/watch?v=36NLN_jI2C4.

—. *Immemory One*. Paris: Éditions du Centre Georges Pompidou/Les Films de l'Astrophore, 1998. CD-ROM.

—. *La jetée* (1962). In *La jetée/Sans soleil*. DVD. Dir. Chris

Marker. Irvington, NY: Criterion Collection, 2007.
—. *Le fond de l'air est rouge* (1977). DVD. Dir. Chris Marker. New York, NY: Icarus Films, 2009.
—. *Le tombeau d'Alexandre* (1993). *The Last Bolshevik*. DVD. Dir. Chris Marker. New York: Icarus Films, 1998.
—. *Leïla attaque* (c. 2006). In *The Case of the Grinning Cat*. DVD. Dir. Chris Marker. New York: Icarus Films, 2006.
—. "Les pingouins ont pris le pouvoir." *Libération*, February 11, 2004, http://next.liberation.fr/cinema/2004/02/11/les-pingouins-ont-pris-le-pouvoir-par-chris-marker_468585.
—. *Level Five*. DVD. Dir. Chris Marker. New York, NY: Icarus Films, 2014.
—. *Owls at Noon Prelude: The Hollow Men* (2005). Video installation. Created by Chris Marker. Installation: two-channel, eight-screen CD-ROM-based video (text composed in Javascript); color, 19-minute loop with sound; with excerpts from T.S. Eliot's "The Hollow Men" (1925).
—. *Sans soleil* (1982). In *La jetée/Sans soleil*. DVD. Dir. Chris Marker. Irvington, NY: Criterion Collection, 2007.
—. *Silent Movie, Starring Catherine Belkhodja* (1994-1995). Multimedia installation. Created by Chris Marker. Installation: metal stand; 5 20" SONY video monitors; 5 Pioneer laser-disc players; computer interface box; 5 video discs with 20-minute sequences; 18 black-and-white film/video stills; 10 computer-generated, semi-sarcastic film posters (*Bow to the Rain*; *Breathless*; *Hastings*; *Hiroshima mon amour*; *It's a Mad, Mad, Mad Dog*; *Owl People*; *The Quicksands of Time*; *Rambo Minus One*; *Remembrance of Things Past*; and *The War That Wasn't*); and soundtrack, "The Perfect Tapeur" (18 solo piano pieces lasting a total of 59 minutes and 32 seconds) and/or 20-minute soundtrack by "Michel Krasna" (Chris Marker).
—. "Six lettres à Alexandre Medvedkine (*Le tombeau d'Alexandre*)." *Positif* 391 (September 1993): 49–54.
—. "Till the End of Time." *Esprit* 129 (January 1947): 145–151.
—. *Une journée d'Andrei Arsenevitch* (1999). *One Day in the*

Life of Andrei Arsenevich. DVD. Dir. Chris Marker. New York: Icarus Films, 2011.

—. "Zapping Zone: Proposals for an Imaginary Television" (1990). Multimedia installation. Created by Chris Marker. Installation (1990): 14 color-video monitors; 13 laser-disc players; 13 loud speakers; 13 video-disc recorders; 7 computers; 7 computer programs; 4 light boxes, with 20 slides each; 11 color photos; 10 black-and-white photos (originally 50 images were intended, but reduced to 10); and 7 photomontages (40 x 80 cm.).

Marker, Chris and Pierre Lhomme. *Le joli mai: Mai 1962* (1962). *Le joli mai: The Lovely Month of May*. DVD. Dirs. Chris Marker and Pierre Lhomme. New York: Icarus Films, 2013.

Marker, Chris and Raymond Bellour. *Chris Marker: Owls at Noon Prelude: The Hollow Men*, eds. Robert Leonard and Ben Wilson. Brisbane: Institute of Modern Art, 2008.

Masciandaro, Nicola. "Conjuring the Phantasm." *Theory and Event* 13.3 (2010), http://muse.jhu.edu/journals/theory_and_event/v013/13.3.masciandaro.html.

Mayor, Chris [Chris Marker]. "Les vivants et les morts." *Esprit* 122 (May 1946): 768–785.

McCollum, Dannel Angus. "Tea with Bertrand Russell in 1961." *Escarpment Press*, n.d., https://escarpmentpress.org/russelljournal/article/download/1476/1503.

McDonough, Tom, ed. *Guy Debord and the Situationist International: Texts and Documents*. Cambridge: MIT Press, 2002.

McGuckin, John Anthony. *The Book of Mystical Chapters: Meditations on the Soul's Ascent from the Desert Fathers and Other Early Christian Contemplatives*. Boston: Shambhala, 2002.

—. *Prayer Book of the Early Christians*. Brewster: Paraclete Press, 2011.

Mian, Marzio G. "Nel Paese delle creature selvagge." *Rolling Stone Italia*, October 2014, 140–142.

Monk, Ray. *Ludwig Wittgenstein: The Duty of Genius*. New

York: Free Press, 1990.

Moore, Alan, with Eddie Campbell et al. *From Hell*. London: Knockabout Comics, 1999.

Moore, Alan, with David Lloyd et al. *V for Vendetta*. New York: Vertigo/DC Comics, 2005.

Nabokov, Vladimir. *Speak, Memory: An Autobiography Revisited*. New York: Vintage, 1967.

"The Next Supermodel." *The Economist*, February 2, 2013, http://www.economist.com/news/leaders/21571136-politicians-both-right-and-left-could-learn-nordic-countries-next-supermodel.

Nietzsche, Friedrich. *The Portable Nietzsche*, ed. and trans. Walter A. Kaufmann. New York: Penguin, 1976.

—. *Thus Spoke Zarathustra: A Book for All and None*, trans. Walter A. Kaufmann. New York: Modern Library, 1995.

—. "Truth and Lies in the Non-moral Sense" (1873). In Friedrich Nietzsche, *Philosophy and Truth: Selections from Nietzsche's Notebooks of the Early 1870's*, ed. and trans. Daniel Breazeale, foreword by Walter Kaufmann. Atlantic Highlands: Humanities Press, 1979.

—. *Untimely Meditations*, trans. R.J. Hollingdale. 2nd edn. Cambridge: Cambridge University Press, 1997.

Oreskes, Naomi and Erik M. Conway. *The Collapse of Western Civilization: A View from the Future*. New York: Columbia University Press, 2014.

Parry, Richard. "Episteme and Techne." *The Stanford Encyclopedia of Philosophy*, Fall 2014, ed. Edward N. Zalta, http://plato.stanford.edu/archives/fall2014/entries/episteme-techne/.

Pasolini, Pier Paolo. *Il Vangelo Secondo Matteo* (1964). *The Gospel According to St. Matthew*. DVD. Dir. Pier Paolo Pasolini. Santa Monica: Legend Films/Genius Entertainment, 2007.

—. *Mamma Roma*. Milan: Rizzoli, 1962.

Passages de l'image, eds. Raymond Bellour, Catherine David, and Christine van Assche. Paris: Éditions du Centre Georges Pompidou, 1990. Exhibition catalogue.

Passages de l'image. Barcelona: Centre Cultural de la Fundació Caixa de Pensions, 1991. Exhibition catalogue.

Phillips, Adam. *Becoming Freud: The Making of a Psychoanalyst*. New Haven: Yale University Press, 2014.

Piketty, Thomas. *Capital in the Twenty-first Century*, trans. Arthur Goldhammer. Cambridge: Harvard University Press, 2014.

Rancière, Jacques. *Film Fables*, trans. Emiliano Battista. Oxford: Berg, 2006.

Régent-Susini, Anne. *Paul Éluard: Capitale de la douleur*. Rosny: Bréal, 2000.

Reisz, Karel and Gavin Millar. *The Technique of Film Editing*. 2nd edn. Oxford: Focal Press, 1968.

Resnais, Alain. *L'année dernière à Marienbad* (1961). *Last Year at Marienbad*. DVD. Dir. Alain Resnais. Irvington: The Criterion Collection, 2009.

Resnais, Alain, Chris Marker, and Ghislain Cloquet. *Les statues meurent aussi* (1950-1953). Dirs. Alain Resnais, Chris Marker, and Ghislain Cloquet. In *Hiroshima mon amour*. 2-disc DVD. Paris: Arte Vidéo; Argos Films; Gaumont Columbia Tristar Home Vidéo, 2004.

Ricoeur, Paul. "L'écriture de l'histoire et la répresentation du passé." *Annales: Histoire, Sciences Sociales* 55.4 (July-August 2000): 731–747.

Rossellini, Roberto. *Francesco, giullare di Dio* (1950). *The Flowers of St. Francis*. Dir. Roberto Rossellini, assisted by Federico Fellini. DVD. Irvington: Criterion Collection, 2005.

—. *Roma città aperta* (1945). *Rome, Open City*. Dir. Roberto Rossellini, assisted by Federico Fellini. DVD. Chatsworth: Image Entertainment, 1997.

Roth, Laurent and Raymond Bellour. *Qu'est-ce qu'une madeleine? À propos du CD-ROM "Immemory" de Chris Marker*, ed. Christine van Assche, English trans. Brian Holmes. Brussels: Yves Gevaert Éditeur; Paris: Éditions du Centre Georges Pompidou, 1997.

Roud, Richard. "The Left Bank." *Sight and Sound: Interna-*

tional Film Quarterly 32.1 (Winter 1962–63): 24–27.

Ruskin, John. *Modern Painters*. 5 vols. New York: John W. Lovell Co., 1885.

—. *The Poetry of Architecture: Or, The Architecture of the Nations of Europe Considered in Association with Natural Scenery and National Character*. London: G. Allen, 1893.

—. *The Relation Between Michael Angelo and Tintoret: Seventh of the Course of Lectures on Sculpture Delivered at Oxford, 1870-71*. London: Smith, Elder and Co., 1872.

Sanborn, Keith. "Shades without Colour." *Artforum* 43.10 (Summer 2005): 79.

Sand, Michael, ed. *Aperture 145, Surface and Illusion: Ten Portfolios* (Autumn 1996).

Scemama-Heard, Céline. *Histoire(s) du cinéma de Jean-Luc Godard: La force faible d'un art*. Paris: L'Harmattan, Paris, 2006.

Schefer, Jean-Louis. *The Enigmatic Body: Essays on the Arts by Jean-Louis Schefer*, ed. and trans. Paul Smith. Cambridge: Cambridge University Press, 1995.

Scott, A.O. "On a Mediterranean Cruise Ship Steered by a Godardian Crew: *Film Socialisme*." *The New York Times*, June 2, 2011, http://www.movies.nytimes.com/2011/06/03/movies/film-socialisme-by-jean-luc-godard-review.html.

Selwyn, Benjamin. "Neoliberalism is Alive and Well." *Le monde diplomatique*, December 2014, http://mondediplo.com/blogs/neoliberalism-is-alive-and-well.

Shabistarī, Sa'd Ud Din Mahmūd. *The Secret Rose Garden*, trans. Florence Lederer. London: J. Murray, 1920.

Shaffer, Peter. *Amadeus*. New York: Harper & Row, 1981.

Shields, David. "Autobiographic Rapture and Fictive Irony in *Speak, Memory* and 'The Real Life of Sebastian Knight'." *Iowa Review* 17.1 (Winter 1987): 44–54.

Smith, Patti. *After the Gold Rush*. Music video. Lyrics and music by Neil Young, montage by Jean-Luc Godard. *YouTube*, June 6, 2012, https://www.youtube.com/watch?v=wLqcClh3qKQ.

Sólstafir. *Ótta*. Audio CD. Season of Mist, 2014.

Sólstafir. *Fjara* (2012). Music video. Lyrics and music by Sólstafir. Dir. Bowen Staines, Gunnar B. Guðbjörnsson. *YouTube*, January 23, 2012, https://www.youtube.com/watch?v=XmGdSOhBx8E.

Sólstafir. *Lágnætti* (2014). Music video. Lyrics and music by Sólstafir. Dir. Bowen Staines, Gunnar B. Guðbjörnsson. *YouTube*, October 7, 2014, https://www.youtube.com/watch?v=GL3LVlDtoUY.

Sontag, Susan. *On Photography*. New York: Dell Publishing Co., Inc., 1977.

Subcomandante Galeano. "Between Shadow and Light." *Roar Magazine*, May 2014, http://roarmag.org/2014/05/subcomandante-galeano-between-light-shadow/.

Subcomandante Marcos. "Carta del Subcomandante Marcos a ETA." *Rebelion*, 2002, http://www.rebelion.org/hemeroteca/spain/021212marcos.htm.

—. "The Library of Aguascalientes," trans. Cecilia Rodriguez, National Commission for Democracy in Mexico, *Flag Blackened*, n.d., http://flag.blackened.net/revolt/mexico/ezln/marcos_library_jan95.html.

"Tacita Dean." Press Release. *Marian Goodman Gallery*, 2009, http://www.mariangoodman.com/exhibitions/2009-04-02_tacita-dean/.

Tagore, Rabindranath. *Sādhanā: The Realisation of Life*. London: Macmillan and Co., 1913.

Tarkovsky, Andrei. *The Mirror* (1975). DVD. Dir. Andrei Tarkovsky. New York: Kino International, 2000.

—. *Nostalghia* (1983). DVD. Dir. Andrei Tarkovsky. New York: Fox Lorber Home Video, 1998.

—. *Offret* (1986). *The Sacrifice*. DVD. Dir. Andrei Tarkovsky. New York: Kino International, 2000.

Taubin, Amy. "Wiping the Slate Clean: *Film Socialisme*." *Film Comment*, September-October 2010, http://www.filmcomment.com/article/film-socialisme-review.

Temple, Michael and James S. Williams, eds. *The Cinema Alone: Essays on the Work of Jean-Luc Godard, 1985-2000*. Amsterdam: Amsterdam University Press, 2000.

Therborn, Göran. *From Marxism to Post-Marxism?* London: Verso, 2008.

Van Assche, Christine et al., eds. *Collection New Media Installations: La collection du Centre Pompidou Musée National d'Art Moderne*. Paris: Éditions du Centre Pompidou, 2006.

Varoufakis, Yanis. "How I became an Erratic Marxist." *The Guardian*, February 18, 2015, http://www.theguardian.com/news/2015/feb/18/yanis-varoufakis-how-i-became-an-erratic-marxist.

Wetzel, Michael. "Acousmêtrie: On the Relationship between Voice and Image in the Films of Chris Marker." *Media Art Net*, 2004, http://www.medienkunstnetz.de/themes/art_and_cinematography/marker/1/.

White, Hayden. *Metahistory: The Historical Imagination in Nineteenth-century Europe*. Baltimore: Johns Hopkins University Press, 1973.

Williams, Jeffrey J. "Prodigal Critics." *The Chronicle Review*, December 6, 2009, http://chronicle.com/article/Prodigal-Critics/49307/.

Wittgenstein, Ludwig. *Philosophical Investigations*, trans. G.E.M. Anscombe. New York: Macmillan, 1953.

—. *Preliminary Studies for the "Philosophical Investigations," Generally Known as The Blue and Brown Books*. Oxford: Blackwell, 1958.

—. *Tractatus Logico-philosophicus*, trans. C.K. Ogden. London: Routledge and Kegan Paul, 1922.

Wood, Michael. "A Preference for Torquemada." *London Review of Books* 31.7 (April 9, 2009): 8–10.

Wright, Jonathan Kent. "Review: Jonathan Israel, *Democratic Enlightenment*." *H-France Forum* 9.1, Winter 2014, http://www.h-france.net/forum/forumvol9/Israel1.pdf.

Yates, Frances Amelia. *The Art of Memory*. Chicago: University of Chicago Press, 1966.

—. *Giordano Bruno and the Hermetic Tradition*. Chicago: University of Chicago Press, 1964.

—. *The Rosicrucian Enlightenment*. London: Routledge and

  Kegan Paul, 1972.

—. *Theatre of the World*. Chicago: University of Chicago Press, 1969.

"Zapping Zone, Chris Marker, 1990, coll. Centre Pompidou AM 1990-160." Nouveaux Médias Archive, Centre Georges Pompidou, Paris, France. Archival document.

Zeffirelli, Franco. *Fratello Sole, Sorella Luna* (1972). *Brother Sun, Sister Moon*. DVD. Dir. Franco Zeffirelli. Hollywood: Paramount, 2004.

www.ingramcontent.com/pod-product-compliance
Lightning Source LLC
Chambersburg PA
CBHW031311150426
43191CB00005B/184